EXPLORING LOCAL HISTORY

James Griffin

and

Tim Lomas

D0104918

TEACH YOURSELF BOOKS

For UK orders: please contact Bookpoint Ltd, 39 Milton Park, Abingdon, Oxon OX14 4TD. Telephone: (44) 01235 400414, Fax: (44) 01235 400454. Lines are open from 9.00–6.00, Monday to Saturday, with a 24 hour message answering service. Email address: orders@bookpoint.co.uk

For U.S.A. & Canada orders: please contact NTC/Contemporary Publishing, 4255 West Touhy Avenue, Lincolnwood, Illinois 60646-1975, U.S.A.. Telephone: (847) 679 5500, Fax: (847) 679 2494.

Long renowned as the authorative source for self-guided learning – with more than 30 million copies sold worldwide – the *Teach Yourself* series includes over 200 titles in the fields of languages, crafts, hobbies, business and education.

British Library Cataloguing in Publication Data
A catalogue record for this title is available from The British Library

Library of Congress Catalog Card Number: 98-67260

First published in UK 1997 by Hodder Headline Plc, 338 Euston Road, London, NW1 3BH.

First published in US 1998 by NTC/Contemporary Publishing, 4255 West Touhy Avenue, Lincolnwood (Chicago), Illinois 60646–1975 U.S.A.

The 'Teach Yourself' name and logo are registered trade marks of Hodder & Stoughton Ltd.

Typeset by Transet Limited, Coventry, England.
Printed in Great Britain for Hodder & Stoughton Educational, a division of Hodder Headline Plc, 338 Euston Road, London NW1 3BH by Cox & Wyman Ltd, Reading, Berkshire.

Impression number   10 9 8 7 6 5   4 3 2
Year   2004 2003 2002 2001 2000 1999 1998

Dedication

To Hannah, Elizabeth and Alice; may their generation be as entranced by the past as we are!

Acknowledgements

We are indebted to many people. First, to Anne Thorn, Alan R. Woolworth (Case Study 7, copyright © 1996 by the Minnesota Historical Society; used with permission), and Peter T. Lubrecht for contributing case studies. These are particularly valuable in showing different approaches, especially the studies involving the United States of America.

We are most grateful to the late David Kennedy for drawing Figures 9.1, 9.2 and 11.2, and for general advice and help. The following sources are acknowledged for permission to use illustrations: Hodder Headline PLC for Figure 2.1; Oxfordshire Photographic Archive, Oxfordshire County Council for Figure 9.4; and Essex County Council Libraries; Trustees of the Town Library, Saffron Walden, H.C. Stacey Collection for Figure 11.11.

Thanks too to Michael Cox and Raymond Gillespie for checking our text technically regarding Scottish and Irish sources respectively; also to David Eddershaw for many useful corrections and suggestions, and general encouragement. Without their help this book would have been much the poorer.

It would be unwise to single out particular local reference librarians because many throughout the country have extended a great deal of courtesy and patience to us. We are, however, particularly grateful to the staff in High Wycombe and Saffron Walden.

Without Helen Coward's enthusiasm and support, the project would not have come to fruition at all; and we are also grateful to Joanne Osborn and Helen Green for their help and support in the later stages.

Finally, Fiona's diligent and timely prodding was necessary to complete the work. We extend thanks to you all.

James Griffin, Saffron Walden, England
Tim Lomas, Lincoln, England
January 1997

CONTENTS

PREFACE

All our lives we have collected the past. Anything relating to family history tends to find its way to us. However, when our forebears were alive they were real people: living, working and eating. So, what was life like for our ancestors? Studying places, and the way they change, helps us to reveal the world that people lived in.

Local history is exciting. There is a magic in handling centuries-old objects and documents and making new discoveries from them. They provide a point of contact between us and people who lived a long time ago. We are in very different circumstances, but perhaps have similar feelings and motivations.

Part of the interest of local history consists of the huge variety of things you can study. The story of Curry Load (Somerset) or Grisedale Pike (Cumberland) may have been written, and it may be on the bookshelves next to biographies of those places' famous sons and daughters. But who has written about their duck ponds? Who has studied the back lanes? Whatever you choose to look into and write about may well be as interesting to those who live there now as it is to you. Indeed, your work may even be historically important, contributing perhaps to some nation-wide study of duck ponds or back lanes. So, how do you go about it?

This book provides a starting place. It begins by answering several general questions.

- Can we find out about people? Or are we limited to places and artefacts?
- Why should we bother to explore this place as it used to be?
- Who am I doing this for?
- Need I study a whole village or town?
- Where can I search to find out about people in the past?

The first chapters set the scene and describe the commoner sources. Chapters 3 to 10 cover particular themes, each contributing to the recognition of the place you are studying. For each source we give:

- what the record consists of
- why it was made
- over what period, and
- what problems we might meet in trying to use it.

Part Two ends with a collection of case studies. Taken from very different geographical and subject areas, these illustrate the results of real studies that have used some of the themes described in the book. They show how a more complete picture is revealed when several themes and sources are woven together; inevitably, several are incomplete (as local studies normally are!)

Most of the examples we include, describing historical events and sources of information, refer to England and Wales. Both Scotland and Ireland had and still have separate legal and educational systems. They had 'regional governments' for long periods and, since 1921, Ireland has been divided into two separate entities. Methodology for research by readers living in Scotland, Ireland, and even North America (see the case studies in Chapter 11) is the same, however. Although this book will be of greatest use to those living in England and Wales, a number of people from Scotland, Ireland and North America have historical connections with those countries. Nevertheless, one should remember that the sources and places to visit for information can vary across differing cultures, and those are referred to at appropriate places. Books referring specifically to Scotland and Ireland are noted in Further Reading.

The final chapter explores ways to present your findings. It offers some pointers to what you can achieve, perhaps in collaboration with like-minded people, for you may well feel that your project could be advanced by being able to discuss it with other local historians. Joining a local history society could widen your interests and help in the eventual publication of your efforts.

In considering your project, do not overlook recording the present: today's humdrum routines and ways of life are tomorrow's history. We owe it to our descendants to record what we can, to preserve what we can and, above all, to inspire the next generation into a love of their roots.

We hope that readers will become as fascinated by the past as we are. The more of us that discover and use the body of resources that exist, the better they will be understood and preserved. Good hunting! We look forward to reading your study one day!

1
WHAT SHOULD YOU STUDY AND WHY?

In this chapter we will consider the following ideas.

- Why should you be undertaking local history research and who for?
- Your study can cover any sort of subject.
- It cannot cover everywhere (after all it is 'local'), but your research may cover small or larger sized areas.
- What sources of information can you search?
- Cautionary words about perception and accuracy.
- How to proceed: read – plan – research – present.

The idea of researching may have arisen when a question occurred to you. Your question might have been like one of the following.

- Could someone really make a living selling nothing but songsheets?
- Why does the Archbishop of York sign himself 'Ebor'?
- How could 12 people live in that little cottage?
- Why is the church two km from the village? And why do they say that a ring hung from its door handle? (See Case Study 2 in Chapter 11 for some ideas on this!)
- How can this be the main road? A car couldn't even pass a bicycle in a lane like this!
- What kind of transport did the people of the past use on it?
- I wonder what it was like to live here in the seventeenth century?

Studying this book should help you to devise and carry through some research to answer your own questions. The more you study the past, the more questions there are to ask. As you work out one situation it leads to another, then another assumption, and more questions. Yes, this *was* the main road, and a hundred years ago it wasn't even met-alled. Also, it was even narrower in places, for example there used to be a cottage on that corner. So, how did traffic pass? Go back another hundred years, and there were no hedges here: vehicles passed by going up on to the edge of the field. How many vehicles needed to pass anyway? What trade was there between the two settlements this road links? How self-sufficient were they? And so on.

─────── # Why bother at all? ───────

Should we be studying the past anyway? There are, we suggest, many reasons why we should.

- Today's scenario was built on yesterday's. As we study the past, the disciplines and skills we use help us understand our own world better, through constraints and similarities with the past.
- To help appreciate and value our surroundings; not just heritage sites, but everyday streets and fields.
- Maybe we are simply interested in some aspects of our particular place for its own sake. We now live in Stocksfield (Northumberland), or Newtownabbey (Co. Antrim), and part of our appreciation of the place is who founded it, or what trade used to go on here, or who used to live at the cross-roads.
- Never forget that local history is as much about people as places. It is not just about streets and houses, but about the lives of those who lived in them, their problems and challenges.
- Perhaps we are fascinated by family history. It is all very well discovering who your ancestors were, but how did they live? (If four-greats grandfathers was a cordwainer, what did he actually do? If the nearest town was ten miles away, what happened when toothache become unbearable?)

POINTS TO CONSIDER

Although local history can be approached at different levels, good local history is more than just fact grubbing. It is a study that has a technique, although the scope is enormous. Nor, paradoxically, is local history just local. Good local historians do not just collect information on their areas, they need to know something and read something about other places too, or they will not know if the facts they have gathered are significant. This book deals extensively with techniques. However, each locality is unique, and what is local to you cannot easily be taught in a book; there is no substitute for learning on the job.

—— Who are you researching for? ——

Unless you are particularly philanthropic, you are probably learning about your area because it is something you enjoy doing. Because it is so immediate – local history starts with your own house, your road, the fire station round the corner – it appeals at different levels.

On the one hand, your interest may be quite superficial. Why is your area called what it is? Why *Hanging* Langford (Bedfordshire)? Why *Fleet* (several countries)? Why The *Shambles* (various places)? Reference books quickly establish answers: there was a long ford near a sloping hill (Old English *hangra*, a slope); an Old English *fleot* was a creek; and a *sceamel* was a stool, especially one on which meat was butchered: the bloody piles of offal, scraps, etc. soon explain today's meaning of 'shambles'.

On the other hand, you may become a very dedicated student of your area, or some aspects of it. Indeed, you may become the local expert. There are no limits; anything, anybody, any date, any process that interests you had its equivalent somewhere in the past, providing you with an aspect of local history to study.

There is nothing freakish about wanting to know what our ancestors lived through. It is a natural longing and inquisitiveness in most of us: humankind is naturally nosy. After all, they are our neighbours, separated only by a curtain of time. Local information gleaned by researchers like us is wanted by others. Local history is a communal activity: this is not just our locality.

You might say: 'Hang on, though! My interest is in cars and computers; how can I research those, when a hundred years ago nobody had even invented them?'

There are two answers to this. First, it is you who should decide what to study: you set the terms of reference. So, to take the case of cars not being in your area in 1897, valid ideas you could follow up might include the following.

- What were the reactions of people in your area when they did come in?
- Pick a different area to study than the one in which you live. How would family life have differed in a car-making town from any other town?
- What difference did cars make to your area and life in it?
- How did the arrival of cars affect transport systems and roads in your area?

The second answer relates to time. Don't forget that history is a curious concept: the very act of reading this is history by the time you have finished. One important aspect of local history involves the recording of the present for future researchers. Bear in mind that changes happening in the 1990s in the world of information technology are already part of the overall history of computing. Of course, computers actually **were** around in 1897: Pascal invented a calculating machine in the mid-seventeenth century, and Babbage another in 1821, but we know what you meant!

For your computer interest, you might choose similar projects to the ones mentioned above concerning cars. What was the impact of computerisation on some local facility or company (electoral register, perhaps, or a local newspaper)?

Another beneficiary of your energies is your community. Village, town, county and national local history societies are full of energetic groups with an interest in researching and preserving the past. We hope you will decide to join one; much of what you do will then benefit other people.

One outlet for your enthusiasm is: write a piece for the local paper to develop your neighbours' feelings for the past. When you reach the 'expert' stage, people may commission you to write articles, even books, or give talks on your particular subject. For local history is not just a pastime, and even amateurs can contribute important work if they do their research properly.

What should be the scope and size of your project?

There are a few restrictions on what constitutes 'local'. You might study every aspect of one place for a particular period of time. In considering the area of that place, you might find it hard to devise an interesting study of one semi-detached house on a modern housing estate; and by definition you wouldn't normally classify a national study as 'local'; though it is necessary to think about the national scene in which your locality is set. Almost any area in between is fair game, however.

There are some natural boundaries that can determine an area for investigation. For example, hills and rivers; a street; an estate; a manor;

a hundred; a town; a district; a parish; a school; a railway line; even an industry. Again, there may be more nebulous determinants, such as areas in which present or past people felt some sense of community.

Local history by definition relates to a 'locality', that is concerning a place; but why should people consider themselves to be 'of' one particular place and not another? As people are by and large social, the spirit of community might be defined as 'the relationship between people who came from the place they call home'. There have been many attempts to define 'community', and this is a problematic subject.

Many of the examples we give in this book describe what people did to establish and strengthen the bonds with their neighbours. Laws and the resulting actions, maps, histories and pictorial representations all play their part in establishing a community as well as a physical place.

Figure 1.1 presents some ideas of various scales that might be involved. The rest of this book may give you more ideas.

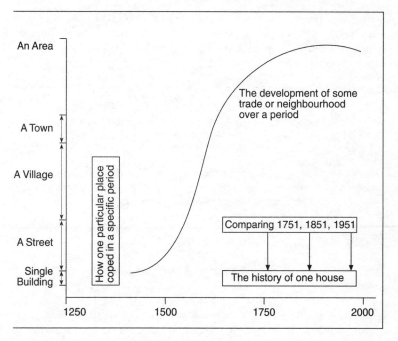

Figure 1.1 Local research at different scales

Where should you research?

This is likely to be influenced by different factors.

● Where you live or work. You will probably be most interested by this
area, and it makes sense to research somewhere you can get to easily.
● The particular subject that interests you may have occurred only in a
specific locality. If it is the mass manufacture of shoes, for example,
you might need to study a specialist town such as Northampton, even
if you lived elsewhere.
● The survival of records may be limited. One local place may pos-
sess records that answer the questions you wish to ask, and be
worth studying if not much has survived from your own area.

Once again, the decision is yours.

Should you research with a group?

It may well be that what you want to study would be better as part of
some larger project. So contacting a local group, or establishing an
informal one of your own, might be a good idea. There is another reason for making such a contact, which we will deal with later.

POINTS TO CONSIDER

There are many groups investigating history nationally or locally. These
include the internationally respected Cambridge Group for Population
Research (who conduct research into every aspect of social history,
and whose publications are well worth seeking out), and several uni-
versity-based groups studying the records of particular trades. At a
more local level, there are many town- or country-wide societies. You
should ask at your reference or local studies library for information.

What are you actually studying?

The sources mentioned in this book are your raw material. From
these sometimes fleeting glimpses of the past it is possible to build up
a picture – albeit incomplete – of what you are trying to imagine. It is
a bit like pointing several narrow-beamed spotlights at different parts
of a painting, switching them on and off one at a time, and trying to
work out what the whole image depicts. Sometimes all you have as a
source is part of the picture reflected in something else. You may still
be able to deduce something from such surrogates (for example,

records of heads of household may be indicators of total population). Unfortunately, not every age has a spotlight pointed exactly where you want it; so your overall impression may have to be based partly on flashes from nearby places or images from other dates.

To help you there is a bewilderingly large number of sources, and you must try to find the most useful ones. Remember that you are trying to imagine your predecessors living ordinary or extraordinary lives, within their environment. So the scope is very wide: almost anything you can discover is of interest. Since history ranges backwards from 'now', everything around you is evidence. All your senses are involved; everyone you see, meet or read about is part of the story. What they say, where they live and work, their leisure and their public service – everything will have its place in your reconstruction.

Whatever we examine tells us something of the past; but only with good luck and a lot of researching can one recreate anything like a full picture. It is like going to a museum and trying on suits of ancient clothing. All may give you a sense of period, but only one or two will fit you really well.

POINTS TO CONSIDER

* There are nearly always some clues about most aspects of a community in the past.
* There are, however, never enough to know the whole truth. We are always left asking for more.
* Clues rarely come in a form that can simply be plucked out and reproduced.
* When we think we have finished, there are always new questions to ask.

Some words of caution

Sources come in many forms, such as those compiled at the time and those compiled later; written, pictorial, artefactual, visual; first hand and second hand. With any of them, the problems of distortion and hindsight are perhaps the main challenge. Understanding the mind and values of the authors is a particular difficulty. Sources were almost never written for local investigators' benefit; so you need to find out as much about the compilers as the topic they are writing about. That they may have been written after the events adds to the difficulty.

Before going into any detail, there are two general comments to bear in mind, whatever historical material you are studying: perception and accuracy.

Perception

People interpret their surroundings differently. So bear in mind that when you and your neighbours consider your surroundings, you will not 'see' the same things. What is of importance to them may not be to you, and vice versa. As a digger into the past, remember that those who created the records you are using (writers, artists, photographers, etc.) also saw their world in a different way.

Accuracy

Accuracy is a duty rather than a virtue, although being accurate is not the same as being pedantic and dominated by isolated fact. Apart from the need to make your own notes and maps carefully, there are many reasons why you should bear this in mind when looking at historical documents. This is true of anything we read or look at, but is particularly important if we wish to draw general conclusions.

Mistakes in records

The person making the records may have made genuine mistakes. We all do this from time to time:

- Spelling errors or the wrong use of grammar.
- Incorrect assumptions: 'It's the third on the right', we say, forgetting about the newly built access to a housing development.
- Unconsciously passing on someone else's errors. In the days before printing, everything had to be copied (you have bought a 'copy' of this book). Publishers employed teams of writers to copy from existing copies. This led to variations in handwriting, and subsequent problems in interpretation. For example, Cinderella's original slipper was of *vair* (French: fur); this was later misread or misheard as *verre* (glass).

Approximations in records

The writer may have been approximating. If I wrote to an acquaintance: 'I live in Bishop's Stortford, in Hertfordshire, a town 20 miles south of Cambridge' this might include several inaccuracies. The statement is acceptable for my purpose but taken out of context –

perhaps being paraphrased or translated 50 years later – other people may be misled.

- I do not live in a town; I really live in a village just outside a town.
- I actually live in Manuden, not Bishop's Stortford at all: but I knew my reader wouldn't have heard of my village.
- I don't even live in Hertfordshire but in Essex; it just happens that the nearest town, Bishop's Stortford, is in that county.
- My house is not 20 miles from Cambridge (nor is Manuden; nor is Bishop's Stortford): this was only a rough approximation. If a later writer converts this to 32.19 km that would be wrong.

I have said enough to show how 'suspect' my statement was. Yet it was perfectly adequate for my original purpose.

POINTS TO CONSIDER

While on the subject of accuracy, there are pitfalls in reading and using premetrication measurements. The problems are threefold:

- ◆ The measure may not be familiar. Apart from those that are not used now but would probably be recognised in Britain (such as furlong, cubit and tun) historical documents may contain references to things that require the services of a good dictionary to identify! Like runlet and tierce, which are both liquid measures; or last and coom, which are dry measures.
- ◆ The measure may not have been the same at different dates (or even in different places at the same time). A good example of this is the rod, pole or perch, a measure formally defined for each area by random sample. The first 16 people leaving church were to stand in a line heel to toe, and the result is a '16-foot' measure.
- ◆ Converting old into new measure may actually be misleading. For example, reading that a field is called 'ten acres', means 'about ten acres', so translating it as 40.4686 hectares is not accurate.

Biased views in records

Most importantly, the originator may be biased in his views. If you are reading about the provision of hospital services, for example, is the writer:

- a patient, eager to stress the inadequacies of the system?
- a hospital manager, as eager to emphasis that all is well?
- a journalist, analysing the status quo? If so, the report may be biased by his paper's political slant.

Why was the record created?

Why was the record written? Whatever you are reading, think why? Who for?

- Was it created for a purpose? If so, maybe only one side of the story is being told.
- Was it written for someone 'on the same side' as the writer? Or to convert the reader?
- At what level was it written? For those uneducated in this particular field; or for specialists?

How to proceed

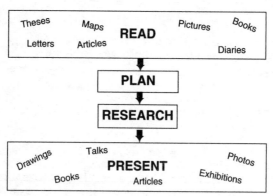

Figure 1.2 A programme of research techniques

Good researchers use tried and tested techniques for their research; this we can simplify to: **read**, **plan**, **research** and **present** (see Figure 1.2).

Read

Finding out about a place and life in it should begin with your own bookshelves, followed by a visit to your local library. Read as widely as you can before beginning your research; it is not just knowledge that should be checked, but the kind of questions previous researchers have tackled and their suggestions for further work. It is also usually necessary to read about localities away from your locality, to be able to put your findings into a wider context.

Making notes

Read as much as you can, making notes on the sources you have looked at. Whenever appropriate and not over-expensive, make photocopies: if you make selective notes, what interests you now may lead you to exclude information about other subjects – and these may become important later if your research takes an unexpected turn. When you take notes, do so in as full a form as you conveniently can. Abbreviations may actually baffle you later!

Here are some potential problems that might arise from entries from *Kelly's Directory of 'Sometown'*, and the notes taken from it:

Printed record:	**Your notes:**
J. Smith, 14 High-street, Anywhere	J Smith, 14 High St, Anywhere
Hy. Brown, 22 High-street, Anywhere	Hy Brown, 22 "
Josh. Robinson, 6 East-street, Anywhere	Jos. Robinson, 6 East St
Robt. Joanes, 41 Church-lane	Rob. Jones, 41 Church La

Henry Brown lives in a district of 'Sometown' known as 'Anywhere'; Kelly's use this formula for areas within towns, or nearby villages. You may later misread or overlook the ditto marks in your notes. But in this case they are wrong anyway, as they only appear below 'High Street', and aren't repeated for the 'Anywhere' part of the entry as they should be.

Joshua also lives in the district of Anywhere, and again it has been overlooked. More seriously, however, Kelly's standard abbreviation for 'Joshua' has been replaced by 'Jos' in the notes, and this is actually Kelly's shortened form of 'Joseph'.

Finally, Robert Joanes's surname has been incorrectly spelt. If in doubt, write '[sic]' in your notes after unusual words, impossible dates, etc. This tells you later that it was shown 'as such' in the original. Square brackets are a useful way of telling you later that the note is yours, and was not made by the original author.

Sources of information

Other places to search and read include:

- your reference library's subject index

- the local newspaper's subject index if there is one
- the index of your local history society's book and journal publications
- county records, not forgetting those of the local family history society.

It is quite likely that your local library will hold all these. What you are seeking, of course, is published work similar to your planned project. However, anything describing the place you are researching may be worth investigating further. Such published material will also put you in touch with other people working in your field. Follow these references up; authors will probably have gathered a lot more material than they have published, and some of this may be vital to you.

Plan

Deciding what you want to study may sound a bit obvious; but if you don't have a particular aim in mind it is easy to be side-tracked. While there is nothing against being side-tracked – people have made some of the most important discoveries that way – all research needs to be organised.

If you have no particular ideas, but want to undertake some local study, contact your local History Society; your library will have their address. The themes covered in this book should give you some ideas.

Research

Exactly what methods and records you use will depend on what you are researching. Chapter 2 contains brief descriptions of a few of the most widespread sources, summarising their scope and explaining where to find them.

Each of the thematic chapters that follow describes the sources in more detail. There we suggest what questions you might ask of them.

Careful preparations for your research is most important. Professionals, such as local studies librarians and archivists, are busy people. They will be helpful, but will appreciate you knowing what you want and actually doing the mundane and basic searching.

Present

The most important topic: what you can do with the material you have gathered, is discussed in Chapter 12.

Summary

- There are many good reasons for studying the history of a local place or some aspect of it.
- Everyone can gain from what you find, but the main beneficiary should be yourself.
- There are few restrictions on the size and type of study.
- Whatever you look at, however, must be put properly into its original context.
- Beware of bias and inaccuracies of various types.
- Research much be preceded by a proper plan. This should include as much as reading as possible.
- The end result must be properly presented so that everyone can benefit.

2

AN INTRODUCTION
TO SOURCES

❛ One can read history, but one cannot understand history, except
through those who have experienced it ❜
   Robert Daniel 'If Only Stones Could Speak', *Family Tree Magazine*, 1995

In this chapter we will think about the sources available for pure
research and examine them briefly. We will consider, under 'General
Information':

- surrogates: where we make do with less-than-ideal sources
- the variety of evidence types open to us
- where we can find this evidence
- preparing for research
- tips when using microfiche and microfilm readers.

The chapter concludes, under 'Types of Source', with individual
descriptions of different evidence:

- the landscape and built environment
- written and printed evidence
- pictorial evidence
- artefacts
- oral evidence.

Paradoxically, evidence for local historians is all around us, yet what
we are looking for is often irritatingly unfindable. Our interest is
usually sparked off by a known fact, a real place, or something that
occurred at a particular time.

- You know, for example, that the sea barriers of East Anglia were
  breached in 1953; then someone tells you that your own village
  was affected, and you want to know how.

- You move into what you guess was an old wind mill: but can you prove that is what it was?
- What happened to your town during the Second World War?

General information

Surrogates

The local history detective must learn how to use existing evidence; to 'read between the lines' in extracting material. As well as making its own statement, a record is a clue which may be interpreted in other ways. Furthermore, it may be all you have: you want to know something, but all that is available to you is something slightly different. Making proper reservations, you may be able to use the different record to cast a side-light on the problem you want to solve.

Let us see what a published military muster of 62 names in 1798 can tell us about the parish of Fawley in Buckinghamshire. Several facts are involved, each giving rise to questions we can answer, and assumptions we can then make. Here we expand just one fact and see what hidden information can be extracted.

Fact
Fawley included 62 men of military age.

Questions
What was military age? Were women ever involved?

Answers
The age range is stated in the record to be from 15 to 60 years. The survey calls for 'All persons residing in [the area]'; though no women are listed anywhere in the military-service part of the survey. A few are given in a second part, however, which listed those who owned draught horses, waggons and carts; again it happens that no women were involved in Fawley.

Assumptions
Women were not called upon to fight. Also, if there were 62 men, a little research in general demographic books suggests an approximate total population for the parish, of between 240 and 300.

One of the 'proper' reservations we must make is that this is a survey of the parish, not the village, of Fawley. So any conclusions we draw about today's village must be qualified: the 1798 survey included outlying farms and hamlets as well. Another thing we must be careful about is to check that the parish's boundaries have not changed.

Our **assumptions** are 'surrogates' we have taken from the military data and are only a few of the tentative conclusions we could draw from the Fawley data. Almost every source has the same potential. However, it is vital to check this evidence, using as many other sources as possible.

What kind of evidence?

Historians usually concentrate on written records – often these are all that have survived the intervening years. They can be consulted relatively easily from the comfort of a central record office or local studies library; and as we have seen, they can generate a great deal of information. But you must not forget that there are many kinds of source. These are often divided into five groups.

1 **Physical evidence** The built landscape; surviving canals, roads, bridges, etc.
2 **Written evidence** From printed books to graffiti; from learned publications to local newspapers.
3 **Pictorial evidence** Sketches, paintings, maps, photographs, films; in all cases, both amateur and professional.
4 **Artefacts** Any objects, from flint implements to half a modern teacup buried in a landfill site; or a 50-ton quayside crane.
5 **Oral evidence** Recent memories; sound recordings (which may date from as far back as the 1860s, so in theory they could carry the voices of people born late in the eighteenth century). Even local traditions and football crowd chants are kinds of oral evidence. To this group **eye-witness evidence** is often added.

The picture you build up will use several of these evidence types, each one hopefully helping to confirm some of the others and adding new information. Because many records are to be found in the same place, however, here are some general comments on where to find them.

Where is the evidence?

The first record type – the landscape – as well as being all around us, is also well described in the written literature. We can therefore concentrate first on the location of documentary evidence.

In England and Wales, over a period of time, many records were collected together, ultimately into the care of County Record Offices. Thus Quarter Sessions records, for instance, joined parish registers, called in from the thousands of superbly made parish chests, many of which survive. (Henry VIII had required the construction of such chests in 1538, to protect the registers and other documents that his new legislation required parishes to keep.) The records were checked, catalogued, repaired and then properly housed.

County Record Offices (CROs) exist across the country, and many large cities have an equivalent. Local record offices, often outposts of the CROs, carry duplicates of the main records as microfilms and microfiches covering their own areas. They also house good selections of printed records, and originals of more ephemeral local documents.

Another name for 'records' is 'archives'. Some English counties call the places where documents are stored 'County Record Offices' whilst others called them 'Local Study Centres'. In all of them the public have a right of access. In Scotland and Ireland much of the archival material will be found in the national Record Offices.

Each county and large city also has collections of vital sources for the local historian with a special interest. Almost every subject you may choose to study has a society associated with it. These are extremely diverse (from places to place names, occupations to pastimes), and will be important in your research, especially local history societies and family history societies. They are not only likely to hold their own records, but they will consist of members who will be useful contacts. Your local reference library will have a list of such groups.

Another whole range of material will be held by your local, county and regional museum services – not just artefacts, but much reference material as well. Almost every museum holds huge collections that are displayed to the public only when specialist exhibitions are mounted. So ask about your particular interest.

Do not overlook local art galleries. As well as keeping large collections of pictures, they too will hold many books of reference. From time to time they will hold thematic public exhibitions. There are publications which list forthcoming showings. Again, ask at your local gallery or tourist information bureau.

Finally, do not underestimate the expertise of the staff in such places as tourist information bureaux and Citizens Advice Bureaux, who can often give useful leads.

Any of these sources may hold a vital piece of evidence for you.

Preparations

Most repositories keep detailed catalogues, so you should plan visits carefully. Browsing in such places can be fascinating, but may easily side-track you!

Staff are friendly and helpful, but often busy. You may need to make an appointment to see the smaller and more specialist collections. Some collections only open at certain times, for many are run by amateurs. You may also need to book a microfilm reader.

Before going to the library or Record Office (RO) you have chosen, think about the evidence you need. Which source is the best starting point: parish records? censuses? births/deaths? What are you actually looking for? What surrogates might also be helpful? Were any unexpected sources used by earlier researchers into your subject?

Having established contact with the collection and worked out what is held (by asking staff and looking at catalogues), take a few moments to plan your time. When do they close? What time does your train go? How is the library and RO laid out? Would it be best to use a first visit to plan for later, longer ones?

Microform

Increasingly, original records are being photographed in reduced size, then stored away from public access. Once technical equipment had been developed it was much better to let the public use the copies.

Using powerful and precision equipment, original material can be reduced such that 10,000 pages of original can be stored on one microfiche card, and whole volumes can be reduced onto a single microfilm reel.

Practical tips

Microfiche readers
When putting the fiche back, note the **fiche number** is usually printed in quite large figures on the label. It is often easier to find the right place to return your fiche to using this number sequence than to sort by reading a series of words. Don't forget to switch the fiche reader off as you leave!

Microfilm readers
There are several types of reader, but all run the film from left to

right. Power readers are often self-threading. Poke the loose tail of film into the first pair of rollers, and press a 'load' button; the reader does the rest of the threading for you.

If the image is upside down or in mirror writing ask for help: the film is loaded incorrectly. It may also be at right angles to your viewing position. In this case, the whole carriage – lenses, reels and all – usually rotates to achieve the position you need.

The content of the films should be fully described on their boxes, and the first few frames on the film inside will carry a title. Check that you are looking at what you intend, and see how it has been paginated. Since microfilms may contain several documents, each with its own page numbers, such films probably have their own sequences of pagination, which are likely to be the ones used in cataloguing them. After a few moments study, you will be able to speed through the film to the right place, before slowing down to examine the image frame by frame.

Picturing the evidence

As you compile your own research material, acquire copies of as many pictures and maps as you can. Do not underestimate your own photographic and sketching skills, though. If you cannot get a photocopy, it is better to have a rough record in your files.

Further research

After a useful period of searching, your notebooks (one for information, one for a record of sources and one for books etc. to be consulted) should contain not only primary and secondary information, but ideas to follow up. Books you consult may mention other books, and magazine articles, as useful sources together with examples of places to visit, things to look at and people to see. Note down as much information as possible about such references. For written material note as a minimum the author, title (books, papers, journals), date, publisher and a brief summary of what the source contains.

Identification

It is just as important to include details of records which did not yield the information you hoped. This will save you searching records twice. So keep a note of all the records you search; a sentence or two saying what the record contains may be useful information to you later.

Finally, don't forget to **label** and **date** everything, and record the **place** where your evidence was found.

Types of source

Built environment

The most obvious evidence that survives all round us are buildings. It is often useful to note the size of settlements and their boundaries, the features that join them (roads, canals and railways), and many miscellaneous features, from milestones and manhole covers to weirs and warehouses.

Questions you might ask include the following.

- Why is this feature here and not over there? For example, what is this milestone doing by a track side running through the middle of a wood?
- Why does the structure face the way it does? Buildings not parallel to a road or boundary may suggest an earlier line.
- Why does the road bend here? Did it curve to avoid something? Was it part of a settlement's defences?
- Why is there a ditch here? Was it a defence or a boundary?

Central to the study of buildings is their date. Furthermore, since almost every building will have been altered over the years, one must learn to recognise and date different features – windows, bricks, chimneys and so on. It is beyond the scope of this book to give details of building types; there are many general books on architecture and some are listed in the bibliography.

Built features which have now disappeared may still be detectable underground in some form or other.

- Mounds and dips in the ground, perhaps detected by aerial photography.
- Crop marks (see Figure 2.1).
- Foundations revealed in a workman's trench.
- Evidence of other kinds brought to light during an archaeological excavation: post-holes, rubbish pits and fireplaces, for example.

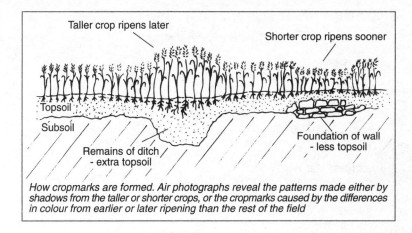

Taller crop ripens later

Shorter crop ripens sooner

Topsoil

Subsoil

Remains of ditch - extra topsoil

Foundation of wall - less topsoil

How cropmarks are formed. Air photographs reveal the patterns made either by shadows from the taller or shorter crops, or the cropmarks caused by the differences in colour from earlier or later ripening than the rest of the field

Figure 2.1 How crop marks occur

Evidence may be domestic or industrial, and it may reveal the presence of moats, fishponds, sluices, water supplies (see Figure 2.2), or drains.

Figure 2.2 Channel for Sir Walter Raleigh's Plymouth water supply in the hills above the city

Exploring sites

POINTS TO CONSIDER

Permission
- **Always** ask the landowner before exploring private land.
- **Never** use a metal detector without the landowner's permission; you will not be allowed to use one at all on a scheduled site.
- Agree with the landowner about things you may find: what you may keep; what must be reported to the police to establish if it is Treasure Trove or not; and what must be turned over to the owner.

Searching
- Never dig on any archaeological site, whether it is being dug professionally or not, unless given written instructions to do so by an archaeologist present on site.
- Never disturb crops or animals.
- Always leave sites exactly as you found them.

Finding
- Whatever you find on private land belongs to the landowner (or the Crown), even if you have received permission to search.
- If you find relatively trivial things (pottery, bottles, buttons, etc.) you will probably be able to keep them (but see below).
- Findings should be reported to the County Archivist, even if not found on a known site, and not apparently of value. It may indicate a previously unrecorded site. This is not mere bureaucracy but safe guarding the past for the future.
- If you find more important artefacts (single coins, jewellery other than gold or silver, etc.), the landowner may wish to keep them or sell them.
- If you find gold or silver it is subject to a coroner's inquest to establish if it is Treasure Trove – valuables which were deliberately hidden rather than just lost. If the court rules that it is Treasure Trove, it belongs to the Crown, and will probably go to a musuem. The finder will be given an *ex gratia* payment to the value of the object. However, the law relating to treasure is about to change, so see below also.
- You must by law report any possible Treasure Trove to the police, who will see that it is brought before a coroner. It is also a good idea to inform your local museum of anything you find.

The 1996 Treasure Act

Under the new Act (which came into force during 1997), 'Treasure Trove' is redefined as 'Treasure'. A coroner's court must still decide what is Treasure, but some of the definitions have been changed. The following are all classed as Treasure:

- objects less than 300 years old which would have been classified as Treasure Trove
- two or more gold coins (ten or more silver ones) if they are found together (the ideas of objects being 'hidden' or 'lost' are dispensed with)
- any objects other than those with a gold content of 10% or more
- any objects deemed by the act to be of 'outstanding historical, archaeological or cultural importance'
- objects not otherwise classified as Treasure may be ruled to be so if they are found with items which are Treasure.

Finally, it is a criminal offence for the finder not to report anything found to the coroner within 14 days.

In Scotland, all finds of ancient objects belong to the Crown, whatever their material.

Written evidence

We have selected a shortlist of 21 written records. These are described briefly in alphabetical order. Our chosen sources are those most commonly found and the ones offering the best clues to help build up a good general background. There is, however, an extensive literature describing sources, and we have space to mention only a few of them. See the Further Reading list at the end of this book for some helpful books to continue such descriptions. (Many further references will be cited in these books' bibliographies.)

Apprentice records *(1710–1811)*

Indentures (so called because the documents were cut in a toothlike wavy line, one half being held by the apprentice and the other by the master) covered the terms of agreement by which masters taught girls or boys their trade. A stamp duty was imposed, which was why the records were originally kept. The Society of Genealogists holds a large collection of these records.

Problems
No examples in your area, or examples are outside the date-range of your research.
Value
Between 1710 and 1750, the fathers' names of apprentices were recorded. All indentures gave apprentices' names and addresses, and

masters' names and trades. From these one may be able to piece together information on migration, the balance of trades, and much about how a trade was learnt.

Censuses *(summary data, every 10 years, from 1801 to date.)*

Note: *only some data were collected in 1941. Details about individual people are available from 1841 to 1891 (a new census is released after 100 years have passed). In Ireland detailed information on people is available for 1901 and 1911 – virtually all previous census material has been lost.* Prior to 1851 local clergy collected information, which after processing was published as summary totals. In 1841 local clergymen collected the data, but from 1851 an enumerator was centrally appointed for each town district of about 200 houses, or country area with a total distance to cover of about 15 miles. Censuses have been taken in the spring since 1851, (in 1841 the census was carried out in June, but missed many people who were sleeping rough). Forms had to be completed by householders, with or without help from the enumerators, the questions varying from year to year. The enumerators then took their household forms, and copied them into books, adding up various totals as they did so. These books were then returned to the Registrar General's office in London, where they were checked and their data extracted. Checking resulted in some classification corrections; and certain categories were ticked off as they were extracted; these operations explain the 'crossing out' found on the records available to us today. See also 'Surveys'.

Problems
There are such a lot of data that extracting particular details can be laborious work. Enumerators' handwriting sometimes needs getting used to. Birth parishes are sometimes difficult to identify.
Value
A huge body of material including (for the 1851–1891 period) personal and some place names, relationships, occupation details, ages, birth places, and more besides.

Churchwardens' accounts *(16th century)*

Note: *the office of churchwarden is medieval; the records date mostly from the sixteenth century.* Two, or four, representatives of the parish were elected annually by the vestry. (The vestry was originally any parishioners who chose to attend a church meeting. Later, when the vestry had greater financial responsibilities, the larger landowners owned the right to more votes at vestry meetings than ordinary people.) The CRO is the place to go to for these records.

Problems
The handwriting may be difficult. (This, as with many problems, can be overcome by consulting a good textbook, see Further Reading.)
Value
As churchwardens were in charge of many things – the parish's property, the upkeep of the church fabric, accounting for the spending of the church rate (money levied by the church on land owned in the parish), being responsible for the control of vermin, and so on – these detailed account books give a rich picture of daily life. They include details of vagrants, for example, the provision of arms and attempts to discover the fathers of illegitimate babies.

Civil registers *(from 1 July 1837 in England and Wales; from 1855 in Scotland; and from 1864 to 1921 in Ireland, 1921 onwards in Northern Ireland)*

Note: *some overseas records predate the above, see below. Registration of adoptions began in 1927.* All births, marriages and deaths had to be registered; though for the first few years in England and Wales there was no actual penalty for not registering; also a fee had to be paid. Inevitably, in this early period some gaps exist. Local registrars entered details in their books (as they do now), and once a quarter these books were copied and sent to the General Record Office (GRO), where indexes were made. Today, you can see these indexes at the GRO, and increasingly on microfiche at large libraries; or you can consult the local registrar's own indexes. Copies of the certificates can be bought from either source. Scottish records, now computerised, are available in New Register House, Edinburgh. Irish records are somewhat scattered, and contact should be made with the heritage centres being developed throughout Ireland, and the Ulster Historical Foundation. All registry offices charge search fees.

Problems
A few events slipped through the net in early years but not many.

Until penalties were introduced for non-registration, poorer people may have been tempted not to register. Indexes group surnames by registration district, so a large scale map may be needed when place-names do not appear to tie up.

Value
Certificates give details enabling studies of families (the building blocks of communities) to be built up. Records of those born, married or died overseas including armed service families – some dating from the late eighteenth century – are held. Even the indexes can supply a certain amount of information.

Court rolls *(from Saxon times through to the middle ages and later in England and Scotland)*

Courts leet and Courts baron were the means used by landowners to rule their communities. They made decisions on land successions, the way the common fields were managed, the interaction between the lord and the people, the administration of frankpledge (whereby each member of a tithe stood security for the good behaviour of the other nine), and many other matters. The rolls are the records of these court judgements. The National Register of Archives publishes a list of records held by County Record Offices and elsewhere. In Scotland the Scottish Record Office (SRO) will be able to help.

Problems
The rolls were in Latin until 1732, and the handwriting may be difficult to read. Modern translations are the best option. (Consult such books as Eileen Gooder's *Latin for Local History*).
Value
The range of coverage is wide, and contains many interesting human reports, often covering the activities of quite ordinary people.

Directories *(1677 to date in London and later throughout the British Isles)*

Early trade lists were alphabetical by name, with trade details following the names; this style was used for small communities and is often only to be found in county directories. In towns, such lists were later augmented with trade-by-trade lists. Information also given includes general data about the place; its services (churches, schools, postal arrangements, etc.) and a so-called 'court' directory of the wealthier inhabitants. Street-by-street lists of house occupiers were given for most towns by the middle of the nineteenth century. In addition to the lists, there are usually several pages of advertisements.

Problems
The information is neither as complete nor as accurate as it might appear. Early directories do not necessarily list every business; and the individuals given are only the heads of households. Inclusion in one year's directory is likely to have been collected the year before. Watch for street-name changes.
Value
Groups of trades show the specialisations of an area; advertisements give a wealth of colourful description. Street lists are a check on town boundaries and development.

Domesday book *(1086 for England excluding the present northernmost counties)*

In the winter of 1085, King William I ordered a survey of land in England. Commissioners were sent out during 1086 (a second set following the first as a check), and were required to ask about 20 very specific questions. These were to be put to a preselected and particular group of people: the Sheriff; the barons and their French tenants; the priests, the reeves, and six villagers from each village. The results were collected and transcribed into two books (*Little Domesday* covers East Anglia, while *Great Domesday* covers most of the rest of England.) The original transcripts are held in the Public Record Office, but modern reprints are available cheaply.

Problems
Not all places were covered: some were exempt, some counties (the northernmost ones) were not in England at all at the time. The transcription of some returns was either not done, or have not survived. The language used was Latin, and heavily abbreviated at that. Moreover, the scribes were Norman, and many of their questions were asked of Anglo-Saxons, so some mistakes must have been made just from hearing the answers incorrectly.
Value
The questions to be asked were: The name of the place? Who held it before 1066? Who holds it now? How many hides? (In other words, What is its area? See Glossary.) How many ploughs does the land support? How many people (of various ranks)? How much woodland,

meadows and pasture? How many mills and fishponds? Have the borders changed? What is the total value? Has that value increased since 1066? Is there potential for a greater value?

Inventories *(1529 to mid-18th century in England)*

Probate inventories are lists of goods owned by a deceased person, with an idea of their value. The inventory had to be approved by the court proving the will, with which it is usually kept. Four 'honest persons' – normally neighbours of the deceased – worked their way round the house, listing everything they considered to be of value. Inventories are today found in CROs, and may usually be photocopied. (A different system operated in Scotland, and inventories were not made in Ireland.)

Problems
Handwriting from this period is difficult, but one gets used to it.
Value
Since the neighbours' idea of what should be listed probably reflected their own sense of what was important, a very good picture of how quite ordinary people lived can be built up. Often the record is divided room by room, adding the extra information of how people lived in their houses.

Memorial inscriptions *(14th century to 20th century)*

Note: *from about the fourteenth century to the seventeenth centuries memorials are found on brasses; from the seventeenth century: on gravestones and memorial plaques inside churches; after major conflicts: on war memorials; at various dates: on tablets on buildings.* At one extreme, wealthy people could afford lavish memorials, often including their own worldly achievements. At the other, most of the poor could not afford a proper burial, let alone a permanently inscribed stone. Many larger buildings have foundation stones, or dates, initials, etc. on stones set in the wall, or on the hoppers at the top of gutter downpipes. Keep your eyes open for other memorial plates, which may be found almost anywhere (a monument to a violent death by the roadside; the dedication of an altar screen, for example).
Problems
Dates on buildings should be treated with caution: they may remember a conversion or rebuilding rather than an original date. The context

may be enough to make this obvious. (However, nobody is likely to have used a totally meaningless date, so make careful notes, take sketches or pictures and check the evidence from other sources.)

Value

Use the evidence as a detective would, building up a set of alibis. (This building was definitely here in 1752, but that one over there was not built or converted until 1820; was there anything else here at those dates?) The value of information such as names or initials, let alone particular pieces of information, is obvious. A memorial stone at Wattisham, near Ipswich, Suffolk, refers the reader to a report in the *Transactions of the Royal Society* for 1762. The pages of that journal reveal not just the sad story of a very poor country family, but the tracking down of the deadly disease which had afflicted them. See the section 'Rich and Poor' in Chapter 5.

Newspapers *(provincial papers: a limited number until 1855; national papers: The Times from 1788; others: 1896 onwards)*

Note: *broadsheets are available from particular periods such as the Civil War, elections, etc.* Only a few newspapers existed before 1855, when the stamp duty of up to 4d (perhaps £2 today) on newspapers was repealed. One of the earliest was the *Belfast Newsletter*, founded in 1737 and which continues to the present time. Lists of papers that survive are published. The format of most papers remained fairly standard through the eighteenth century, with local news restricted to the last page. Reporting normally covered the gentry, who largely represented the readership. By the early nineteenth century, births, marriages and deaths were being grouped together, and more details were given about all levels of society. Papers dated from 1801 are held at the British Library's national collection in Colindale, north London; earlier papers in their main library in central London. The National Libraries of Wales (Aberystwyth) and Scotland (Edinburgh) house their collections.

Problems

Finding your area has no extant local paper for your period is frustratingly common. Locating the particular evidence you seek in a local paper may be time consuming (but it is rewarding, since it helps to build up your overall picture of the communities it describes). Watch out for bias and inaccuracy in reporting.

Value

If your research involves a nationally important event (like a state visit or an air raid) the local paper will naturally go into much more detail than the national press has room for. Even middle-class weddings may give full guest lists and their relationships to the couple. Don't overlook the letters page, which will include personal experiences as well as comments on weightier issues. Advertisements are a mine of information on housing, staff and services.

Overseers' accounts (1555 to 1925, England)

These records are of the expenditure made by those responsible for looking after the poor, and the highways. Overseers of the poor took over the monastic duties of the collector, who was responsible for raising money to look after those who could not work. The overseers relieved those who were born in the parish or who held settlement documents allowing them to live there. Their account books give details not only about the poor, but until 1834 expenses of running the workhouse, and some general parish schemes to provide work (such as road widening, or putting men to work digging fields instead of ploughing them). From 1555 (Highways Act) citizens were required to give their actual labour for the repair of parish roads. By the middle of the 1600s, the wealthy could made a payment instead, or pay someone else to turn up in their place. The 1835 act abolished the call for physical labour from everyone, and commuted it to a set charge. The overseers (or surveyors) of the highway were annually elected parishioners who had to check roads three times a year, and then had the unenviable job of organising repair work. Enquire at the CRO for local holdings.

Problems

Your area may have poor records or none at all.

Value

Details, however fragmentary, about the poorest section of society are always hard to find. Those who contribute to such funds are at the richer end, but details about them are always useful too.

Parish registers (from 1538)

The 1538 Act required Anglican priests to keep records in lockable chests to be provided for the purpose. (Roman Catholic registers date from 1563.) Copies of the records were made at regular intervals and sent to the diocesan records. These bishops' transcripts are vital cross references for the registers themselves. Details often vary, the difference frequently representing extra information given in the transcripts. The main registers were kept as single sheets, until the stipulation of a properly bound book (1598), and ultimately separate registers for baptisms, marriages and burials (1812). Nonconformist registers date from the late seventeenth century and banns registers from 1754. Registers can usually be accessed locally in the CRO or reference library; but a huge number of births (and some marriages) have been extracted by the Mormons and are accessible (in the same places) in the form of the International Genealogical Index (IGI). In Scotland these registers are in the SRO.

Problems
There are gaps in the records, especially in the early years. The Civil War period disturbed some parishes more than others. Watch out for dates, especially for calendar changes from 1752. In that year, New Year's Day was transferred to its present date from 25 March, and in September, 11 days were removed from the calendar, so that 1 September was followed by 12 September. Some records may be Latinised. Remember too, that the recorded baptism and burial records are not births and deaths, although as time passed, records of these events were added to the required details.

Value
Changes to the population (by addition, and subtraction through births, marriages, deaths and migration) can be traced in these registers. Interesting studies of family lives can also be generated from the records themselves: finding out preferred names, days and dates for baptisms and marriages, average ages of the marriage, etc.

Poll books *(1696–1868 as poll books; thereafter as electoral rolls)*

Poll books listed people eligible to vote, street by street, and recorded how they actually voted (secret polls only began in the mid-1800s). They may be consulted in CROs and reference libraries, and large collections are held by the Institute of Historical Research (University of London), the British Library, and the Guildhall and Bodleian Libraries.

Problems
Availability for your area of study. Also remember the restrictions on

who was entitled to vote (for example, until 1832 the eligibility varied from place to place; after that date only some male landowners could vote until later in the century; and women were not enfranchised until the twentieth century). Most people are not in these records.

Value

Although restricted, these listings give useful confirmation of who lived where and when, and give an indication of their politics.

Quarter Sessions records *(1361–1889, England)*

These are the records of the highest provincial civil courts, to which magistrates and assize courts referred the more serious cases for trial. They do not cover crime alone (for which they could award punishments that included transportation and death), but also the issuing of various licences required by taxation systems through the ages (e.g. alehouses and gamekeepers), and various transactions relating to the upkeep of roads, bridges, and so on.

Problems

Availability and completeness in your area.

Value

The records are so varied that almost any entry that happens to relate to the area you are studying could be most helpful, giving details of names, places, sums of money, etc.

Sasines *(1617 on, Scotland)*

In Scotland legal transactions covering hereditable property are recorded in the Register of Sasines. They are held in the SRO. Indexes for most parts of Scotland up to 1780 have been published; after that the registers are easier to search.

Problems

You need to know the place where the property was, or you cannot look it up.

Value

Because every transaction is described, sasines provide an unequalled record of details about living as well as deceased people.

School log books *(from 1862)*

Note: *a 50-year rule is imposed by most CROs to preserve personal* *details*. Head teachers were required to make entries, recording not just absences, cautions, illnesses, etc., but also 'ordinary progress'. Local archive offices will hold examples; some schools retain their own. In Scotland many log books are located in both national archives as well as schools. Always check with the nearest primary school established in the late 1870s.

Problems
Not all schools are old enough to have usable records. Not all that are old enough have survived.
Value
Despite being told not to include 'reflections or opinions of a general character', many interesting comments are made. For educational and genealogical studies, they can be a mine of information.

Surveys *(any date)*

'Censuses' are counts of every person in a particular population. 'Surveys' are enquiries made for some particular purpose. They may be complete overviews (like the Domesday survey, or examinations of the population for all of military age), or they may be samples, from which generalisations about the whole population are made.

Problems
A survey of the people you are interested in at a particular date may not be available.
Value
Names of individuals, or trends of behaviour in the community as a whole, may provide useful information for local history studies, provided one takes due note of possible bias in such samples.

Town records *(medieval onward)*

These include civil court records; charters granting rights to the community; details of street improvements and maintenance (e.g. paving after 1836). They may be deposited in CROs, (national record offices in Scotland and Ireland) but may still be held in town halls. Your local reference library will be able to help.

Problems
Early records often produce details about individuals which are only

fleeting glimpses. This information may be little more than frustrating!
Value
Useful references to boundaries, community rules, punishments and
changes in the built environment can be given (e.g. pg.138).

Turnpike trust records *(1663–1888)*

Between 1663 and 1773, individual acts of parliament were required
for major road improvements. After 1773, such road making was covered by one General Turnpike Act, and after 1888 control passed to
county councils. Maps and descriptions of the proposed changes were
published with individual acts. It is also worth checking local newspaper coverage (especially from the 1850s) of meetings and details of
toll-house proceeds sales. CROs usually hold trust records. These are
a more limited feature in Scottish and Irish history.

Problems
Locating the records relevant to your particular area of search.
Value
You may be lucky enough to find a very complete picture of a road
improvement, including objections, suggestions, costs, etc.

Wills *(from 1393 to date)*

These had to be proved before a church court until 1858. Often accompanied by a list of the goods involved (see 'Inventories' above), they
were produced before the local bishop's court (if the property was in his
diocese); or in the relevant archbishop's court (York or Canterbury), if it
was in two or more sees; or in the Principal Probate Registery (PPR) in
London if it lay in both archbishops' provinces, or involved property
abroad. Searching at all three levels is worthwhile, however, because to
appear wealthier than they really were, some people applied to a higher court than was necessary. After 1858, all wills were proved at the
PPR. If the deceased had property but made no will, an administration
(or 'admonition') was sworn. It adds little to one's knowledge of the
deceased, beyond confirming that no will was made. Wills may be
inspected at the PPR. In Scotland the ancient system of proving wills
was through one of 22 commissary courts superseded by the sheriff's
court after 1823. The records are kept at the SRO. In Ireland the system was similar to that of England and Wales, being based on church
dioceses until 1858. The new Principal Registry then took over but the

records were destroyed in a fire in 1922. Varying collections of wills have survived and are located in the national archives in Dublin and the Public Record Office of Northern Ireland.

Problems
Locating wills is the main problem. Sparse details and sometimes difficult handwriting once you have found them. Note that wording such as 'All my plate, pictures, books, glass...' may only be legal language meaning 'everything I have' rather than implying that the deceased actually owned 'silver' or 'pictures'.

Value
A long will (and the longest one ran to many bound volumes!) can be a mine of information. It may relate not just to people's relationships and what they owned, but include addresses, jobs, particular valuable artefacts, and so on.

Workhouse records *(1722–1894 in England; 1838–1894 in Ireland; 1845–1894 in Scotland)*

The Poor Act of 1722 required the overseers of the poor to provide accommodation for the homeless and those who needed parish protection through illness, etc.; and the 1834 Poor Law Amendment Act abolished outdoor relief, but workhouses were made as unpleasant as possible to encourage inmates to find work for themselves. Not every institution was run as harshly as Dickens depicts in *Oliver Twist*, however, but life in the best of them would be considered cruel today. Minute books and accounts are sometimes held by CROs.

Problems
Availability.

Value
Glimpses of the lives of the very lowest stratum of society.

Pictorial evidence

Many written records are illustrated. However, a number of libraries and museums also hold large collections of maps, pictures, photographs and aerial photographs, and films. For example, the photograph collection at the Centre for Oxfordshire Studies contains nearly a quarter of a million images (many being from surrounding counties), though not all are topographical.

Aerial photographs *(1920 onward)*

Following the successful use of aircraft to photograph enemy lines in the First World War, the Ordnance Survey and others were instrumental in systematically recording crop marks. Most of the country has been surveyed in this way, and copies can be bought from Wildgoose Publications and Aerofilms Ltd (see Useful Addresses). Your library and CRO will probably hold local examples. In Scotland the National Monuments Record of Scotland holds a large collection.

Problems
There may be a few gaps in coverage. These photographs are not cheap, and the cost may be quite high if a large area is involved (not least because sites are usually photographed from several angles).
Value
Crop marks and humps in the ground reveal themselves as roads, houses, walls and other features. So tracing settlements or buildings etc. which have apparently disappeared on the ground may be feasible from aerial views.

Film and video *(from 1895)*

Many early films of English subjects, of about two minutes length each, are held by the National Film Archive, and for Scottish subjects the Scottish Film Archive, Glasgow. Some surviving material from this date deal with local subjects. Your museum, library and RO is more likely to hold – or know the location of – useful local examples dating from the 1920s and 1930s.

Problems
Availability and extreme brevity. The identification of unnamed locations may also prove difficult.
Value
Once identification of places, dates and perhaps people is established, changes (or stability) should provide useful evidence.

Maps and plans *(16th century onward)*

County maps (from sixteenth century) were often aerial views, and early ones showed no roads. Estate maps (from c. 1570) may contain accurate field shapes and sizes, but the built landscape may be roughly sketched in and out of scale. Enclosures of open land date from the early 1600s, but most occurred in the period starting in 1760. Maps were produced to establish ownership of newly divided fields. Transport maps and itineraries date from the late seventeenth century. Town plans (from seventeenth and eighteenth centuries) often began by being mere decoration. Ordnance Survey maps (one-inch series from 1801; 6-inch Townland maps in the 1830s in Ireland; 6-inch, 25-inch and 50-inch scales from the late 1850s for the whole of the British Isles) were originally produced by the army. Tithe-award maps from 1836, to effect the commuting to annual payments of the earlier tithe system (itself based upon land ownership and occupation) are the earliest detailed records of many towns.

Problems
Availability; although many maps survive, not every place is represented at every possible period. Changes of name may cause confusion.

Value
As well as the obvious checking of settlement growth, road directions, etc., the names of places, streets, farms and fields for example paint useful word pictures (e.g. on ownership, land use etc.)

Photographs *(1840s onwards)*

Callotypes (1839 invention of Henry Fox Talbot) and Daguerrotypes (mid-1830s in France), and the various improvements which followed, provide invaluable records – with certain reservations. When roll film and more portable cameras were introduced in the late nineteenth century, both hobbyists and professionals increased their output still further. Huge numbers of photographs and postcards on every subject survive (your library, museum, art gallery, will know of local collections), including series on the local landscape.

Problems
Local scenes often contain figures posed by the photographer. In the nineteenth century, exposure times were extremely slow; as a result subjects had to sit or stand in unnatural poses (often with neck braces). Bias in personal, and professional, portraits may not be obvious. Yet the majority of photographs suggest that Britain is a sunny place by the seaside, occupied mostly by very well-dressed people!

Value
Buildings before alteration; customs; work practices, etc.

Pictures *(from about 1600 onward)*

Landscapes developed during the seventeenth and eighteenth centuries, having previously only occurred as (often not very helpful) backgrounds to portraits. Some exceptions can be found, like the Bayeux and similar tapestries. From the eighteenth century, a large number of useful records exists, including some almost systematic series, such as the work of Hogarth. Local paintings will be known to, or held by, art galleries, museums and libraries, and probably the local council. Do not underestimate the value of amateur paintings.

Problems
The availability of subjects in the period of your research; and the suitability of subject matter for your purposes may not be ideal.
Value
As for photographs.

——— Artefacts (any date) ———

Museums may be the obvious place to look for examples of manmade things. But artefacts are everywhere, so keep your eyes open in country houses, shop window displays and friends' houses, for example. Manufacturers of today's equivalents sometimes have collections or catalogues from the past.

Artefacts are any objects made by people, in any age, whether surviving whole or not. Their value to a local history study is obvious, since they represent something made, found or used in your locality. Wherever they come from, artefacts should not be examined by asking 'What is it?' or 'How old is it?'. Instead, investigate its physical features (What is it made of? Is it inscribed? etc.); its construction (Is it machine-made? Is it in several parts? How are they fixed together?); its function (What could it have been used for? Has its use changed?); its design (Is it decorated? Is it well designed?); and its value (What would it be worth when it was made? What about today?)

Problems
The fragment that has survived may be too small to give us many clues. Its use may defy our imagination. Both these problems may be overcome by consulting your local museum.
Value
Provided artefacts are asked the correct questions, for bias and reliability as well as those outlined above, they may provide detailed information about our study period.

Oral evidence

Recordings of oral evidence exist from the 1860s and since some are of people who were elderly then, this means that in theory we have some oral evidence from nearly 200 years ago. Museums and sound archives hold recorded collections, and local radio stations may also have material. Recordings made as part of language studies may contain useful material for local historians. It is usually ordinary folk who retain their dialect longest, and it is their lives which are the most difficult to learn about. In Scotland a major source is to be found at the School of Scottish Studies, University of Edinburgh.

Interviewing people yourself about their lives, now as well as in the past, requires careful planning, but may be extremely rewarding.

Problems
The availability of what you want covering your period; the quality of the recording itself; and words or phrases used may not be known to you. If you are making your own recordings, remember that some people may become confused with the passage of years.

Value
Talking to the right person, using a series of carefully prepared questions and prompts, may result in a unique record. For interviews covering 'technical' subjects, find someone who has the necessary specialist knowledge to ask appropriate follow-up technical questions.

Conclusion

The store of sources is huge and varied. We introduce a few of these – albeit the most commonly found and useful ones. But always bear in mind the points raised in 'General notes'.

- You may need to use a less-than-ideal record to investigate some characteristic.
- You need to get used to varied records and modern technology to consult them.
- Don't forget to keep full and adequate notes.

3
BIRTH TO DEATH

In this chapter we will be considering:

- the concept of change
- how typical our study area is
- measuring the area we are studying
- ways of counting the number of people living in it
- how the population is made up
- births, baptism, marriage, deaths, burial
- migration.

Your local community

As you consider the people in an area, the following are the kinds of question that may occur to you.

- How have the area and population of your community changed over time?
- Are the population level and density of your area typical of the surrounding communities?
- What influences caused population variations between your place and others?
- How did the number of children born to the average family in one age compare with other ages?
- How do average family sizes compare between rich and poor?

Background

Whatever your local study, you must always bear **change** in mind.

Underlying the historian's attempts to reconstruct from single moments in time and place are the differences between those scenes and the ones before and after them. Using such differences, you can see whether your subject society was growing or not.

Sources

A number of sources are useful, including maps, parish and civil registers, censuses, and published statistics, like the 1641/42 Protestation Returns and the Inland Revenue's Land Tax Redemption Quotas of 1798. Histories too play their part, by drawing together other people's work on the subject.

You must consider two ideas in studying your subject area.

1 Is your area typical? How does it compare with its neighbours? The county? The whole country?
2 If it is not typical, what influences have produced this difference?

--------------- **Population** ---------------

You must work out the overall population in your area, its make-up by families and by sex at different ages, and as accurately as possible work out how large the area is. This basic information will help you make statements about how crowded the place was; whether there were more elderly people than the average for a place of its size; how many men and women were of working age, and so on.

At various points in your study it is also a good idea to compare your historical area with its present-day equivalent. Often you will be surprised at the amount of space we seem to need today, and at the average age of the study population compared with the present one.

Area

The starting point is to establish the area of your subject population. This may present little problem if the study is limited to one street, say. Large-scale maps will supply the raw materials, although defining an area in the distant past is not always possible in this way. It may be necessary to fall back on the number of houses or families, from polls, listings, and so on.

Depending on what you are studying, the area may be changing as well as its population. For example, the historian may be looking at 'Sedburgh, North Yorkshire'; 'Irish settlement in eighteenth century Shoreditch, London'; or 'Nonconformist worship in the Sands area of High Wycombe, Buckinghamshire'. In such cases, the boundaries at different ages need to be established in order to derive area.

Take care to check that the boundaries of your area have not been changed artificially, in rationisations such as English county changes in 1974 and others in the 1980s and 1990s. Changes took place in Northern Ireland and Scotland in 1975, and again in Scotland in 1996. For example, many old maps show remnant islands belonging to neighbouring counties within them.

Numbers

Censuses and surveys yield the information you need on absolute population numbers. From the second half of the nineteenth century, good statistics can be drawn from the censuses (except in Ireland between 1841 and 1891), while earlier numbers have to be worked out using various sources.

POINTS TO CONSIDER

If you are using a nineteenth century census, take special note of the first handwritten page of each enumeration book. On this preliminary page the enumerator has written the route he took in taking the census. Draw this out as carefully as you can on to a tracing of a large-scale map nearest in date to the census year, and then on to a modern map. It may not be quite straightforward, because the enumerator could take whatever route he chose in covering his area. He might zigzag down part of one road and then cover a side road before coming back to the first one; or work from one end of a road to the other on both sides like a postman.

Your research may involve more than one book even if you are studying just one street (see Figure 3.1). Suppose you were studying the fictional Cow Lane, your statistics would have to be drawn from part of three books in the 1861 and 1871 censuses. Streets were not numbered in most towns until the mid-1800s.

Producing a total population from a published census may not mean counting every name, however, since each page of an enumeration book is carefully totalled. Also, statistics for parishes, boroughs, etc. have been published as totals since the 1801 census.

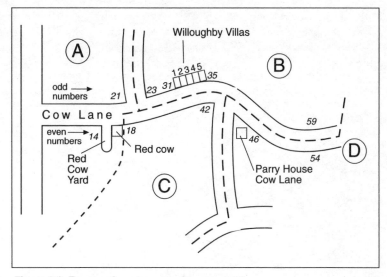

Figure 3.1 Enumeration areas covering one street

Parish registers can also be used to derive a total population, provided suitable account is taken of migration in and out. Studying the numbers added by births/baptisms (and sometimes marriages where one partner is known to have migrated into the area and stayed), and subtracted by deaths, ultimately produces a rough working total.

Directories and surveys often list heads of households (though not necessarily all of them), and approximate total populations can be derived from these if suitable reservations are made. For example, the total population of a place as listed in the 1851 census, say, divided by the total number of households, gives an average unit figure. For example, Figure 3.2 shows how an appropriate population might be derived from several possible statistics.

You need to use methods like these for your area at different dates. Plotting these on a graph will give a fairly good idea of population changes for the 1841–91 census years.

The published census summaries add data for 1801–1991 as far as whole parishes are concerned. Most local reference libraries and CROs will hold printed histories of your area, and the largest of these should contain some approximations about earlier populations. But there will be gaps, and often different figures will be given for the same year.

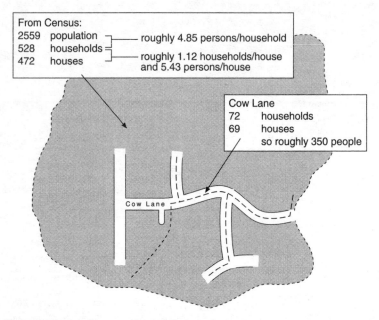

From Census:
2559 population — roughly 4.85 persons/household
528 households =
472 houses — roughly 1.12 households/house
and 5.43 persons/house

Cow Lane
72 households
69 houses
so roughly 350 people

Cow Lane

Figure 3.2 Population statistics for Cow Lane

For earlier periods, individual surveys are often of householders. They may be counting the people religiously inclined in a particular way, such as the protestation returns; or for taxation purposes, such as the land tax quotas; or for military purposes, like the Fawley example quoted in Chapter 2.

Add curves to a graph to represent the populations for the county and the whole country. These are, in effect, 'smoothed' curves for you to compare your figures with. The important element in a graph such as this is the shape of the curve.

Populations rise and fall in most areas of the country, going up when masses move in, and down when they move out. In your area, rises may be caused by a burgeoning industry; by the influx of people due to the process of centralising and urbanisation; by people living longer; or, paradoxically, by private houses becoming slums. Falls may be caused by the ceasing of some trade; by the population moving out due to the process of urbanisation elsewhere; by a slum clearance – to make way for a new park, a by-pass or larger houses.

Population composition

It is not just the overall numbers you need to think about, but how the population was made up. For most populations, the ratio of males to females will be roughly equal. It may not be, and one of your enquiries may need to be: 'Why are there more men than women here?'

By the same token, you also need to consider age groups. Are there more babies than one would expect? Are they equally divided into girls and boys? What about older children? How many of the community are of working age? Are there many more elderly men than one might expect?

A careful analysis of the whole community is needed. Having produced the complete population of your particular area, you must now divide it into age bands. Read other workers' reports on such studies to decide what these age divisions should be. Often, ten-year bands are used, and the results are presented using population trees, which are particularly good ways of comparing populations, since differences show up well; see Figure 3.3.

POINTS TO CONSIDER

Some final thoughts on population; for we need to imagine what our ancestors thought about population.

❝ Be fruitful and multiply, and replenish the earth [with inhabitants to be begotten by you] ❞.

Holy Bible, with annotation by Rev Matthew Poole, (d. 1679)

❝ If world population began with a couple in, say 10,000 BC, and grew at 1% per year, the population today would form a sphere of living flesh round the earth many thousands of light years in diameter, and expanding at a rate many times faster than the speed of light. ❞

Cipolla, quoting Putnam (1950)

It is possible to fit the whole population of the earth on the Isle of Wight.

Popular saying

This last idea was investigated mathematically by the author of *Teach Yourself Basic Maths*, 1995, who proved that, if one could get ten persons into one square metre, the statement is untrue. However, when the saying was first made, it probably was possible.

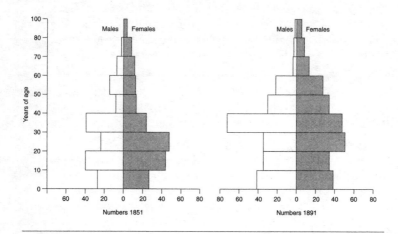

Figure 3.3 Population trees for Cow Lane, 1851 and 1891

While we are about it, there is another anomaly which may have struck you. You have two parents, four grandparents, and so on. In theory over a billion 28-great grandparents related to you were alive at the time of the Norman Conquest. However, since the total population of England was about 1.3 million in the fourteenth century, such a conclusion is manifestly impossible. The answer lies in (relative) immobility.

The further back you go, the less mobile populations can have been. This means that families lived relatively close to each other. It is the resulting cousins marrying cousins which provides the solution to the paradox.

— The factors affecting population —

Four factors affect population:

- additions by birth
- additions by in-migration
- subtractions by deaths
- subtractions by out-migration.

Civil and parish registers are our sources for these statistics, but it is not just a question of numbers. Ages at marriage and death are important too.

Marriage

In theory, women can bear children for about 30 years. In practice, from a physiological point of view, the ideal age range is probably the 14 years between 22 and 35. Pressures from society and day-to-day living (largely financial) have tended to push the age of marriage up. For example, in the 200 years between the sixteenth and eighteenth centuries, the average age of first marriages rose about three years in noble and well-to-do families, and was actually higher in the lower classes.

Studying marriage registers by themselves can yield interesting data on overall numbers; but by combining this with baptism/birth and burial/death registers, figures can be put together on family size and the gaps between children. Remarriage after a partner's death is another factor to be investigated.

Until the civil registers began (in 1837 in England, 1855 in Scotland, and 1864 in Ireland), details given in parish registers gradually increased, until from 1812 a standard format was introduced, (see Chapter 2).

The data given on certificates after 1837, however, are matched in their detail by only a handful of parish registers before that date. The basic information on marriage registers has not changed since 1837. Researchers in Scotland will find more information on certificates than will their counterparts in England.

Tomorrow's historians will find life more complicated when they study today's marriage practices. While some couples have always lived together without getting married, the number increases every year (with or without children). Many genealogists will be able to confirm that in the past some first-born children arrived before their parents got married; the difference today, though, is that unmarried couples who decide to have families often stay unmarried. Problems over naming, parenthood and length of partnerships are just some of the extra complications future historians will meet.

Divorce

Before 1857 to get a divorce meant applying for a special act of parliament. Naturally, this was out of the question for most people, who either continued to live together in disharmony, or simply separated.

In the period 1858 to 1887 over 7,000 divorces were granted in England; by contrast in the twenty years from 1867 to 1886 the number exceeded 320,000. Only recently has divorce become relatively easy, and thus so widespread in the United Kingdom.

Births

Most early societies required sons to inherit and daughters to provide for old age. The importance of sons is shown on medieval English monuments and in wills, for example. Here sons and daughters are grouped together, with even infant youngest sons taking precedence over older sisters.

As medicine improved survival in the nineteenth century, the need for large families reduced somewhat.

POINTS TO CONSIDER

It is easy to lose sight of real people when studying registers and their totals. One does well to remember that a child's death was as poignant and distressing to families in the past as it is today.

Parish registers do not mention births as such until 1644, since they are essentially church records of baptisms. From that date, however, birth dates were to be included, along with details of both parents.

Deaths

In parish registers, age at death was not required until 1813. Before that, the record was not of death but of burial. (One important difference between the births/baptisms question and that of deaths/burials, is that burial must be undertaken within a few days, whereas baptism can happen at any age, or not at all.)

Civil registers give an address and a cause of death; parish registers only the parish name, though extra details are to be found in many registers, where incumbents felt expansive. Usually these were restricted to odd statements: 'a traveller' or 'a soldier'. Occasionally, though, a register may be found which yields most rewarding general information.

Migration

Inexperienced genealogists often hope to trace their ancestors' origins back to one remote rural parish, making a study of the registers a simple matter. Life is seldom so simple: populations moved!

It is instructive to compare the family names when studying an area with those of another date. You will find that, after 100 years or so, a large number of surnames present in the earlier list will have disappeared. After 200 years almost all the surnames are different. Note, too, that comparisons like this are not saying 'A particular family called "Grant" has moved'. They are actually saying that where the surname Grant was present at one date, no families at all of that name were present at the later date.

So, where are in-coming names from, and where are out-going ones off to? The answers to these questions are many and varied, and there is no simple formula. Some useful ideas, however, are as follows.

- The surname may have died out. This is a statistically sound statement, not just a vague idea. Only a few women marry men of their own surname, all the others will have families with different surnames. Among the men, a number will not marry and some of those that do may not have children for one reason or another.
- In the past, probably most families on the move will have gone only into a nearby parish, rather than moving long distances in one go.
- Marriage may account for some movement. A bride often goes to her husband's parish; a new husband may move in to look after his in-law's business.
- A specialist trade may draw people in from (or push them out to) quite distant places. For example, established railway towns supplied specialist workers for new railway towns.
- Lack of work probably accounted for more moves than any other reason. This will have led to in-migration as well as out-migration, both permanent and seasonal.
- The need for merchant sailors and the recruitment of armed forces must also have occasioned moves in the past.

One can analyse the reason for migrations into two categories, which might be described as:

1 Betterment migration: involving many unmarried men, travelling long distances to places like America from Ireland.
2 Subsistence migration: often involving whole families travelling relatively short distances.

How, then, can you check? There are ways, though they may be laborious to follow through.

- Families which die out will be exhibiting a strong reduction of numbers over a period of time. You may find evidence of males dying in childhood, for example; of a whole crop of daughters being born, rather than the 50:50 ratio you might expect.

- Families which move (in and out) must come from (and go) somewhere. Checking all nearby parish records may reveal them. Often the drift is towards a nearby town or city.

- From 1754, banns registers were introduced for Anglicans. Provided these survive for your area, a study may show the missing names, for banns must be said in both the bride's and groom's parish churches. If marriages are by licence, these too will state both parishes.

- From 1851, census records state parishes of birth as well as trades. By plotting the parishes of birth of parents and children, a rough guide to the in-migration results.

- Studying the local trades before a family 'disappears' will establish any specialist work that went on in your area. If one of those trades ceases at about the same time as the family leaves, at least you may have a clue as to what they may have done to earn their living. A study of nearby places may then reveal that particular trade increasing (if you are lucky), perhaps suggesting where your 'missing' people might have gone to. Unfortunately, however, most people were 'ag. labs.' or 'lacemakers', which means you need to fall back on checking nearby parish records instead.

- Court records of transportations do exist, as do those of the army and navy.

- Shipping lists give the names of emigrants. Often the best sources for these are the genealogical societies in the country of destination of the emigrants.

In considering the number of people in the community you are studying, it is essential to bear migration in mind, as well as births and deaths. Like changes in the age at marriage and of bearing first-born children, length of life, etc., it affects the make-up of the whole community you are researching.

4

TOWN AND COUNTRY

In this chapter we will consider the following:

- a background history of the countryside
- a background history of towns
- finding evidence of your community's history
- studying the effect of a significant event in your community
- studying changes in your community.

— The countryside: background —

The British countryside can yield evidence of thousands of years of occupation. The changes wrought to the rural landscape have been many with most of the landscape in England in particular less than 1,500 years old.

It needs to be remembered that the main reason for changes to the countryside has been the need to make a living. Although some developments are the result of other factors such as increased leisure, agriculture has been the main economic activity for much of this country's history and the main changes largely reflect this.

Early farming

The earliest evidence for farming is not written but goes back at least 5,000 years with scratch marks made by the plough having been found. Life for many people up to 2,500–3,000 years ago was at least semi-nomadic.

Farming seems to have become a little more settled after 500 BC. Surviving evidence can be found of such communities at places such as Chysauster in west Cornwall (English Heritage). Here the inhabitants of the eight surviving houses had both small garden plots and small arable sites. Remains such as this are more prominent in the 'Celtic' parts of the British Isles and in the south and south east.

Gradually cultivation moved from higher ground to the heavier but more fertile soils associated with river valleys. What needs to be remembered though is that the population of the British Isles was so small, even after the Roman conquest. Few serious researchers estimate the population to be more than 1% of the present numbers. It is perhaps not surprising that large swathes existed in the form of marsh and forest.

Roman times and their successors

The Roman landscape is probably better known for its roads than its farming. These main Roman roads opened up access to the heavier and more productive soils. Roman villas represent the country estates and reveal that the Romans continued to clear the landscape. Some of these villas were the centre of large estates with fields and often a corn growing economy.

For many years it was thought that the civilisation created by the Romans was cruelly wiped out by the Anglo-Saxon and Viking people. There is much evidence to suggest that this was not always the case. It is a truism, however, that the vast majority of the countryside in many parts of the British Isles starts to take shape only from the period following the departure of the Romans. The majority of names of settlements emanate from this period. It was in the years between the fifth and eleventh centuries that villages sprung up of different sizes and shapes.

The period is also associated with the formation of the large open field system often with two or three large fields divided into elongated strips. Occasionally open field system survivals can be found such as those at Laxton in Nottinghamshire but heavily altered. Other remains are the ridges and furrows formed by frequent ploughing of the strips although it cannot be assumed that all ridges and furrows are of this antiquity.

Further changes were taking place. Huge swathes of woodland were being cleared, fenlands reclaimed, isolated farmsteads and hamlets were appearing and village organisation was becoming more structured. Understanding of the countryside in this period can be helped by written evidence such as Saxon land charters, many of which have been published. The Vikings from the late ninth century also continued to clear forests in new areas, establish farmsteads and found some villages.

The medieval period

After 1066 the structure of the English countryside became more organised and one of the effects of this was an increase in documentation. This is of great assistance to the local historian.

Perhaps the best known of this new documentation is the *Domesday Book* (1086) which provides the earliest detailed account of the villages, land ownership and economy for estates in many parts of the countryside.

Such sources reveal a population that was still minute by today's standards. East Anglia was the most densely settled part of the kingdom but, even here, there were probably an average of fewer than 50 people to the square mile. Many parts of the countryside still remained unclaimed at the time of the Domesday Book although the improvement to moors, marshes and fens continued apace in medieval times. Moreover, most villages that exist today had appeared by 1086.

Although there were many variations, most villages farmed land on strips in large open fields, often doing labour service on the lord's land (demesne) although this was often commuted to money payments in the later middle ages. There were, however, regional variations. Villages and communities became more organised with regular courts, land transfer procedures, by-laws and licences enforced by elected or chosen officers. Books on estate management advised on husbandry.

Although in law many of the villagers were legally unfree, this did not always indicate economic poverty. There were extremely wealthy people who were technically of unfree status. Others faced appalling poverty struggling to produce enough to feed their families.

There were periods of especial hardship such as the great famine of 1315. The problems of the rural village were compounded by the great plagues and pestilences of which the Black Death of 1349 was the best known and probably the most cataclysmic event to hit the British Isles, but it was not an isolated occurrence. Epidemics of plague caused serious depopulation of towns and villages.

However, it was not all a time of gloom and doom. The eleventh to the fifteenth centuries provide many examples of rural prosperity although it did not affect everyone equally. In corn and wool growing areas the evidence provided by the splendid churches and buildings shows that at least some were doing extremely well. Elsewhere there is plentiful evidence of woodland, marsh, fen and moor clearances.

The sixteenth to eighteenth centuries

Amongst the greatest landowners were the churches, especially the monastic communities: the great Cistercian and other religious estates in places such as Rievaulx and Fountains.

The big sixteenth century development was the enclosure of land. This was partly a response to new demand: population was rising after the declines of the middle ages. Not all of the enclosure was of the large open fields. Some was direct from woodland but its effect was still enormous in many areas: some counties such as Devon were left with hardly any large open fields by the end of Tudor times.

The reason for enclosure was nearly always to accommodate sheep for there were large profits to be made from the wool trade. Landlords continued this enclosure process for much of the seventeenth century. It is a pervasive myth that the present landscape of enclosed fields dates from the nineteenth century. In many areas, the enclosure movement was well advanced by the seventeenth century.

There were other effects due to the sixteenth century enclosures, notably a certain amount of disruption, depopulation and movement to towns. The houses of many of the rural dwellers were rebuilt with the result that very few surviving cottages are older than this period. Many villages were also rebuilt in this period, the result both of prosperity and a desire for more privacy than that afforded by medieval buildings. The countryside also saw the escalation in construction of the great stately homes with their accompanying parklands.

Although much enclosure occurred prior to the late eighteenth and nineteenth centuries, that does not mean it did not also happen at that time. On the contrary, thousands of parishes were affected after 1750, largely for corn rather than sheep to feed a rapidly expanding population. Those later centuries saw the use of parliamentary acts, rather than simple agreements, to regulate enclosure and these acts are an indispensable source of information on life in the countryside.

The nineteenth and twentieth centuries

Historians disagree on whether the small farmer was really the loser by these enclosures. Although there was extensive migration and many poor country people suffered, it is not true to state that many rural areas emptied. Many actually grew but at a much slower rate than the new industrial towns.

In some places, however, the rural population was significantly reduced. The Highland clearances and the Irish potato famines are the best known examples but it happened on a small scale in other places.

Yet the adverse social effects on large numbers of rural dwellers went hand in hand with improved efficiency. These were the days of enthusiastic landlords and scientific developments which improved livestock, crop yields and agricultural implements. The industrial transformation of the United Kingdom not only produced more mouths to feed but also provided the industrial infrastructure to mechanise farms.

Improved transport opened up opportunities for fresh products such as milk and vegetables from market gardening. Such responsiveness was not enough to prevent much rural poverty in the later nineteenth century, a situation not helped by foreign competition.

The rural inhabitant of 1700 would not have recognised their community 200 years later. New field systems, crops, employment, transport, machinery, cleared forests, hedges and the like and many fewer self-sufficient communities. Differences between the rural community of 1900 and the 1990s are even greater. The decay of country estates, commuter villages, diversification, destruction of hedges, further mechanisation, the decline of rural trades, a situation where farming contributes only a small proportion of the gross national product, destruction of rural areas by new roads, airfields, towns and suburbs, the effect on the landscape for European Community quotas and the like would have been unimagined three generations ago.

Towns: background

Pre-Norman towns

A few towns predated the Romans especially in the south-east of England and were later taken over by Romans on identical or near identical sites. The Romans then founded many more. Although these towns were well laid out with regular street patterns and public buildings, they were relatively unimportant both in the landscape and in terms of population. Roman London was an exception with an area covering over 300 acres.

Not all of these towns survived the Roman period and more soon became derelict following the barbarian invasions. It was not completely moribund, however. Saxon kings such as those in Wessex had fortified 'burhs' and the excavations of Viking York reveal a fairly sophisticated urban life with tradespeople and merchants. Such urban settlement was all on a fairly small scale.

Medieval towns

The *Domesday Book* demonstrates clearly the paucity of urban settlement around the times of the Norman Conquest. Only five places were listed with more than 1000 burgesses.

Thereafter borough development proceeded apace. The twelfth, thirteenth and fourteenth centuries witnessed a large number of charters to establish or re-establish towns often under the control of the king or an important magnate. Some were on virgin sites but others used existing lands. Some developed into successful market towns in later years but many others failed.

The fourteenth century onwards seems to have witnessed the appearance of a host of small urban centres often serving a radius of a few miles, possessing features such as markets and sometimes castles and connected by roads in varying states of repair. The period also saw the growth in importance of seaports especially on the east coast.

A sizeable number of towns went into decline from the mid-fourteenth century often resulting from plague and economic difficulty. The rise of London was phenomenal and it grew into one of the greatest cities in the world.

Industrialisation and urbanisation

By 1851, for the first time, the population in towns was greater than that of the countryside. Many towns grew up without real planning until nineteenth century legislation, especially in the field of public health, improved the situation. A few towns were built as planned towns, for instance Middlesbrough, but many more resulted from the expansion of market towns. Much of the rise was in the north and midlands.

The old image of row upon row of back-to-back houses did indeed characterise many towns along with cellar dwellings, filthy courtyards, appalling sanitation and overcrowding but there were huge variations. Towns of all kinds existed connected with different industries, transport, agriculture, the sea and leisure. Facilities varied but the majority were connected to good transport networks especially railways. Many had trams and buses which facilitated the development of the suburb, a feature which was magnified in the twentieth century. Local government reforms in the nineteenth century often improved civic pride and many became distinctive communities with their own buildings, theatres, hospitals, schools, police forces and the like.

Shops and retailing often followed along with leisure facilities such as parks, sports grounds, pavements, lighting, theatres, music halls and cinemas. The twentieth century has seen major changes. Some have lost populations, inner cities have often decayed, others have become commuter towns. New towns have also grown up. The distinctive styles of 1930s architecture and that for the 1950s and 1960s can be recognised in many urban communities helped by legislation to provide council housing. The rise in home ownership and changes in transport facilities has also altered the nature of urban development. Other recent changes have been the development of retailing, out of town shopping, multiple stores, facilities such as sports centres and, some would argue, urban squalor and poverty existing alongside the gentrification of some parts of towns.

Finding evidence for your community's early history

'What did my local community look like in its earliest days?'

'Earliest days' for many communities are likely to include the period up to the thirteenth century when documentary evidence often increases for many places.

Before Domesday

Before the *Domesday Book*, written information is likely to be severely limited but it does exist. A number of Anglo-Saxon land charters survive giving information about the distribution of land and the rents and services which had to be given to landlords. Their format and style ('diplomatic') is not always easy to follow and there can also be problems with dates and indeed with the accuracy of the boundary clauses.

Place names, not just of communities but sometimes of streets and fields, can also provide you with snippets of information. The volumes of the English Place Name Society can be a mine of useful information and there have been many similar publications.

The bulk of pre-Norman evidence is likely to come from archaeological remains. Clues can also come from historic sites marked on Ordnance Survey maps.

Groups such as Cadw, University archaeological departments and English Heritage have investigated many sites such as Roman towns and Saxon remains. Sometimes, a specialised museum or research unit may have produced extensive documentation.

Starting with Domesday

The real starting point for many investigators may well be the justifiably-famous *Domesday Book*. You can go straight to this source, or at least to the transcribed versions and pose certain questions. Did my community have a local entry? What did it say?

It also provides a mine of information on rural life for a sizable part of the British Isles and you will be greatly helped by both facsimiles and transcriptions of *Domesday Book* entries as well as detailed analyses of different areas of the country. Not all areas of England are covered.

You should note, moreover, that the *Domesday Book* is not the equivalent of a photograph of Norman life. It was almost certainly never envisaged as a full survey of all people; it is largely a tax document listing land subject to geld (tax). It means some land and buildings are excused and it does not list all people. The aims of the survey seem to have been to determine who held the land at the time of the survey, who had held it in 1066, what changes had occurred in size and value, how many different types of people lived on the lands, how many ploughteams and how many mills and fisheries there were.

There are other difficulties for local historians. Detail is richer for some areas than others such as East Anglia and parts of south-west England. A major problem lies in interpretation. It is difficult to know the social and economic position of some of the types of people being described. Units of measurement are not fixed and there are confusions and ambiguities. Some landowners are identified only by first names.

However, the problems should not disguise the real value of the *Domesday Book*. It can provide essential and fairly accurate information about farming, early towns (although sadly London, Winchester and Bristol are absent).

Finding other medieval sources

Many researchers into rural and urban life often jump from the *Domesday Book* to early modern times thinking that the documentary evidence for medieval times is either very deficient or unusable by the non-specialist. In fact, there is a surprising amount of evidence available especially from the twelfth century. Admittedly, many of the archival documents from medieval times are faded and written in medieval Latin, but a large number of documents have been transcribed.

Nevertheless, there are stumbling blocks. Even when documents such as the hundred rolls and charters have been published, they have often been left in Latin. Two strategies which might be employed are firstly looking to see whether researchers before you have done some of the hard work of translation. Another possibility is to consult the *Victoria County History* series.

If this fails, the seemingly difficult task of looking at the Latin document can be partially mastered. Many early documents adopt a similar format which can soon be understood. If the required information is largely in terms of particular names, places or values, these are often easy to extract although you may need help with abbreviations and ways of showing names and monetary values.

The documentary evidence can be very usefully supplemented by archaeological material for many rural and urban areas. Some of the urban excavations have been well-known and publicised, e.g. Winchester, York, Lincoln and London. It is such archaeological research which is likely to provide details of the early history of places such as the existence of mints in Saxon times.

Many towns, counties and districts employ a community archaeologist and the investigations of archaeology teams from universities, national groups and the like runs into thousands over the years. Extensive site records of remains for most early periods of history survive. Roman, religious and deserted villages are just some of the types of rural and urban site producing documentation available to you. The value of aerial photographs has long been recognised. You should be able to gain fairly easy access to such photographs noting features such as crop marks, buildings, former villages, rural and urban morphology.

One aspect of fieldwork which went through a popular period some years ago was hedgerow dating largely following the work of Max Hooper. However, subsequent research has thrown up many pitfalls and potential inaccuracies and you should proceed very cautiously if this is your desired area of study.

Finding evidence for the lives of rich and poor people

The sixteenth century onwards

'What was life like for rich and poor people and how did it differ between the sixteenth to the twentieth centuries?'

Trying to determine the lives led by people 300 years ago throws up more problems than that for more recent times but substantial evidence is likely to exist.

Published works

It may be worth looking at published works. Many case studies can be found in specialised journals such as the *Agricultural History Review*, *Rural History*, *Urban History*, the *Journal of Social History* or *Business History*. A number of industries have published research into their histories, for instance textiles, iron and steel.

Parish and Quarter Sessions records

The sixteenth and seventeenth centuries are well covered by the many local records at parish and town level. The various documents produced by local officials such as churchwardens, constables, surveyors of the highway and overseers of the poor are well worth exploring. Quarter Session records will yield masses of material covering the period from the sixteenth century when the duties of justices of the peace extended to cover aspects such as highway maintenance, poor relief, country finance and buildings. The records can include minor law cases such as assault, theft, bastardy, witchcraft and breaches of the peace alongside petitions from the poor seeking relief, villages seeking help with workhouses, helping wounded servicemen, pregnant women and the mentally ill. Justices acted as administrators before the appearance of county councils after 1889, dealing with issues such as poor relief, roads, wage rates, weights and measures, lunatics, buildings and elections. The Quarter Session records may also include a motley collection of registered and deposited records such as savings banks, friendly societies, charities, gamekeepers, printing presses, roads, gas and water companies, inns, Anglican communicants, dissenter meeting houses, jurors and the like. Most session records were kept on rolls but time can be saved in most cases as many have been calendared, printed or both.

What can appear a formal set of procedures can throw up all kinds of local scandal and provide details of everyday life. The petty misdemeanors, the poor relations between neighbours, accusations, the hardship stories, the occasional riots, the state of repair of buildings and other structures, details of those serving the country in times of war, juvenile problems, punishments including transportation, how people voted in elections, the number of hearths in people's houses, those who served with the militia all add detail to the lives of people at the time.

Parish registers

Parish registers exist for most places by the end of the sixteenth century although they are rarely available for the period when the law first required them after 1538. Whilst entries can be very brief, later ones enable you to piece together clues about the lives of people, the existence of trades, times of epidemic and mortality, life expectancy, marriage patterns and industrialisation. Many have been published but you may be frustrated by careless custody and gaps in entries particularly for the mid-seventeenth century.

Family and estate records

The records of wealthier people are likely to be more numerous for this period. Some family records are kept in archives at the ancestral homes and not all are readily accessible. The earlier volumes of the *Victoria County History* often devoted inordinate space to the genealogies of the local aristocracy as did many parish and local histories of earlier times.

Probate inventories

Details of homes, businesses and possession can often be gleaned from probate inventories associated with wills. These may be enormous documents handwritten by appraisers who visited every room noting and valuing everything although the accuracy in monetary terms sometimes needs to be questioned. Few stones were left unturned and outside buildings such as workshops, barns and stables were not ignored. A particular attraction for you as the amateur local historian could be the large numbers which have been published or are available in typescript.

Taxation records

Taxation documents can also provide a wealth of detail about rural and urban life. For example, the Valor Ecclesiasticus of 1535 on the eve of the dissolution of the monasteries was a *Domesday Book*-type survey of ecclesiastical lands with values attached to the house, gardens, orchards, arable land, woods, pasture, meadow, rents, services and tithes. Taxation documents had appeared fairly regularly through the middle ages and these continued into the sixteenth century. The 1523 Tudor Subsidy, for instance was a tax levied on goods, lands or wages worth at least £1 a year. Taxation records followed into the seventeenth century and can reveal the rise of the yeomen classes and periods of wealth and instability. Another useful source is the glebe terriers of the sixteenth and seventeenth centuries recording lands held by parsons. It can also be useful for dating early enclosure and listing field names.

Records of mortality

One area of interest to many rural and urban historians is mortality. It seems that disease and famine were relatively common well after the medieval period. For example, sweating sickness seems widespread after about 1480, work has been done on flu outbreaks in the mid-sixteenth century, measles and later typhoid and cholera. London Bills of Mortality can be useful sources for those working on the English capital. Local researchers could also look for evidence of famine: 1527 in Essex, 1623 in Lancashire, the Highland potato famines of 1836–50 and the well-known Irish famines of the early nineteenth century.

Travellers' accounts and county surveys

Travellers' accounts can also be regarded as possible sources for this earlier period. Leland provided good descriptions of towns, country and industry soon after Henry VIII's dissolution of the monasteries.

Maps and plans begin to appear and from the later sixteenth century local historians and topographers begin to do their work. Surveys of counties and maps by people such as Lambarde, Norden and Saxon and Dugdale may well be worth your scrutiny in any investigation. Few counties did not have a monumental survey or history in the seventeenth centuries although they were not equally good and their interests and concerns were not identical to those we may have today. These early histories include both counties and towns with London attracting a history as early as 1598. Most English towns though had to wait at least until the eighteenth century and often later.

Town records

The best place to look for urban changes is likely to be the town's own archives. Some towns may have minute books of relevant bodies such as the assembly book for Southampton or the leet book for Coventry. Order books often list orders and acts passed by councils and the proceedings of council meetings are often available in journals. Publication of council minutes was made compulsory by the Municipal Corporations Act of 1835 but some places kept them well before this date. All boroughs kept annual financial accounts listing incomes from lands and buildings, profits from markets, entry fines for freemen, investments, sums borrowed as well as sums expended on properties, salaries, festivities and charities. All boroughs also had legal courts. Many towns generated masses of records especially from the late eighteenth century onwards.

What all this means is that urban records are very likely to provide useful information about trades and industry, local social classes including the wealthy, parliamentary representation and national legislation affecting the place, public health, education, municipal and other facilities, town planning, charities, the relief of the poor, law and order, markets and fairs. Large-scale maps and plans can add and corroborate information derived from such sources.

The Royal Commission on Municipal Corporations investigated the history of 284 incorporated boroughs and reported in 1835. You may also care to refer to the Boundary Commission's reports of 1837 where details can be found of public utilities. By this time the censuses and trade directories are beginning to provide an almost overwhelming wealth of information for urban areas. This is certainly the case when linked to the tens of thousands of pages of information generated by the commissions and investigations often associated with public health reforms.

Many local and national surveys and investigations shed important light on individual towns. Parliamentary surveys can be particularly useful such as the 1840 'Select Committee on the Health of Towns', and the 1845 'Report of Commissioners for Inquiring into the State of Large Towns and Populous Districts'. Public health sources can be useful for providing information about aspects of life such as housing.

Enclosure records

The countryside is generally as well-covered by source material as the towns. The documentation is extensive for most counties with records providing information on the distribution of land ownership, types of tenure and the decisions made about redistributing land. It is the maps accompanying the records which may offer you invaluable details. It should be noted though that it was enclosure done through acts of parliament which generated the documentation.

Farming surveys

Interest shown in improving farming led to a mass of published works in the late eighteenth and early nineteenth centuries, many of which have been republished. Perhaps the best known are the 'General Views' sponsored by the Board of Agriculture and usually consisting of two reports per county, one for 1793–96 and one for 1805–17. Also useful and again republished are the tours of Arthur Young in the 1760s and 1770s, Cobbett's *Rural Rides* and Caird's *English Agriculture in 1850–51* which contains both county descriptions and a few detailed accounts of individual farms.

Land tax assessments

Land tax assessments exist for many areas for the period 1780–1832 and note the names of landowners and occupiers, rateable values and assessments. However, local historians have learnt to treat these assessments with care; tax burdens varied from county to county, some people were placed in the wrong columns, some returns are for quarterly periods and others for years and some exonerated themselves through a lump sum. Coupled with inevitable avoidance, the cross-referencing difficulties across counties and the inability to relate the taxes paid to acreage held mean that you need to use such information sensitively.

Tithe records

The other large-scale maps which exist for many places alongside the enclosure ones are the tithe maps. Following the Tithe Commutation Act of 1836–60, the 12,000 remaining tithes were converted to a money payment. The commutations resulted in surveys and maps. The maps are nearly always large-scale (13–27 inches to the mile) and include fields and plots. Accompanying these are often tithe apportionments containing the agreements and details of areas, arable land, grassland and a schedule listing landowners, occupiers, a description of the premises and the state of cultivation. This includes names and boundaries.

Parliamentary papers

Another source often worth scrutinising are the varied collections of Parliamentary Papers dealing with so many aspects of rural (as well as urban) life. For example, there were reports made by committees on agricultural distress in the 1820s, 1830s, 1880s and 1890s. Parliamentary and other surveys cover a wide range of statistical and personal detail about migration, health, poverty, life and working conditions such as for children and female workers, particular industries, agriculture, sanitation, etc. and yield masses of evidence although the information is sometimes slightly distorted.

Local business and transport records

Since many urban and rural communities were predominantly economic units, you should not ignore the information which you might find in local business and transport records. It may be worth browsing through indexes of public undertakings such as transport companies, company records and those for small craftspeople and tradespeople, fire insurance records, trade catalogues and contracts.

Rate books and other housing records

Another source for the town historian are the rate books for the nineteenth century listing names, addresses, occupiers, descriptions of property, rates, arrears and whether their property is occupied or not. The better ones are arranged by streets which helps date new streets and can identify street locations. For recent times, one might also look at sources such as recent housing survey returns, building control plans and documents related to clearance areas. Few towns employed street numbering until the mid-1800s.

Letter and diaries

Local archives may house letters and diaries rarely intended for public consumption, and thus more likely to reveal feelings. The many diaries connected with rural people are becoming increasingly available to researchers through publication either by local societies or commercial publishers. There are too many to list but the following can give a flavour – Dorset Record Office examined farming in Dorset through the diary of James Warne, 1758; John Edgson left a Buckinghamshire farm diary of 1787–1808, and the diaries of Henry Hill of Slackfields Farm, Derbyshire covering 1872–96 have been published by Nottingham Adult Education.

Personal letters though can be very useful; for example the letters sent by a Gavin Scott, a Lanarkshire farmer to his son in 1916–17, have been privately published and shed useful light on everyday practices.

Twentieth century rural and urban life

Photographs and films

Twentieth century information about rural and urban life can come from a wealth of sources including ones not available for earlier periods. Photographs, available in some quantity from the mid-nineteenth century, are supplemented in this century by archival film. For many areas, archive film of farming, industry, important visitors, leisure including holidays and celebrations may exist in photographic collections, including then and now pictures, specific themes or period collections and published postcards. The published collections, however, rarely represent more than a fraction of those available.

Oral history

Sometimes it is possible to get far into the attitudes and minds of past people. The use of oral evidence and the interest shown in social and economic history and 'history from below' has been in operation long enough to have good recorded evidence of people's lives 100 years ago. Transcripts of interviews exist in many museums and archives as do tape recordings.

Advertising and surveys

Properties and facilities may be chased up in the records of estate agents and auctioneers. Advertisements can show aspects such as farms, stock, equipment and prices. The catalogues and advertisements of agricultural engineers such as Ransomes can be useful.

The Land Utilisation Survey of Britain covers the British Isles in the 1930s and can provide you with a good general view of the state of British agriculture. During the Second World War, a National Farm Survey resulted in the compilation of a database of every farm in the country but you should check about access to these documents.

Scotland

Much of the information given above applies for Wales, Scotland and Ireland but there are clearly differences. Scotland, especially the Scottish Record Office, houses some very useful material amongst its family papers: court records dating from the seventeenth century, rentals, leases, estate accounts, plans and correspondence. The Records of the Department of Agriculture and Fisheries date from 1866 and Scotland is fortunate in having the Register of Sasines, a property register which has been described as a continuous *Domesday Book* noting all land transfers since 1617. Other sources might include the Register of Deeds dating from 1554, farmhouse tax records and parish summaries of agricultural statistics since 1866. The Scottish Office was created in 1885 and keeps records on agriculture. Also useful could be the records of heritors and local committees of landowners, which exist for 800 parishes in the Scottish Record Office.

Many Scottish burghs have also deposited their records in the Scottish Record Office, including lists of properties, court books, council minutes, accounts and guild records. Urban information can also be obtained from family papers although some of these might be found in the National Library of Scotland. Edinburgh, Glasgow, Dundee and Aberdeen have their own archives.

Wales

Wales is more likely to have had similar structures to England but there have been particular documents focusing exclusively on aspects of Welsh rural life which can be useful to the historian especially for more recent times. These include royal commissions. For example, the 1894–96 Report of the Land Commission dealt with issues such as land hunger, rural depopulation, changes to rural society and evictions and another Royal Commission in 1894 on Labour shows clearly the plight of the Welsh agricultural labourer.

Identifying significant community events

'What have been the most significant events to affect the local village or town?'

You may have such a passionate interest in your community that you want to note all the major events that have occurred. This may appear attractive but can often prove unmanageable. In some respects, it is preferable to focus in detail on some of the major events which have affected your community. Look at what happened and at reactions and effects both in the short terms and longer term.

Starting points

Certain events are likely to have a direct effect on many communities. Not all of the following will yield vast quantities of information but many often repay further research:

- the effects of early settlers, e.g. Iron Age, Romans, Anglo Saxons, Vikings
- Norman events, e.g. laying waste, manorial structures, castles
- religious events such as churches, monasteries, religious rebellions, the dissolution of the monasteries, Pilgrimage of Grace
- medieval political troubles such as war in the reign of King Stephen; Peasants Revolt, Welsh, Scottish and Irish factions; War of the Roses
- major acts of God such as plagues
- civil war
- acts of union and coming together politically of component parts of the United Kingdom
- industrial, agrarian and transport changes
- eighteenth to twentieth century political developments, e.g. extension of franchise, riots, working class movements; suffragettes; Irish independence;
- involvement in recent wars, e.g. Boer War, First and Second World Wars including loss of men, life on the home front such as preparing for war, blitz, evacuation.

The overall effects of such events can often be gleaned by reading general books or articles on the events themselves. You may find it more helpful to begin with the wider picture analysing the main issues and the significance of the events before looking in detail at the events from your local angle. A good starting point would be to read some of the general county histories.

Pre-Conquest sources

Momentous events in pre-Conquest days often depend for recognition on snippets of written information or clues extracted from archaeological excavations. Sometimes isolated facts can come from tombstones or accounts produced by well-known writers such as Tacitus. For details of Viking raids one can glean pieces of information for some areas from sources such as the *Anglo-Saxon Chronicles*.

Again sensible conjecture can be based on place names but this period has not been called the Dark Ages for no reason. One could be fortunate in some areas with chance survivals such as the Sutton Hoo ship burial or Anglo-Saxon poems such as 'The Battle of Maldon'. Even where written information is available though, the information needs to be used with some care.

Medieval sources – chronicles

Following the Norman conquest, local and national records can provide information for specific places. Besides the value of the *Domesday Book*, some places are referred to in the 'chronicles' which became relatively common from the twelfth century. The bulk of these chronicles were compiled by monks and there is thus a need to question both the accuracy and the possible bias especially with issues affecting the power and influence of the church. Many chronicles were based on plagiarism from earlier writers enlivened with rumour and imagination. Nevertheless, the chronicles such as Roger of Wendover, Matthew Paris, Florence of Worcester and William of Malmesbury have their uses. Some writers were better on local events such as Hugh Candidus who focused on the Peterborough area. Some had a career which involved frequent travel such as Gerald of Wales, chaplain to Henry II.

Royal and judicial records

Royal and judicial records can also help enlighten us about communities in medieval and Tudor times. The crown issued hundreds of charters for many purposes to people and institutions all over the country granting lands, offices and privileges. These letters patent and close and libertate rolls have been printed in calendars arranged chronologically and provide good local information especially about social, economic and political events. Inquisitions post mortem were inquisitions on tenants-in-chief providing details about local lands, heirs, tenants, etc. Royal accounts can also deal with local events and issues such as the cost of building and maintaining castles.

Early letters

Letters and diaries become more common as literacy increased. These can often give a human and local view on national events. Many letters survive from the fifteenth century such as those of the Paston, Cely, Stonor and Plumpton families. They cover East Anglia, the Cotswolds, Oxfordshire, Buckinghamshire and West Yorkshire. Whilst such letters are often valuable for giving insights into family matters, local gossip, estates and households, they also deal with political events.

Sixteenth century sources

By the sixteenth century writers including travellers such as Polydore Vergil were describing localities in various parts of the country. Stow also produced his well-known *Survey of London* in the early sixteenth century.

Many of the events associated with the Tudors are well documented. Local events such as the dissolution of the monasteries can be studied in some detail through using the Valor Ecclesiasticus of 1535 listing the buildings, lands, tithes and other income possessed by churches, cathedrals and monasteries, but some counties are missing. The various religious changes associated with the Tudors can also be followed through at a local level by using documents as diverse as wills and those dealing with the purchases and changes recommended by churchwardens in their accounts. It is also possible to glean details of national events in a local context from sources such as parish registers, records of the lord lieutenancy and Quarter Session documents dealing with issues such as looking after injured soldiers and widows.

The Civil War

Accounts of the Civil War exist for many areas. Besides details in state and parliamentary records, local records exist in the form of town archives, letters and diaries. Some areas are fortunate in having good accounts by eyewitnesses and those caught up in action such as

Lucy Hutchinson. Good collections of letters exist from attackers and defenders such as those from Brilliana, Lady Harley to her son Ned when defending her husband's castle at Brampton in Herefordshire from Royalist forces. Contemporary prints and pamphlets can often add detail although their reliability needs to be questioned.

Diaries and autobiographies

Memoirs and diaries increase in number in the seventeenth century especially among the more wealthy. Many have been published and some are extremely well known. Pepys gives a very good account of life in London. Likewise, John Evelyn began writing his diary in 1631 and maintained it until 1706. He was closely involved in many of the events of the time.

Not all diarists recorded events from a national perspective. Local ones can be equally valuable. Nicholas Blundell, for example, a Lancashire Catholic squire, describes his world and social, economic and cultural life in the early eighteenth century. The Presbyterian, Richard Kay, was able to record the Jacobite army's march through Manchester. Local parsons and ministers are good sources for diaries; perhaps the best known is James Woodforde but there are many others.

Many of those prominent in life in the nineteenth century wrote autobiographies, journalists wrote accounts of national and local events and letters survive from many of the politicians and industrialists. People of all social classes kept details of life and events such as Cardinal Manning, Fanny Kemble, Thomas Raikes, a Yorkshire Tory in London in the early nineteenth century, William Cobbett, the Reverend Benjamin Newton of Yorkshire and Francis Kilvert in Herefordshire. John O'Neill, a Lancashire trade unionist, kept a diary as did Ellen Weeton who ran a dame school.

Newspapers

Newspapers began in the early seventeenth century in England and Wales. They become much more useful from the eighteenth century although you may be disappointed by the quantity of local history in the earlier editions. By 1800 some 100 provincial titles existed. Copies of many can be found locally although sometimes a visit to the Newspaper Library at Colindale may be necessary. It is sometimes difficult to keep track of newspapers in the earliest days as there was a great deal of coming and going of titles.

The main interest of these newspapers was in national events such as high society scandals, stock markets, wars and parliamentary debates until the later eighteenth century although property information can be found in advertisements. These newspapers are also excellent for criminal trials. Details of local births, marriages and deaths are rare before 1750. They can also be regarded as good sources for tracing industrial and agricultural developments in an area including strikes, lock outs, industrial conditions, accidents, prices, wages, transport networks and bankruptcies.

Later newspapers can overwhelm. The advertisements hold a fascination for many and they should certainly not be ignored. However, much more can come out – births, marriages and deaths, farming, industry and trade, houses, local crimes and policing, transport issues, religion, schools, public utilities, pastimes and sport, libraries, cinemas and theatres, inns, costumes, emigration and immigration, pollution, architecture, local concerns and attitudes, music, local personalities, local governments, markets and fairs, food and drink, museums and heritage, recipes and weather.

Industrial records

The rise of many industries can be traced in company accounts and letters, maps, plans, sketches and descriptions of the industries from visitors and those involved in the industry. Many of the working class movements have been well documented in official government correspondence.

Explaining the forms of community today

'Why has my local town or village emerged in the form it has?'

You may be particularly interested in the growth of your community. There are many aspects which can be examined to provide answers to this question – population, buildings and facilities and economy to name but a few.

Population

Estimates of populations in various communities are fraught with difficulties but it is possible to make sensible deductions in the days before the census started. However, the further back one goes the more uncertain the figure is likely to be. Those interested in the demographic aspects of their community are advised to look at journals such as *Local Population Studies* which often contain both information about particular localities and the techniques employed. The work of the Cambridge Group for the History of Population and Social Structure may be worth examining so that you can see the types of work it is possible to do on historical demography.

Medieval times

The problems with trying to get an accurate impression of the size and growth of communities is that only a proportion of the inhabitants of a place appeared in the documents. Since so many of those documents were concerned with taxes, compilers included only those liable for the tax. Even this figure is suspect because of evasion and inaccurate compilation. Sensible guesses thus have to be made about proportion of marriages, numbers of children, average family size and the like. Not surprisingly it has led to considerable variations in estimates.

Parish registers

Things improve somewhat after the appearance of parish registers following the 1538 Act although only around 800 of 12,000 parishes have original returns. As industrial expansion led to new urban development, parish registers tended to become more inaccurate and those dying before baptism, common law marriages, criminals and suicides were just some of these who may have escaped recording.

Pre-1801 counts

Contrary to common belief, other sources exist to help with population details before the advent of the census in 1801. For example, chantry certificates listed 'housling people' receiving communion in 1547, Protestation Returns of 1641–42 recorded males age over 18 signing an undertaking to support the rights of Parliament and those refusing to do so, Compton's Census of 1676 listed Anglican communicants along with Protestant and Catholic dissenters, muster rolls listed all men between the ages of 15 and 60 in local communities liable to be called up to fight. It will be readily apparent that these help with details about people in a local community but there are omissions especially of women and children.

The census

This is where the census becomes so important. The 1801 census set out to show the number and distribution of people living in Great Britain, the number of houses, including uninhabited ones, and the number of people in agriculture, commerce and manufacturing. Names were not sought in the earliest censuses but detail increases, especially after 1841. The 100 year rule restricts access to the full detail of those recorded after 1891 and none was compiled in 1941 but the value for so many aspects of a community's growth is enormous. The margin of error is likely to be relatively small.

They are an indispensable source for total populations but they are also invaluable on the growth of towns, depopulations, occupations and migrations. Supplementary census details provide extra information about schools, churches and chapels, age structures, blindness, dumbness and mental deficiency.

Maps, guides and directions

Population figures though are unlikely to provide the necessary details about the factors explaining changes and the features associated with the growth. Other sources can prove useful for this purpose.

Early maps and atlases

Early atlases and maps such as those of Saxton or Norden can show the relative importance of towns, types of land and even pronunciation of places at the time. A few late sixteenth century town plans exist; for example, the Civitates Orbis Terrarum has plans for various cathedral cities. Ogilby's maps of 1675 are based on fairly accurate measurements and note fields, houses and other buildings. Speed's maps from the early seventeenth century included 64 town plans. By the end of the eighteenth century practically every county had a good large-scale map even if the accuracy cannot be guaranteed.

Ordnance survey

Official ordnance survey work did not begin suddenly. It gradually evolved and slowly superseded the private mapmakers. The systematic publication of the inch to the mile maps began in the first decade of the nineteenth century. The last sheet – the Isle of Man – was not completed until 1873. You can easily obtain these early maps as they have been reprinted. You may find that a very useful adjunct to these maps is the large-scale town plans beginning with St Helens in 1844 on a scale of 60-inches to the mile. 50 years later 400 plans on a scale of 120-inches to the mile had been produced. 25-inch to the mile surveys were also completed in the later nineteenth century for almost all areas. For many local historians, the scales most in demand are likely to be the 1, 6 and 25-inch maps.

Guides

Maps can be supplemented with many other sources especially for more recent times. However, the earlier periods can be aided by using the accounts of travellers such as Leland, Fiennes, Camden and Defoe. County volumes did not necessarily involve personal tours but the county societies especially in the later nineteenth century provide masses of detail of the growth of communities within their counties. More microcosmic studies became popular, often at parish level.

Directories

These can give a good idea of the growth of a settlement in recent times and they are likely to be easily obtained.

Their existence can be largely explained by the need of business people to know where to find customers as trade between towns increased. Although the earliest directory for London is 1677, they appear in bulk from the late eighteenth century. The most well-known ones are the Post Office, Whites, Kellys and more recently Thompsons. They lose their prominence after the Second World War although many places will have up to 20 directories. They can be of various types such as street ones, commercial and trade ones and even court ones for London which began by listing the better off but ended up more or less as a street directory. The type of work which can be done by using directories though can include the development of neighbourhoods and suburbs, the growth of facilities, changing employment and the socio-economic aspects of particular areas in town and countryside.

Most local libraries have copies which will enable you to trace the trades, transport services, post offices, facilities such as schools and the principal inhabitants. The publication of guide books increased from the mid-eighteenth century and, although contents vary, some can be excellent for details of industrial and commercial development, e.g. *Pictures of Newcastle upon Tyne* in 1812. Industrial and commercial information becomes more common in the nineteenth century. The best guides were revised frequently such as *Picture of London* which was revised yearly.

Migration research

A topic which interests many historians is migration. The concerns are likely to include who migrated, where from and to? Why? Numbers? Families or single? Ages? The effects of migration on existing populations and newcomers? Census and parish registers can give good indications of this and much useful work has been done in this field. There are some clues to pre-census materials in the emigration registers kept by the British Government in the later eighteenth century. This would be useful for Scottish and Irish researches. It is estimated that between 1760–75 some 2.5% of the Irish population and 3% of the Scots emigrated to North America. Not everyone migrated and another theme for research could be place loyalty by looking at surnames over a period of time, although findings will need to be treated with some caution.

Housing and retail development research

A tremendous amount of development has taken place in recent times sometimes caused by wartime reconstruction. It has been an activity of research groups to trace housing development and reconstruction using a range of evidence such as maps, directories, censuses, municipal records and field evidence. You may find that it pays to narrow the focus to make a manageable area for investigation. Some people like to focus on particular aspects of development such as retailing or council housing in urban areas.

In some instances it is possible to trace buildings and sites over the centuries by using sources such as current and past title deeds, OS maps, directories, registers of voters, advertisements and sales particulars, photographs and, in earlier times, tithe and enclosure maps, surveys, rate books, tax records such as land, hearth and window taxes, old drawings, date stones, fire insurance records, probate inventories and wills.

5
HOME LIFE

In this chapter we will consider the following:

- the difference between house and home
- the difference between rich and poor
- land
- houses
- house design
- domestic duties

- servants
- who lived at home
- privacy
- pressures
- work at home
- groups at home.

As you think about the theme of home life, the following are the kinds of questions that may occur to you. Maybe the community you are studying will enable you to answer one of them in a research project.

1 What was the difference between the daily lives of people from various levels of society in your area?
2 What elements of 'traditional family life' survive today?
3 Did people rent or buy their homes in the past?
4 How long did a family live in the same house? (And how **did** they all fit in?)
5 Where did newly-weds live?
6 How varied was the diet of ordinary people?
7 What kind of family supplied servants to work in other houses? Did the supplying families themselves have servants?
8 How have incoming populations (Irish, Jews and Europeans as well as 'ethnic minorities') affected the British population in your area as a whole?

Throughout history, the difference between the lives of rich and poor can hardly be better summed up than in their living conditions. Before the nineteenth century, only the rich could afford time and expense of writing about their daily lives; almost everyone else was too busy trying to scrape a living.

However, many of the records that survived before 1800 about the lives of ordinary people suggest that these were times of what we would consider to be great poverty and distress.

House and home

As soon as what Cipolla has called 'the agricultural revolution' occurred (about 10,000 BC), communal and family dwellings were built and their remains occasionally survive. Home life is behavioural, however, and depends on people rather than buildings.

Tribal groups still exist, even in the UK, in the form of extended families. Even if they rarely live under the same roof today, it is still quite possible to find three or more generations acting as one loose unit from a few streets in the same area. Until the twentieth century this unity occurred more often, although there were clear differences between the various strata in society.

Until this century too, most people in the UK lived in rented accommodation. Even the upper class often 'took a house', as the novels of Jane Austen confirm. For most people who had capital, to buy a home was not an option: their funds were tied up to provide a regular income. For the vast majority of society, however, there was no question of investing capital. Their sole aim was day-to-day survival.

Sources

From the nineteenth century, when all records proliferated, national statistics (such as censuses and church records) and private sources (like diaries, photographs and artefacts) are available. Before that, we need to look where we can. For example, diaries, inventories, letters, a few paintings and miscellaneous references in Quarter Sessions records may give us glimpses into the homes of ordinary people. Wealthier men and women are better evidenced; their home life can be found in the same source, but also in books.

Many museums and visitor centres offer reconstructions of rooms, houses, streets and even villages. These can be very instructive to visit. But it is rather too easy to forget the smells, the cold and the general lack of space when viewing such displays. Above all, most are shown in a blaze of light. While this is helpful in enabling us to see the smallest details, we must try to unthink the electricity!

So, viewing the next display you see of a working man's living room, do so through grey tinted glasses! You must imagine the corners to be in darkness; the backs of your legs are cold as you stand looking at the fire; small-print books are difficult to read; every now and then the smoke blows back down the chimney; and though it is 2pm on an autumn day, the window reveals a swirling cloud of yellow-black fog.

Rich and poor

POINTS TO CONSIDER

❝ Though I am a bachelor, [said one of Sherlock Holmes' clients], I have to keep up a considerable staff at Hurlstone, for it is a rambling old place, and takes a good deal of looking after … Altogether, there are eight maids, the cook, the butler, two footmen and a boy. The garden and the stables, of course, have separate staff. ❞

(A. Conan Doyle 'The Musgrave ritual' in *The Memoirs of Sherlock Holmes*)

❝ They lived, as the country people do, on dried pease, pickled pork, bread and cheese, milk and small beer.

Water   This they have taken out of a ditch or pool of standing water, at their own door, as is common in this clay country…

Kitchen utensils   They have two small iron pots which have long been in use. In these they boiled their pork, pease, etc. They have likewise two brass skillets, rather old, in which they boil milk…

Meat   In this part of the country there is a great deal of ewe-mutton killed between the 1st of November and January, some of which is very poor and rotten, and is usually sold at three halfpence or perhaps one penny per pound [about half to one kilogram for 1p]. ❞

January 1762, report by the Royal Society

(On the case of mortification of the limbs ... Charles Wollaston, Vol. 83, p. 523.)

This concerned the way of life of a labourer, his wife and six children, stricken by an unknown disease, which in follow-up papers in *Phil. Trans.* was established as ergotism, caused by diseased grain.

What a contrast! Compare the equipment that would have been needed by the staff serving Conan Doyle's bachelor, with the poor man's battered iron pots and 'rather old' skillets serving a family of eight.

Sixteenth-century inventories of ordinary people were similarly stark. For example, one man's utensils comprise 'one pot & a pan'; he also had '4 platters'. Another man owned '2 pots, 3 cauldrons and a pot hanger'; his equipment was completed by '2 old platters'. As usual, richer people fared better, with one wealthy woman leaving 'pewter of all sorts'.

What held for cooking was just as true for other things. The richer man kept a stable, while the poor man walked. The well-off had clocks and watches, the poor lived by the sun and the church clock. Above all, the rich could afford to run a huge house, while the labouring man occupied two or three rooms.

Land

It is in the nature of man, a gregarious and hierarchical animal, that while groups should live together, ownership is in the hands of a dominant few. Despite peaceful or bloody revolutions through history, in most societies the division of land is linked to an individual's position in society.

At various times in history, groups have elected to live a communist life. Cases like the Diggers in the English Civil War period, who set up camp on what is now a golf club in Surrey and began to dig and plant. Local landowners objected, and brought the law in to clear them away. Similar groups settle in various quiet places today. As far as the local historian is concerned, records of such groups are not easy to locate, if they ever existed as formal documents.

Researching the ownership of a block of land or a single building today, therefore, involves and reveals details about people's position in society.

The earliest surviving records deal with the rights of kings and nobles. One of the first and, as far as accessibility today is concerned the most useful, is William I's *Domesday Book*. Here the make-up of most of English society is set out, and the feudal ownership of the parishes involved are explained (both before and after the Conquest).

❻ The archbishop himself holds in demesne [i.e. his private land] Mortelege [Mortlake]. In the time of King Edward it was assessed for 80 hides. The Canons of St Paul's hold 8 of these hides, which have paid and do pay geld with the rest. Now they pay geld 25 hides

altogether. The land is for [sufficient to support] 35 ploughs. In
demesne there are 5 ploughs; and (there are) 80 villeins [villagers
owning up to 30 acres each for themselves] and 14 bordars [small-
holders owning a 'bord', a cottage, and farming up to five acres] [i.e.
villein and bordars owed duty to the lord] with 28 ploughs. There is a
church; and 16 serfs [full time servants working for the lord as
ploughmen, shepherds, etc.]; and 2 mills worth 100 shillings; and 20
acres of meadow. From the wood, 55 hogs from the pannage [rent
levied on every tenth pig, indicating a total of over 500]. In London
there were 17 houses rendering 52 pence. In Sudwerca [Southwark] 4
houses worth 27 pence... The whole manor in the time of King
Edward was worth £32, afterwards £10; now £38. **9**

From published historical works, we know that a heirarchy of duty
and ownership existed, each level of society owing its position to the
benefaction of the group above it.

POINTS TO CONSIDER

Conquest and inheritance both play their part in ownership, so when
tracing the history of a piece of land – or the fortunes of a group of
people – you must bear both in mind. American settlers divided their
newly discovered land into states, townships, claims, etc., but these
overlaid previous Indian tribal areas. We can generalise to a certain
extent. As time passes:

♦ records about people show evidence of land in different places
♦ records about land show evidence of ownership by different people.

It is also in the nature of man to be entrepreneurial, so the land and
other property, although always owned by someone, may be occupied
by someone else. Rent is paid, though not always in the form of money.

The records of land registration are basically older in Scotland and
Ireland than England. The Return of Heirs and the Register of Deeds
cover land transactions in Scotland in the sixteenth and seventeenth
centuries; Irish records date from the beginning of the eighteenth century. In England, full registration did not happen until the second
half of the nineteenth century (with the exception of Middlesex and
Yorkshire records which are older).

—— The construction of houses ——

Upon the land which their position in society gave them, people built
or adapted houses to suit their particular wealth and needs.
Researching buildings, to reconstruct the life that went on in them,

needs a book of its own. Our list of further reading makes some suggestions. However, the lower people are in society, the less substantial their houses, and the less likely these are to have survived. In considering Figure 5.1, there are three points to bear in mind.

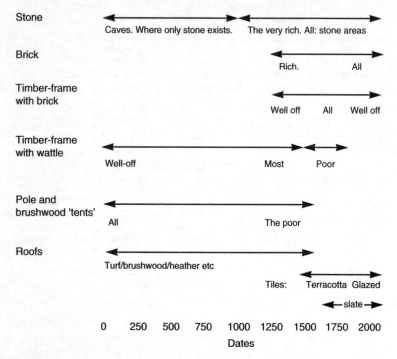

Figure 5.1 Building materials in different ages

Materials

In some areas, stone is common, so wood may be at a premium. Here the normal rule (the rich will build in a more permanent material than the poor) is less valid.

Adaptation

Through the years, buildings are changed in two ways. (a) Rich people add on to their existing structures and so change them (often so much that it may be difficult to recognise in which period the building originated); (b) poor people take over buildings vacated by the rich.

There is a recognisable cycle in the use and reuse of land surrounding

---

POINTS TO CONSIDER

The proven existence of an 'outlier' material within a building usually points to a rich owner. Who but a well-off landowner could afford to bring in slate posts to mark the boundaries of his fields? Short stretches of fields with 6 to 8 ft (2–2.5m) slate fencing survive in Bisham, near Marlow, Bucks.

---

provincial English town centres. The land would originally have been occupied by wealthy traders, whose houses would gradually have been upgraded over the years. The 'great rebuilding' of the seventeenth century, often using brick, was followed by what might be called the 'great refacing' in the Georgian era, when the done thing was to clad the front of an older structure with a classical brick front. Round the outside of these early rich areas, the wealthy Victorian tradesmen and manufacturers built their grander houses. Most of these were still within the area we now think of as the 'town centre'. But then, as populations rose, the rich moved out to small villages outside the town, or to the edge of the countryside. Later these too were to fill in, of course, and the rich moved still further out. But studies of the large houses they left show a gradual decline, first into flats, then into ruins and today often taken over as offices.

Survival

When we look at our landscape today, we see modern buildings with a few older ones amongst them. These are seldom from one particular period. Some old structures may form the inner core of later buildings.

How can we find out about the past landscape of houses, then, if most of what we can see now are new? Maps and land records, newspapers and directories, should help. Field visits, especially if you can go inside buildings, are also essential.

Plot the outline of your area of interest on to your own working map to a convenient scale, and copy this a few times. Devote one map each to appropriate periods – what is appropriate will depend on what you are studying, but if your area was, say, a few streets today situated about half a mile from a town centre, you might choose 'Post Second World War', '1900 to 1945', 'Victorian', '1700 to 1840' or 'Pre-1700'.

Sketch on to the appropriate map houses that survive today which you can date. Look at any dates on buildings (compare the opening of Chapter 9 of this book), and study as many maps as you can in the local library (see Figure 5.2).

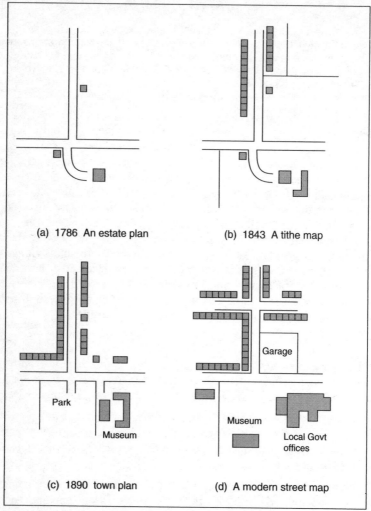

(a) 1786 An estate plan

(b) 1843 A tithe map

Garage

Park

Museum

(c) 1890 town plan

Museum

Local Govt offices

(d) A modern street map

Figure 5.2 Maps showing buildings accumulating in an area

In the fictional example in Figure 5.2, one original building survives until after 1890; we could imagine that the owner sublet or sold land between 1786 and 1843, and the owner of this built a house which today is used as a museum. Late Victorian town expansion led to a terrace of artisan's cottages being built, some of which survive today.

———————— **Life at home** ————————

The earliest homes housed a man's stock as well as his family. The nineteenth century cow shed is a throwback to the days when everything was under the same roof.

William Cobbett in his *Cottage Economy* dares not advise his readers on such a fundamental thing as a cowshed: 'To pretend to tell a country labourer how to build a shed for a cow, how to stick it up against the end of his house ...or to dwell on the materials...' [is a vain enterprise, because any such man who didn't already know such things] 'is not only unfit to keep a cow, but unfit to keep a cat'.

Who lived at home?

Besides immediate family and relatives, many tradesmen had apprentices, journeymen and servants living in the house, while labourers often occupied outside accommodation. In ordinary homes, the four-room cottage might well contain more than one family, a lodging group paying a small sum for a roof over their heads.

Privacy

There was a steady progression from the earliest communal buildings to today's spacious houses with many rooms. This is helpful in dating houses, but it also tells us something about family life too.

The earliest homes were single spaces, with clan groups and animals sharing one roof. In a primitive home, the warmth from your cow was well worth the inconvenience of its smell and habits!

Buildings evolving from this had centrally placed doors with a passage leading to the accommodation for cattle on one side and people on the other. At this stage the fireplace – originally in the centre of the space – tended to be moved to the side of the room.

In the houses occupied by people who were higher up the social scale, a space in the communal room was curtained-off for the lord and his lady; the next change was to partition this space off permanently. Sometimes an upper storey was created as a bedroom area.

By the sixteenth century even yeomen's homes showed a domestic pattern we would recognise. Inventories produce valuable evidence, not just about what people owned, but in what rooms possessions were kept.

POINTS TO CONSIDER

Until the thirteenth century there were no chimneys, (smoke drifted through thatch, waterproofing it to a certain extent) then merely holes in the roof. These became vents, still sited in the middle of the building. The renovated Barley Hall, in Coffee Yard off Stonegate, York, contains a fine example. From the 1400s brick chimneys were built, even in stone buildings, for brick doesn't crack as stone does. Chimney pots appeared widely only after 1750, when stacks became wide to give access for sweeps.

At this date, space inside houses was still very much at a premium. There was little space for corridors and lobbies. Upstairs especially tended to be a series of rooms opening from one another.

Studying the nineteenth-century census reveals interesting things about families. Victorian families were on average larger than today's; having nine or ten children was not unusual. The idea that nine or ten lived behind every cottage door is not true, however.

- A number will have died in childhood or at birth.
- From the age of eight or nine, some children will have moved to live with their employers (see Chapter 8).
- Some children may be lodging with relatives or neighbours.

A four-roomed cottage, one perhaps containing a weaving loom, could still be expected to house seven people: father, mother, four children and a lodger. Privacy was often restricted to segregation by sex.

Pressures

Besides space, amongst the other areas which would make subjects for local history research, are pressures involving:

- health care
- sanitation and water
- heat and power
- light (which relates to reading and learning as well as seeing)

Suppliers' records for all these survive from the nineteenth century. Whether they can be found from your area and at your date is something for you to research. All these were privately supplied: doctors and hospitals, water companies, coal and oil merchants, gas companies, and so on. Your local reference library and record office should be able to suggest what records have survived, and where they are.

Local newspapers and printed histories and books of reminiscence will also contain useful general information.

Work at home

As explained in Chapter 8, by belonging to protective units, peasants living in a community owed duty to their masters, and ultimately to the lord of the manor. As well as such communal work as farming and community work (like road maintenance), all but the poorest families worked in their own homes. They tilled the ground round their houses and kept some livestock. Often a trade went on in the house as well.

Domestic duties

The duties of the housewife have only changed in the past few decades. Until the Second World War, mothers would hand wash and maintain clothes for their families. Further back this century the family would brew its own beer and keep its own livestock, as well as grow much of what it ate.

For you, evidence is likely to be restricted to finding artefacts used in home life in museums, reading accounts and diaries of daily life and, if you are lucky, finding the odd sound recording of people who remember daily life in the past.

Group experience

The home lives of individual groups of people provide interesting subjects for research.

- **women** amongst possible projects would be: those who stayed at home; those who worked on the land; those who left home to work elsewhere
- **children** of various ages
- **incoming foreign groups** which would include Jews, the incoming Irish into England and the incoming English into Ireland
- the **elderly**.

There are seldom records specifically about such groups, but local studies can extract useful historical insight into what kind of lives they actually led. Only your research will turn up the interesting cases – here is your opportunity to shed useful light on a particular group. Your local records may contain details about a group of women working at home in a local trade, say silk-weaving; the diary of a newly-wed bride; or unusually full information about children's attendance at Sunday school; or have a tradition of well-organised alms houses.

6
EDUCATION

In this chapter we will consider the following:

- the provision for education before 1800
- the provision for education after 1800
- twentieth century developments in education
- how to find out about schools in your community
- finding out about everyday life in schools.

Education before 1800

The history of education for all only really dates back just over a century although schools and other forms of educational provision have a much longer ancestry. Most of the focus on pre-nineteenth century forms of education have been on the grammar and public schools, many founded during the reigns of Tudor monarchs.

The pre-eighteenth century situation may well have seen many more local schools in towns and villages, either run by the church or by benefactors. The descent of these schools is not easy to trace as many petered out following the death of their benefactors.

The expansion of education in the British Isles was much slower than in other countries such as France although it tended to be better developed in Scotland. It was really only after 1833 that educational provision moved beyond the concern of individual, wealthy benefactors, the church and a few interested people. There was a strong feeling amongst many that education for the poor was an undesirable thing.

One early organisation involved in the setting up of early charity schools was the Society for Promoting Christian Knowledge (SPCK and SSPCK in Scotland). They advised that children aged 7 to 11 should be taught reading writing and arithmetic. Another type of school existing prior to the nineteenth century was the Sunday School, often associated with Robert Raikes, although Methodists and others had tried to establish such schools prior to his work in the 1780s. The idea behind such schools was social training with little concern for academic subjects.

The development of education post-1800

The monitorial system

Many early schools were very small and their existence was sporadic. As population increased, the ideas associated with the monitorial system became more prominent. The British and Foreign School Society from 1807 (representing nonconformists) and the National Society from 1811 (representing the Church of England) used teachers to train older pupils who themselves taught younger ones whilst the teacher kept an eye on what was happening. Lessons were largely confined to basic number and writing.

Grammar schools

These monitorial schools were not attended by the children of the more wealthy, although many grammar schools were in decline by the end of the eighteenth century. For example, Leicester Grammar School in 1820 had just four pupils. Most grammar schools, however, had a rigid curriculum concentrating on Latin. It was not until the Grammar Schools Act of 1840 that schools were permitted to enlarge the curriculum.

Public schools

The expensive public schools excluded most people from the middle class. These schools were often harsh places. The curriculum was dull and teaching mechanical. Latin and Greek formed the basis with some mathematics. However, between 1840 and the 1880s many public schools changed with new ones founded such as Marlborough and Clifton. The headships of reformers such as Butler at Shrewsbury and Arnold at Rugby introduced many changes to the public school system such as more subjects including sport, team spirit, religious and moral principles and gentlemanly conduct. The education of wealthier girls also improved during this time following the work of reformers such as Elizabeth Reid, Frances Buss and Dorothea Beale.

Other provision

Dissenting Academies were run by Nonconformists especially Quakers partly because they were excluded from other types of schools. These often provided a curriculum more suited to the world of business. Private tutors existed for a number, more particularly girls.

Universities

Universities did exist for a small number. Edinburgh and Glasgow both had vigorous medical schools. The two English universities at Oxford and Cambridge were the preserve of the wealthy and restricted to Anglicans. Only gradually did things improve. In 1828 University College London was established by Nonconformists followed by Kings College for Anglicans in 1831. Durham followed in 1837 with higher educational institutions appearing in the north in the later nineteenth century. Oxford and Cambridge were only opened up to non-Anglicans after 1871. By 1879 Oxford also had two women's colleges but Oxford allowed no women onto degree courses until 1920 and Cambridge waited another year.

Mechanics' Institutes

Mechanics' Institutes designed for adults also played their part in the nineteenth century. Most taught crafts and skills as well as the '3 Rs'. By 1850 there were over 600 mechanics' institutes in England. Adult education was also aided by the University Extension Movement and the Workers' Educational Association which was founded in 1905.

State involvement in schools

Many historians regard 1833 as a crucial year for education as it saw the start of a government education grant. New schools began to appear. Many were in urban areas. In 1839 a committee decided to extend funds and to appoint two inspectors. It also decided to improve the training of teachers: as late as the 1851 census 500 teachers listed as such in the census had signed their name with a cross.

The six volume report of the Newcastle Commission of 1861 makes interesting reading for local historians. It noted 58,975 schools in England but fewer than 20% of pupils were staying at school after the age of ten and over one third attended school for fewer than 100 days a year. It also concluded that teaching in elementary schools was not well geared to the needs of children and a large proportion of children were not satisfactorily taught the '3 Rs'. The Revised Code began operation in 1862 providing grants based on success in examinations and on attendance. The payment by results had many critics. Costs fell but there is evidence of mechanical teaching, parrot learning and the neglect of subjects beyond the three examined. Attendance figures were massaged. Even so the system continued until 1897.

There was a recognition by the 1860s that things needed to be improved partly because of the advances made abroad, inadequate voluntary schools, the extension of the franchise and the need for a more literate society.

Elementary education

The move to universal education

1870 witnessed the Forster's Act. It aimed to cover the country with good schools and get parents to send their children to school. Voluntary systems continued where 'suitable, efficient and sufficient', but elsewhere board schools were set up managed by school boards. 1,600 board schools were built in the first six years and the number again doubled by 1880. In the same period some 6,000 voluntary schools were built. The efficiency and attendance of boards varied. Many served areas too small to be efficient and many had unsuitable people on the boards.

Further changes followed such as Sandon's Act of 1876 which declared it the duty of parents to send children to school. In 1880 Mundella's Act insisted on full-time attendance up to age ten with no child leaving before 13 unless they reached the required standard. The school leaving age gradually rose: 11 in 1893 and 12 in 1899 except for some agricultural districts. Changes were also made to the awarding of grants with more subjects added. New subjects such as history, geography, drawing, physical education, algebra, geometry, domestic science and craft became more common.

In the 1890s school fees were reduced or eliminated in many places. Conditions in schools though varied considerably. It is wrong to assume that all late Victorians were supporters of education for all. Blind eyes were often turned to absences and conditions of schools were sometimes deplorable. For example, in 1886 an HMI report for Truro British School described conditions as 'dismal, very squalid building, of which total destruction is the only real improvement'.

Attendance often remained poor. The above mentioned British school at Truro had an average daily attendance of 160 out of 300 with school log books listing all kinds of reasons – bad weather, lack of boots, epidemics, stone picking, potato planting, harvesting, helping with washing, market days, tea treats and fairs. Logs show lessons that were far from stimulating and many punishments sometimes verging on the cruel. Classes were often large.

Twentieth century developments in education

The boards were proving increasingly creaky and the 1895 Bryce Commission recommended a more 'centralist' reorganisation of education. By 1901 it was illegal for the boards to use rates for any other purpose apart from teaching the '3 Rs'.

The early twentieth century

The result was the Education Bill of 1902 which abolished school boards and attendance committees and transferred responsibilities and employees to local education authorities. Over two-and-a-half thousand boards were swept away and replaced by 328 LEAs. They received money from local rates and national taxes. In 1904 the Regulation for Secondary Schools required all secondary schools to offer a four year course in English, geography, history, a foreign language which could be Latin as well as maths and science. The Act was opposed by many, again notably along religious lines. The first decade of the century led to further development such as free school meals for needy children, school health services and juvenile employment bureaux.

The status of teachers was also improving slowly. In 1902 55% of teachers had no sort of college training but new regulations after 1905 improved the situation.

Even in the late 1920s, however, 80% of pupils did not proceed past the top class of the elementary school. The poor could still not afford the trapping of a grammar school education even if they won a free place. Technical education was still badly provided for. The idea of a grammar school/secondary modern system first appeared in the Hadow Report of 1926 although little had been achieved when Spens advised grammar, modern and technical high schools 'under a single secondary code' in 1938.

Post-Second World War education

The 1944 Butler Education Act provided the basis of education until the 1980s. Education was divided into primary, secondary and further.

On average one child in five attended grammar schools and they were usually selected on the basis of the 11+ examination. Some places moved quickly to comprehensive schools, e.g. Middlesex, Coventry, Oldham or in rural areas which could not afford separate provision such as Anglesey and the Isle of Man. The numbers increased steadily under both Conservative and Labour administrations. In 1965 the Labour Education Secretary instructed all LEAs to prepare and submit plans for comprehensive education. A few resisted or were slow but by 1970 comprehensive schemes had been approved for 129 out of 163 LEAs.

Dissatisfaction with state education has provided a continuing role for independent schools, many dependent on fees, and since the 1970s by an assisted places scheme. Recent developments especially during the post-1979 Conservative administration have been rapid with a succession of Education Acts creating amongst other things a National Curriculum, new types of schools such as grant maintained and city technical colleges, the erosion of the power of LEAs, increased power for parents and governors, the replacement of the GCEs and CSEs by a unified GCSE examination, national testing at 7, 11 and 14, open enrolment, the development of vocational education and the expansion of higher education both in terms of students and the number of institutions. There have also been changes to teacher training with the demise or merging of many colleges of higher education and radical amendments in the way teachers are trained. More rigorous inspections of schools and colleges have also taken place. The other major changes to affect education have been the establishment of the Open University (1969) and the Open College (1987).

Finding the evidence for your community's schools

'What is the background to my local school?'

A good starting point is either a guide to using educational sources such as the relevant chapter in W.B. Stephens *Sources for English Local History* or C.W. Higson's *Sources for the History of Education* (1967 with a 1976 supplement).

Published works

An examination of a published study on schools may reveal clearly the kind of issues dealt with although there is a tremendous variation in the quality of such documentation. Use could be made of the work of the History of Education Society and the *Journal of Educational Administration and History*.

Much obviously depends on the nature of the school. You may be fortunate in having a detailed account in a volume of the *Victoria County History*. Others may need to go no further than the local archives or even the school itself. Schools have often deposited their material in records offices but some have retained them. Another obvious source is a published history of the school.

Central records

If you are seriously pursuing a project, you may need to seek information from central repositories such as the Public Record Office. For example, files ED 1, 2, 3, 4, 16, 21 and 49 at the PRO contain information on matters such as buildings, attendance, accommodation and staffing especially for the former board schools.

The 'National Society' in London also has records for 10,000 of its schools as well as surveys done for 1846–7 and 1866–7. Official records sometimes contain details of foundation dates such as the 1833 'Abstract of Education Returns' which includes not only the numbers of pupils but also the foundation dates of schools set up or re-established since 1818.

There are lists of public elementary schools published as parliamentary papers for 1905–06 and later as a non-parliamentary paper as 'Board of Education List 21' which was published occasionally up to the Second World War.

The 1818 Select Committee on the Education of the Poor is a useful source for local information. It is likely to contain many local written statements. It will enable you to investigate local attitudes towards education at this time such as complacency about provision or even hostility, inadequacy and who supported it.

Grammar schools

For grammar schools a survey of provision was done by Nicholas Carlisle in 1818 although it is not complete. For very old foundations, A.F. Leach has searched all chantry certificates for the mid-sixteenth century in his *English Schools at the Reformation 1546–8* and Vincent's *The State and School Education in England and Wales 1640–60* lists grammar schools in the first half of the seventeenth century. The 'Educational Register' covers the period 1851–55 listing staff and pupil numbers, buildings, scholarships and foundation dates.

Scotland and Wales

Many Scottish educational records are located in the Scottish Record Office including those for the Education Department. Earlier documents may be found amongst the Kirk Sessions of the Church of Scotland or with the records of the SSPCK which was active in establishing and running schools in some areas such as the Highlands and Islands. There may also be material in local government records such as Burgh Council papers, heriot papers and estate papers. Inspection reports on many Scottish schools exist for the period 1886–1925 although they cover a longer period for higher grade schools. Welsh schools are often covered in the same kinds of sources for English schools such as Welsh sections in the Newcastle Commission papers, but there are some sources with a Welsh dimension or concerned solely with the Principality such as reports concerning the state of education in Wales.

Finding evidence about school life

'What was life like at school 100 years ago and how had things changed by 50 years ago?'

This can be an enormous research topic as there are so many strands. Trying to write a detailed account of school life over a long period of time can prove overwhelming especially if detailed log books exist.

Starting points

You may benefit from reading some of the better school histories, to see the type of things investigated. Amongst the aspects you may care to investigate are pupil numbers, attendance, buildings and facilities, finance, teaching, discipline and standards. There is usually plentiful information about all these aspects.

Central records

The nineteenth century should have produced extensive source material. For example, the records on 10,000 schools linked with the National Society may well contain detailed information about particular schools after 1839. Reports also exist for Roman Catholic and Methodist schools and although many records of the British and Foreign Schools Society were destroyed by German bombs, the annual reports exist to provide useful information about nonconformist schools in the nineteenth century. Unless there are copies locally, however, it may be necessary for you to examine such reports at the headquarters of these denominations in London.

The same may apply to the vast amounts of information which can be found in parliamentary and other official documents. For example, investigations into educational provision for the lower orders were carried out as early as 1817. Other years when there were reports include 1867, 1871, 1888, 1893 and 1899 which can provide details about attendance, fees and financial information.

The various commissions such as Newcastle (1861) do not cover the whole country but there are detailed reports on many areas. There are also many case studies in the Cross Commission of 1886–88. Some large towns had their own investigations into educational provision such as Birmingham, Manchester, Liverpool, Leeds and London.

A tremendous number of official commissions deal with aspects of education such as the 1838 Select Committee on the Education of the Poorer Classes in England and Wales, the 1861 Assistant Commissioner's inquiry into the state of popular education in England and the 1888 Royal Commission appointed to inquire into the workings of the Elementary Education Acts in England and Wales. Sometimes other organisations conducted their own local investigations such as Birmingham Statistical Society's inquiry into education in 1835.

The reports of Her Majesty's Inspectors (HMIs) provide a very useful source for many aspects of education. Another source is the minutes of the Committee of Council for Education and the successor reports which cover aspects such as finances, buildings, equipment, accommodation and attendance for the later nineteenth century although the detail varies from school to school.

Magazines, prospectuses and advertisements may also prove fruitful. Magazines can come in two forms. Official journals were sometimes produced by organisations such as the *Ragged School Union Magazine* for the period 1849–75 and the *School Board Chronicle* exists for the later nineteenth century. However, many schools especially secondary and independent developed their own magazines from an early date.

Local school records

School board records such as minute books, correspondence, circulars, election details, returns and salary books are likely to be useful for the last 30 years of the nineteenth century. Most will be held locally. After 1903 the LEA records should be searched. There may be annual reports, minute books and correspondence as well as details of new requirements such as school meals, medical inspections and architects' plans.

Log books

Log books vary in quality but many are captivating documents probing beneath the officialdom to give a real feel for how schools were operating in practice. The original injunction of 1862 required only a daily 'briefest entry'. A fair number, however, date from before the statutory requirements and headteachers often entered considerable detail although entries were not always daily. Within them, you may find details about achievements, attendance, teaching staff and their problems, purchases such as teaching materials, books and furniture, recalcitrant pupils and punishments, problems with parents, rewards and visits. They are also excellent for lessons and the curriculum taught.

Registers and other written documents

There is a number of other records which may be available locally. For example, attendance and admission registers can provide you with details about numbers, absenteeism, parental occupations, catchment areas, ages and reasons for departure. Punishment books can also be very human documents and shed light on attitudes and values.

School managers' reports, correspondence, letter books and plans can also prove useful. You may also be fortunate in obtaining exercise books completed by pupils which can obviously help determine curriculum and standards. Many schools also have good photographic collections.

The scope for oral evidence is enormous. Practically everyone alive will have attended school. As many elderly people have a good recall of their childhood, many can recount tales of schools up to 80 or 90 years ago.

Post-elementary education

Nor is there any shortage of information for post-elementary education. Commissions such as Taunton (1868–69) and Bryce (1895) contain much local detail about grammar schools. Endowed grammar schools are likely to be documented through the records of the Endowed Schools Commission although a researcher will probably have to use the Public Record Office for the 6,700 files on individual endowed schools for the period 1850–1903.

Parliamentary papers can also be useful for grammar schools including Reports for 1865, 1872, 1873, 1875, 1886 and 1887 and 1891. Nor should you forget details in local newspapers and local education authority records. It is also likely to be worth approaching secondary and public schools direct as many have retained records such as financial information, details of teaching staff, minutes of meetings of teachers and governors, letters, teaching documentation, photographs and magazines.

7
SPARE TIME

In this chapter we will consider the following:

- investigating leisure activities over the centuries
- finding evidence of leisure activities from over 200 years ago
- finding out about nineteenth century leisure activities
- finding out about twentieth century leisure activities.

—— Investigating leisure activities ——

The concept of specific leisure time is a relatively recent one. Nevertheless, the idea of breaks from usual routines date back to earliest times.

Early forms of leisure

There is certainly evidence for Roman, Saxon and Viking games and entertainments. For example, Saxons have left us evidence in verses and pictures of music, ball games, horse racing, hunting and fowling. Likewise, Viking sagas such as the Orkneyinga Saga refers to games such as draughts, shooting and rowing.

Local historical investigations into the ways that earlier societies enjoyed themselves are much less prominent than for many other areas. In part this is the result of a paucity of evidence especially for the period before the nineteenth century. Where work has been done it is often linked to surviving festivals attached to particular localities.

Something can be deduced about medieval pastimes from surviving evidence. Local records, for example, can provide information about the role of the inn and drinking. Other activities are sometimes made transparent when communities exceed the bounds of respectability such as when ball games get out of hand. There are even clues in poems.

Sixteenth and seventeenth century leisure

Records become more extensive from the sixteenth century with alehouses, theatres and strolling players having to be licensed. There are also accounts of less salubrious activities such as bear-baiting, cock fighting, dog fighting and horse racing. Some places owe their development to sports such as Newmarket and racing. The Jockey Club itself dates from 1750.

A useful source for the time is Edward Chamberlayne's *The Present State of England* written in the later seventeenth century. He noted that:

❛ for variety and sports and recreations no nation doth excel the English. The nobility and gentry have their parks, warrens, decoys, paddock courses, horse races, hunting, coursing, fishing, fowling, hawking, setting-dogs, tumblers, lurchers, duck hunting, cock fighting, guns for birding, low bells, bat fowling, angling, nets, tennis, bowling, billiards, stage plays, masques, balls, dancing, singing, all sorts of musical instruments. The citizens and peasants have handball, football, skittles, or nine pins, shovel board, stowball, goffe, trollmadam, cudgels, bear baiting, bull baiting, bow and arrow, throwing at cocks, shuttle cock, bowling, quoits, leaping, wrestling, pitching the bar and ringing the bells. ❜

Eighteenth century developments

The eighteenth century saw new forms of leisure. Cricket became popular in the later part of the century; the MCC dating from 1787. Other places gained a reputation as healthy and/or social places. The origins of many spas date from the eighteenth century. Few areas of the UK do not show evidence of failed attempts to establish spas or health resorts. Facilities developed to support such places such as pleasure gardens. Coffee houses also became popular in the eighteenth century. By Queen Anne's reign there were an estimated 500 in London alone.

It was quite clear, however, that leisure activities were not always of a civilised nature. A modern historian, for example, has said of eighteenth century Britain:

❝ rarely has the world known a more aggressive society .... The amusements of all classes were streaked with blood and cruelty. It is not surprising that the popular sights of London were the lunatics at Bedlam, the whipping of half naked women at the Bridewell, the stoning to death of young men and women in the pillory or the hangings at Tyburn, where a girl or boy might be seen dangling between a highwayman and a murderer. ❞

It was the period after c. 1750 that saw the decline of traditional activities. Magistrates, the evangelical movement and MPs attacked many popular recreations and many had disappeared by the First World War.

Leisure for the masses

By the nineteenth century, the range of leisure activities extended far beyond village entertainments and drink for the poor and some specialised entertainments for the wealthy. Factory workers were given a half day on Saturdays after 1867 and Bank Holidays were introduced after 1871. Further changes occurred with the 1886 Shop Hours Regulation Act and in 1904 the Early Closing Act.

Facilities were opened up for all by the coming of the railways. Resorts such as Brighton, Blackpool, Bournemouth, Scarborough and Skegness owed, if not their birth, at least their expansion as holiday resorts to the railway companies. Factory outings became common and several industrial towns had holiday weeks and fortnights as they were almost emptied. Whilst much of the attention was on seaside holidays with new hostels, piers and entertainments, the holiday trade affected many places such as the Lake and Peak districts and other regions with pleasant countryside.

Other leisure activities existed as a break from the labours of industrial Britain and the accompanying living conditions. A continuing thread was drink. In 1885 it was estimated that the average working class family spent a quarter of their income on drink. The Temperance Movement existed as a part antidote and its activities filled the leisure time of a sizeable number of people. Various laws appeared in the nineteenth century dealing with the control or expansion of the alcohol trade.

Sport

Sport became more widespread and better organised. Cycling expanded and many took up walking and sailing. The growth of soccer is well documented with the first FA Cup in 1871 and the Football League dating from 1882 initially with a strong input from the industrial north and midlands. Other sports also developed. Rugby Union rules first applied in 1871 with Rugby League taking a separate route in the north after 1890. County Cricket championships date from 1873 and the first test match took place in 1876 one year before the first Wimbledon. At the local level many small clubs provided an extensive range of sports for many people. Horse racing remained popular with new race courses developed in many areas.

Music, theatre and cinema

The cinema, theatre and public musical events also expanded considerably in the nineteenth century. Music halls and pantomime belonged to the later part of the century. The cinema took off from the last decade of the century but was preceded by the magic lantern. The music halls provided not just songs but dancing, comedy, magic and other forms of entertainment. Fairs, circuses and other travelling shows were also popular with their varied kinds of entertainments.

Municipal pride

It was also a time of expansion of parks and gardens. The investigation of the municipal park is beginning to be an area of serious study. Other local facilities included swimming baths, libraries and museums. Most towns had their libraries, reading rooms and museums by the early twentieth century. Many places had a range of clubs for men and women such as literary and philosophical societies.

Home amusement

Spare time for many was less organised and often much more personal. Many homes had their own musical entertainment. The piano was not just a feature of the wealthier households. Cheap, ordinary games are referred to in sources. Perhaps at the lowest level was the simple hanging around at street corners as noted in sources such as Robert's 'The Classic Slum'.

Twentieth century leisure

No sudden transformation took place in the twentieth century. Sporting and musical events continued. Theatres, music halls and the cinema developed further. Railways taking people on day trips and holidays only slowly gave way to road transport. In recent years the British holiday faced increased competition from foreign resorts although the short visit to museums, tourist attractions and places of beauty have expanded, helped by the increase in car ownership. The holiday camp business expanded following the opening by Butlin of Skegness.

Recent changes to leisure have been influenced by changing transport and employment patterns as well as changing tastes. Eating out has become more popular and new sports have appeared and others, such as bowling and swimming, have expanded. Leisure time is now often spent in the home especially with the dramatic expansion firstly of radio and then television.

Finding evidence of entertainments – over 200 years ago –

'How did my local community entertain themselves in the period up to 200 years ago?'

As with most investigations, it is more challenging finding out about details of leisure activities for earlier periods of history.

Starting points

As always the best starting point is a look through what has been written to determine the kind of questions historians seem to be asking. Whilst not as well covered as some matters, there are good published works and articles such as Robert Malcolmson's *Popular Recreations in English Society 1700–1850*. There may also be information available from societies such as the British Society of Sports History or the Brewery History Society. Another very useful source which should be checked early on is the *Victoria County History* series which is often strong on early sports.

Medieval written sources

For the earliest period it may be worth checking archaeological reports or collections in museums. Artefacts may include toys and games from Romans, Saxons and Vikings. By medieval times, there may be snippets of written and pictorial evidence. People at play are pictured in some of the medieval illustration but they can rarely be assigned to particular places.

Local manorial records may help. A common local official was the ale-taster whose task was to check the quality of ale being produced. Court rolls can also provide evidence about the occasional game or sport especially where it led to problems. Information about feasting may also come from accounts and household books. Some are excellent in this capacity such as Lady Eleanor Montfort's roll for Odiham Castle in Hampshire.

The local investigator may also be fortunate in having collections of letters which occasionally describe sport. Often reference to sport involves hunting but not always. Eating and drinking are frequently alluded to. It needs to be remembered, however, that such letters do not represent the bulk of the population in fifteenth century Britain.

Personal accounts

By the sixteenth, seventeenth and eighteenth centuries, information about leisure activities increases but there may be a deficiency for a particular locality. There are of course the diaries, especially Evelyn and Pepys for London referring to the plays, music and other entertainments. Gambling and cruelty loom large.

However, there are other writers to refer to, such as John Bufton of Coggeshall and Thomas Cartwright of Chester. The travels of people such as Leland and Fiennes also give clues. Of use might be accounts of foreign travellers who comment sometimes on sports and pastimes such as Misson's *Memoirs and Observations* in the late seventeenth century.

The sixteenth and seventeenth centuries have much more than diaries. You may be fortunate in having drawings, such as scenes of games being played: many scenes exist of hunting. London is well represented pictorially including pictures and paintings of theatres, but similar evidence exists for many other places.

Inns and drinking

The role of inns and drinking comes out clearly in the documents. Travellers describe the facilities and activities for particular places they visit. Probate inventories may also prove of use especially for inns and coffee houses. Such documents obviously have a greater value in that they list other artefacts associated with leisure activities including reading books. Quarter Session records should include alehouse licences. Court rolls continue into these periods and continue to give clubs' pastimes exceeding the bounds of propriety. For example, the court roll for Padstow in 1564 notes that John Burlas kept 'ludos prohibitos' (prohibited games) and at the same place in 1567 John Bragyn was indicted for playing at 'le chards, dises et Tenys'.

The range of pastimes

The local archives may have many other documents which can be used. For example, a glance at documents such as letters and journals in the Cornwall record office will yield information on many of the feasts and holiday sports. There are references to bull-baiting, cricket, cudgelling, skittles, bowling, wrestling, hurling, badger-baiting, stag fighting and cock fighting. Some of these activities were advertised in newspapers. Others had societies established set up with rules and other documents that can be consulted. Gambling was rife if many documents are to be believed. The local records are likely to show that many social assemblies were associated with events such as assizes and other courts, race meetings, local traditions and festivals.

___ Finding out about nineteenth ___ century leisure activities

'How did leisure activity change in my community in the nineteenth century?'

As mentioned above, this was a time when the range of leisure activities expanded, helped by more spare time and improvements in facilities such as transport. It is also a time when the variety of documentary evidence also increases.

Starting point

Newspapers, directories and local society records

One almost indispensable source is newspapers which become more useful as the century progresses. A newspaper index is obviously helpful. You should enquire whether the library or archives has a press clippings file arranged by categories such as sport, theatres, etc. which would obviously ease the task.

Trade directories are also valuable in listing places of entertainment such as theatres. Many clubs and societies have deposited their own documents in local archives such as theatres and sports clubs. For example, Wolverhampton archives include records for the rotary club, opera club, chess club and more political organisations such as the Peace Company and the local branch of the National Council for Women.

Guides

Also useful are the many town and country guides especially for resorts. In 1851 Murray began his British guides beginning with Devon and Cornwall and finishing with Warwickshire when 60 had been produced. A rival firm was Adam and Charles Black in Edinburgh. Many of these early guides are not the tourist brochures of today but even advise about criminal activity and show pictures of industry.

Transport and municipal records

Transport documents may also be useful such as posters and advertisements from railway companies for excursions. Also likely to prove helpful are borough archives for details of municipal facilities such as piers, swimming baths, gardens, parks and other forms of entertainment.

Maps

Maps are likely to supplement information. The Ordnance Survey series, especially the larger scale maps should show individual recreational facilities and enable you to trace developments such as public houses, theatres, cinemas, seaside entertainments, libraries, baths, transport, zoos.

Pictorial evidence

Another nineteenth century source which becomes increasingly widespread is the photograph. Few places will not have photographs depicting recreational activities. A parallel pictorial source is postcards. You may find that your library's or archive's collection of pictorial sources is very extensive. For example, the Local Studies Library in Lincoln has a collection of 30,000 illustrations including 10,000 for the city of Lincoln alone. Many such indexes are now being computerised and should enable you to locate relevant illustrations from more than one repository.

Probing beneath the surface

It may be unnecessary to go this far as a large range of books of photographs and postcards has been published. It is too easy though to see holidays and resorts in idyllic terms and any serious investigation of a resort should probe beneath the surface looking at sources such as poor law, public health, Board of Health and Ministry of Transport sources. Vestry, parish and municipal documents often contain valuable information and sometimes local papers and councils provide visitors' lists. It is worth looking at published books to see the sorts of issues dealt with such as J.K. Walton's *The English Seaside Resort: A Social History 1750–1914*.

Records of individual sports

Few professional football or country cricket teams do not have an official or other history written about them. Centenaries and other anniversaries sometimes generate material. Some sports clubs employ their own archivists. Programmes are useful sources and these sometimes contain archives sections. Major sporting events such as cup finals and race meetings are well photographed. Newspaper reports of major matches are often extremely detailed.

Songs

Although unlikely to be a major source, local folk songs can sometimes give clues to past traditions, leisure activities and beliefs, e.g. about drinking or customs. For examples, there is a collection of eighteenth and nineteenth century Kidderminster ballads concentrating on the workers in the carpet trade.

Official commissions and police records

You may find that the various official commissions are valuable sources. A number investigated the drink trade and public houses. For instance, there was an 1853 report on public houses and another in 1877 on intemperance. Amongst the aspects they deal with are the extent of drunkenness, the possible causes of excessive drinking, the role of the pub and the gin palaces, brewing, licensing hours and rules, variations in drunkenness between areas, social classes involved, immigrants, men and women, the costs of drunkenness in relation to wages, the role of drink at other social events such as race and sporting meetings, the effect libraries and parks had on such habits, when drunkenness tended to occur and police and magistrates' attitudes towards drunkenness. Drinking records are likely to be found amongst magistrates' court documents.

Such records often throw light on other leisure activities besides the pub. For example, the High Constable of Wolverhampton in an 1853 report drew attention to the theatre in the town and the absence of parks. References were also made to the mechanics' institutes and lectures at the Athenaeum which were overcrowded. There were stated to be few public concerts with the 6d charged at the Promenade too much for working people. The decline of some activities can also be noted. For example, the same official noted that dog fighting and bull baiting had diminished recently.

Records of music-making and theatre

In 1866 there was an investigation into theatrical licences which sheds much light on theatres and musical halls. Music halls in particular became significant from the mid-nineteenth century until they faded in the 1930s. The investigators sought local information about licensing arrangements, the capacity of institutions, prices, audiences, stages and scenery, performers. Sometimes the detail extends to an extensive description of an evening's performance. Do look though to see whether work on theatres has been done already. The Society for Theatre Research has been active and many local organisations have looked at early theatres. You may be fortunate in having access to the posters and handbills of theatres and music halls although newspapers often provide back up information.

Finding out about twentieth century leisure activities

'How have leisure activities in my community changed over the last 50 years?'

Many of the sources referred to above continue to provide useful information. Many activities have been well researched and documented and it would be worthwhile searching catalogues for books and articles in local journals to establish whether a particular leisure activity has already been researched and written about. For example, public houses, parks, seaside holidays, piers, music halls, cinemas and theatres have generated many books. Sometimes there are regional research groups on an aspect of leisure such as the Mercia Cinema Society. The same applies to sports.

Starting point

Personal accounts

Oral evidence can perhaps add new detail. Inter-war interviews with employees exist; and have been published for places like Middlesbrough, Clydeside and the Nottinghamshire and Derbyshire coalfields. It may be possible to probe areas not usually covered in other sources such as attitudes towards various types of leisure, personal tastes, the everyday games such as playground and street games, how much spare time there was for different classes, families and ages. There may also be diaries and letters available.

Parish councils

The councils were set up to replace the vestries after 1894. Amongst their concerns could be allotments, footpaths, local celebrations, recreation rooms and playing fields.

Drinking records

The licensed trade is also well covered in recent years, e.g. magistrates' records and Home Office documentation. The latter includes 'Statistics as to the Operation and Administration of Laws relating to the Sale of Intoxicating Liquors in 1921 and 1938'.

Surviving evidence

Finally one should not ignore surviving evidence. Whilst many facilities have been demolished, the landscape is dotted around with evidence of buildings either maintaining former uses or converted to other functions. Old inns, theatres and cinemas have often been converted, and it is possible to trace remains of recreational facilities as varied as old skating rinks, exhibition halls, concert halls, swimming and slipper baths, boating lakes, horse and greyhound race tracks, fairgrounds and zoos, sports stadia, towers and dance halls.

8
OCCUPATIONS

In this chapter we will consider the following:

- the sources which will help
- names
- pre-industrial rural communities
- towns
- guilds
- trade and industry
- the question of scale
- learning a trade
- some typical occupations
- industrial archaeology

As you think about the theme of occupations, the following are the kind of questions that may occur to you. Maybe the community you are studying will enable you to answer one of them in a research project.

1 What did working for your local Lord of the Manor actually involve?
2 How were community services organised in late medieval times?
3 What area did industrial firms in your area influence (by selling their wares or services, and recruiting their workforce)?
4 How far were people prepared to travel to get to work?
5 How did the new industrial manufacturers find their workforce?
6 What 'specialist' jobs were done in your area? Were they part of an overall manufacturing system, (for example, a 'French polisher' who is part of the chairmaking trade)?
7 Why do censuses show certain trades existing together, (grocer and tea dealer; blacksmith and beer retailer, for instance)?
8 How did people in your study area make a living before the Industrial Revolution? How do these occupations differ from the work going on in the area today?
9 What did a family do if its cost of living exceeded its main wage-earner's money?

─── Identifying useful sources ───

At almost all stages of a society's development, labour is divided. As you research occupations in your study area, you must think about the stage the community had reached in the period that interests you. There is no point in trying to find company records for the fifteenth century relating to a cloth mill you know to have been working in the early 1800s. In the middle ages, work wasn't organised that way.

Written and pictorial records

Most records are extensive in modern times and decrease in availability the further back you go. Thus studying the history of say a Sheffield cutlery manufacturer is easier in Victorian times than finding out who made knives and forks for the community 200 years earlier.

Useful sources include: censuses for the 1851–91 period and directories from 1800; also, local newspapers from 1850 are likely to be helpful. Guild records and individual firms' records will contain technical as well as general facts, while town records will yield more general data – cutlers, for example, required town land and public water for their trade. They would also have been represented in civic ceremonial events, no doubt. Apprentice indentures shed light on eighteenth century trade. Local reference libraries will have printed books that cover both your town and the trade in which you are interested. These not only contain descriptions, but also reminiscences.

Art galleries and libraries will contain photographs and other pictorial evidence of trades that interest you. Museums, study centres and large houses open to the public often contain sections which reconstruct local trades. From time to time, demonstrations of old crafts are to be found and are well worth going to.

Names

Place names

Quite a few settlements bear witness to occupations at one time associated with them: Sutterton, Lincolnshire (shoemaker's homestead); Marloes, Dyfed (place where marl is dug); Abbey, Co. Galway; Cobalt, Ontario (Canada). Other words are less obvious, thus 'Chipping' from the Anglo-Saxon *ceap* (to barter) is part of many names (e.g. Chipping Norton in Oxfordshire).

Parts of place names often describe particular kinds of work which once went on there. For instance '-wic' from the Latin *vicus* (a row of houses) is sometimes found at the end of names. Some -wic names originally described early *entrepôts* (like Southampton, originally 'Hamwic', which was the distribution port for Winchester, and 'Londonwic' the original name for the area around the Strand, which served the city). But the word also had another meaning: 'dairy farm'. Your library will contain books on general and local place names.

Street names

Street names provide an even clearer indication of trades. It is common for traders to keep together in a town:

- they may need to share a common resource (such as water power)
- they may need to deal between one another as part of the manufacturing process (for example the chairmaking industry)
- younger members of families may wish to work near their relatives
- it is an economic fact that custom increases if a trader sets up near his rival rather than far away from him. (If this sounds odd, imagine wishing to buy a house. Are you more likely to visit four agents if they are all in a cluster, or if three are in one part of town and one is some distance away?)

Most occupational street names relate to traders clustered together in a market area. Some names are less obvious that others: Billiter Street (where bellfounders lived and worked) and Godliman Street (makers of 'godelmynnes', rather special soft shoes) are both in London. Ancient cities are a rich source of such names.

POINTS TO CONSIDER

Beware of street renaming (which can introduce traces or remove them, as it were); and the names of modern streets (a 'Tanner Street' might be named after someone who just happened to have an occupational name).

Personal names

You should not overlook personal names. At first sight this seems to be a rich source of information about occupations. The obvious Baker, Taylor and Farmer are there in the records alongside the less obvious Caird (a tinker and pot mender), Souter (a shoe mender), and so on. However, surnames were first used so long ago that, unless we are studying the early middle ages, they won't be very helpful.

Attributive surnames were added to single forenames in the period around the twelfth century (although the various levels of society were given extra names in different ages). Moreover, the choice of surnames was a relatively random process. So, in 1150 or so, to help identify which 'John' you meant depended on whether his occupation was more important than, say, his fiery red hair, his father's importance, or the proximity of his house to some notable feature of the landscape.

POINTS TO CONSIDER

In Wales, the practice of adding a trade to a surname, such as 'Jones the Post', continued into the twentieth century; and all surnames are much more recent in Wales than in England.

Records from pre-industrial rural communities

According to their level in society, people were either free or unfree. But both categories, when called upon to do so, had to fight for their seignior and to labour for him. Work like maintaining roads and bridges as well as labouring on the lord's fields was involved.

Even later, when the government of settlements had passed to the communities themselves, parish upkeep work still had to be done. Administration was then by surveyors acting for the community, although actual labour could be commuted by the payment of money. Some records of such service will survive, first in estate records and then in surveyors' accounts.

So, until the nineteenth century, the poorer members of society were bound to labour a certain amount away from their homes. At the same time, most people were self sufficient to some degree.

Early agricultural communities

Celtic and earlier farmers reclaimed small fields from the country in which they settled. Their individual clan-group areas were largely surrounded by waste land. The arrival of the Romans, Saxons, Vikings etc. meant that more and more of this waste land was enclosed. Place name evidence suggest that communities from these different groups often lived alongside each other. Although the latest wave of conquerors might rule the countryside, original settlements were not always entirely replaced with incoming populations.

It is, in fact, the Anglo-Saxons that we have to thank for most place names, for by the sixth century almost all English places had a name. The Anglo-Saxons had carved up the whole of England as they knew it, and parcelled out standard blocks of land to members of their community.

Working in the open-field system

In flattish country, especially in the English midlands and south, parishes used the open field system. Here, all landowners were allotted their share of different fields and other land. Crops were rotated annually in (usually) three large fields bounded by banks and ditches. There were hay meadows, woodland and waste land. Each of these played a part in village life, so all owners needed to share in each element: parishes tended to be formed so that they shared out the available land. So, in poor countryside parishes were larger, and where some difficult feature – such as a range of hills – crossed several parishes, they each had a share of it. Take a look at **parish shapes** in your area. With the passage of time, better farmers prospered, and less able ones sold or moved or died.

The open-field system (the champaign system) was not easy to run. Disputes regarding ownership happened often, as evidenced in court-leet records. It is interesting that the word 'hedge' derives from the Anglo-Saxon *hæg*, meaning 'hay', perhaps suggesting that hedges grew on boundary strips which were once cropped as fodder.

Another problem with the champaign system was that it meant travelling the parish to tend one's crops. Imagine working in one field, to be told about a sudden problem in another one, and having to walk a couple of miles in the rain to deal with it.

Some records of strip holdings survive. These are usually in the forms of maps produced by large landowners, for example the estates made by monasteries to verify and value their holding.

A combination of this general dissatisfaction and the increasing aggregation of strips by better-off landowners, meant that over the medieval period the process known as 'enclosure' began. By the seventeenth century, enclosure was well under way and by the late eighteenth century most open fields had been converted into small, hedged enclosures.

In land less easy to farm than the wide, open fields – that is in the hilly countryside of the south-west of England and in the north – a different allocation of land was needed, and the older system of small individual farms continued. Here, a single family's holding was often larger than that of the open-field worker, for the land was poorer.

Working in early towns and villages

In the newly forming towns, land was parcelled out too. Many market towns expanded into the town-centre sites we know today in the period 1150–1500. Burgesses acquired standard-sized blocks, and the remnants of these can still be seen in many towns today (car parks on land behind main streets often reveal ancient boundaries).

In medieval times, all these parishes were close to being self-sufficient. Their needs were simple: farms provided food, woods provided fuel and building material, rivers or ponds supplied water, and there was often clay to be had for pots and tiles. Any more exotic needs – such as stone for a church or gold for the landowner's wife – relied upon occasional trading with parishes 'in the outside world'.

Part of village life included support services. Thus millers and bakers, smiths and cobblers performed their trades when required, but probably continued to farm their own land at other times.

In certain areas, manufacturing trades provided the extra currency needed to satisfy special needs. Thus, as far back as the earliest settled communities, some commodities were traded. A few of these are still traceable today. For example, Grimes Graves, Norfolk, is a locality rich in flints. The best are underground, and the 'graves' are actually stone age quarries, little more than chambers opening out from vertical shafts. At ground level, the remains of the flint knapping process can be found. Ancient trackways lead away from the site to the north (towards the sea), so these tools were distributed widely into areas where flint does not occur naturally.

Similar trade routes can be traced from salt deposits in Cheshire, and from the rich metal mines in the south-west of England and in Wales.

Guilds

Those skilled in particular trades will have thrived in early communities: would you want to produce a makeshift pair of shoes yourself if you knew your next door neighbour's were comfortable and well made?

POINTS TO CONSIDER

Evidence of overseas trading dates back before AD 1000. In a fascinating Anglo-Saxon exercise teaching Latin (to children), the following exchange is given between a teacher and a merchant:

'Merchant, tell me, what do you do?'

'I go aboard my ship with my wares, and row over parts of the sea, selling my goods, and buying precious things which cannot be produced in this country.'

'What things do you bring us?'

'... precious gems and gold; strange clothes and spices; wine and oil; ivory and brass, ... and many such things'.

Aelfric's *Colloquy*

Such craftsmen in towns formed themselves into groups, the better to:

- fix prices
- teach their trades to the next generation
- defend their expertise generally.

Records survive both of central groups (like the London Livery Companies: from Vintners to Watermen, and Dyers to Fanmakers) and of local town guilds. These are to be found in record offices and libraries, and may be published.

——— Trade and industry ———

From earliest times local materials and conditions have concentrated some trades in particular places. In the eighteenth and nineteenth centuries, however, working at a greater scale meant involving more people and therefore such trades tended to be based in London and the larger towns.

In the seventeenth and eighteenth centuries, the well-to-do began to have leisure time to consider theoretical and scientific subjects. The Royal Society, the Stock Exchange and the first insurance and banking

---

POINTS TO CONSIDER

Until the seventeenth century any town in Europe with a population of over 20,000 was considered a big town. In a country where even a city like Oxford had a population of only about 10,000 (slightly smaller than Berwick-on-Tweed today), the importance of London – 30 times larger – is self-evident.

---

companies were founded at the beginning of this period. The expansion of industry required:

- need
- opportunity
- invention
- expertise
- raw materials
- labour
- money
- power sources.

Given that there was a need, the availability of money and the arts of invention came largely from London. All other ingredients were local, however. Your research is bound to uncover evidence of some industrial activity almost wherever you are. These might include:

- processing occupations – like making steel, glass or pottery
- extractive industries – metals, but also minerals and chemicals
- manufacturing trades – turning materials into artefacts
- service industries – from the harnessing of water and wind, to transporting people and goods.

Everyone was involved, of course, for occupations like agriculture, the merchant marine and the army all provided the 'need'. If, for example, you find that a Civil War army was quartered on an area of otherwise agricultural villages, how did they organise their water supply? Did general trading routes pass nearby? What local fuel supplies existed?

Thus far there is no industrial *revolution*: the growth of trades from prehistoric times was steady if undramatic. The one ingredient so far unaccounted for that comes closest to being a sudden change is – the power source. New technological skills created a need for more power than most places could provide. The first manufactories were sited where fast running rivers could be harnessed as water mills. That is, they were built in steep valleys below hill ranges. Evidence for this industry can be found in some landscape paintings.

Specialist work: a question of scale

Specialist work gradually settled into recognisable categories, but until the seventeenth and eighteenth centuries people tended to work as individuals or in small teams. A man who was a lorimer (a maker of the metal parts of horse harness) worked with other people, but he would be unlikely to have worked for 'a firm of harness makers' in the sense we mean today. The entrepreneurial late eighteenth and nineteenth centuries did bring people together to work in larger units, however.

To appreciate the question of scale, however, consider a trade such as printing in the nineteenth century. A company might consist of one specialist with an errand boy, or employ hundreds of people. Each trade has its rich and poor.

Learning your trade

Almost whatever calling a person followed – be it medicine, teaching or domestic service – consisted of a strict hierarchy.

The guild system, set up in the late middle ages partly to protect industries from the intrusion of untrained men and women, established four levels.

1 **Labourer**. To this we could add 'boy' or 'girl'. Such work required little training beyond obeying everyone else's orders! Pay and conditions were poor.
2 **Apprentice**. Masters and mistresses came to an agreement and an indenture was produced. The agreement was that the master would teach the apprentice a trade for a given period (normally seven years). During this time, apprentices often lived in their master's house, but would have earned very little.
3 **Journeymen.** Once apprentices completed their term, they automatically became eligible for employment by the day. This did not necessarily mean with the master under whom he had been an apprentice. It will have involved attending hiring fairs, reading job advertisements, and walking long distances to find work.
4 **Master.** Only when a journeyman had built up enough capital could he set up on his own. When that did happen, though, he could register with his guild, and as soon as he took on staff to work for him, the cycle was complete – he became a master.

Apprentice records are a rich source of information about trade in the period between 1710 and 1811. These dates represent the imposition and cessation of a stamp duty being required on apprenticeship indentures. Records were kept of apprentices' names and addresses, and the name and trade of the masters. An added bonus is that between 1710 and 1750, the name of the apprentice's father was also required.

Who worked?

The pressures on ordinary people were extremely onerous. Few if any families in the UK today live as the majority of people did until relatively recently. Moreover, the safety net to protect those who could not work was extremely basic or even non-existent. Luxuries (like adequate lighting at night or new shoes) were rare, and finding work to pay for the next meal was the all-important consideration for thousands of day workers. In such circumstances, how did families cope? By mothers and children working too.

Mothers took in washing, made lace or plaited straw. The discomforts of children's work was sometimes drawn by Victorian artists like Frederic Shields (whose portrayal of a six or seven year old girl shivering in the lee of some hay stooks while bird scaring, *One of our Breadwatchers,* is in the Manchester City Art Gallery). The point of such pictures was that every village in the country had families so poor that hand-picking stones from fields scoured by winter winds, and similar work, was all that kept them from starvation. Many more artists went to the other extreme however, idealising rural life.

Typical occupations

The 1841–91 census included occupational questions (varying slightly over those years). Usefully, censuses cover everybody, so women, children and old men are included – they were omitted from, say the *Posse Comitatus* (the 1798 survey of those men of military age). Using such records, a local population can be studied and compared with surrounding areas and with the same places at other dates.

Queen's Square, in the Frogmore area of High Wycombe, described in more detail in Chapter 9, contained 114 people in 1851 and 62 in 1881. Of these, 77 had occupations given in 1851, compared with 49 in 1881. There were 41 different occupations listed in 1851, but only 26 in 1881.

In 1851 the commonest occupation was 'house servant' with nine people involved and the second 'chairmaker' describing five people's jobs. In 1881 the same occupations came top of the list, with 'general/domestic servant' the job of five people, and four 'chair manufacturers'. A china dealer had built up his trade considerably, as had a draper.

Amongst the occupations present in 1851 but gone 30 years later were a blacksmith, two carpenters, a furniture broker, a hat maker, an ironmonger, two publicans, a saddler, two shoemakers, a stationer, and a straw bonnet maker. In 1881 a pawnbroker and an umbrella maker were the only two trades not undertaken in 1851.

The changes suggest a small reduction in houses (as opposed to work premises), with some of the few professional people in Queen's Square in 1851 having moved to a new well-to-do neighbourhood further from the town centre.

The following notes show the varying levels of work apparent in one trade which may be taken as typical of working hierarchies.

Domestic service

Samuel Adams, a one-time servant himself, and then author of *The Complete Servant* (1825), sets out information on servant keeping linked with income level which Table 8.1 adapts.

At the lowest end of servant keeping, single people with a modest income kept one servant to undertake all the general housework. At the other end of the scale, the servants' hall of a large house was a micro-society of its own, with the upper servants being looked after by juniors: in effect having servants of their own within the master's establishment.

Where did the servants come from? Besides the obvious supply from the poorer classes, the tasks of general servants, ploughboys and the like were surprisingly often performed by the sons and daughters of neighbours' families. As these in turn would also keep their own servants and errand boys, the result was to some extent circular. Table 8.1 gives some indication of the levels of income employers needed to support different domestic servants.

Industrial archaeology

After the Second World War, historians intensified their use of archaeological methods into industries from the more recent past. A network of specialists recorded and conserved the building used in manufacturing and a range of service occupations, such as wind and water-mills, transport systems, ovens, forges and mines.

You have a vital role to play in discovering and reporting whatever is to be found in your area. The work of preserving such features as brick kilns, saw-pits, trading posts, even anti-tank defences, can only happen if their sites are discovered and interpreted. No one is better placed to start this process off than local historians – like you!

Income level	Butler	Valet	House steward	Coach man	Groom	Assistant groom	Footman	Gardener	Labourer
Up to £200									
Up to £300									
Up to £400									
Up to £500					1				
Up to £600					1			1	
Up to £750					1		1	1	
Up to £1500				1			1	1	
Up to £2000				1	1		1	1	1
Up to £3000	1	1		1	2		1	2	
Up to £4000	1	1		1	2		2	2	1
Up to £5000	1	1	1	1	2	1	2	3	1

	House keeper	Cook	Ladies' maid	Nurse	House maid	Laundry maid	Still-room maid	Nursery maid	Kitchen maid	Scullion	General servant
Up to £200											1
Up to £300											2
Up to £400		1			1			1			
Up to £500		1			1			1			
Up to £600		1			1				1		
Up to £750		1			1				1		
Up to £1500		1			2			1			
Up to £2000	1	1			2			1	1		
Up to £3000		1	1	1	2			1	1	1	
Up to £4000	1	1	1	1	2	1		1	1		
Up to £5000	1	1	1	1	2	1	1	1	1	1	

Table 8.1 Income level and servant keeping in 1825

9

GETTING ABOUT

In this chapter we will consider the following:

- studying the landscape as we see it
- transport
- maps and names on maps
- town records
- canals and railway records
- directories, newspapers and other printed sources
- the case-study landscape revisited.

As you think about the theme of occupations, the following are the kind of questions that may occur to you. Maybe the community you are studying will enable you to answer one of them in a research project.

1 Did the river always look like this?
2 What purposes have the main through roads served over the years (drove road, stage coach route, etc.)?
3 Would our ancestors have recognised the Market Square?
4 Why were canals efficient for such a short time?
5 What was the town like before the railways came?
6 How did railway closure affect trading in the town?

- Case study: roads in High Wycombe -

Reading the evidence of roads

What can we discover about High Wycombe town, and past life in it, from the small series of crossing routes in Figure 9.1? We will use a

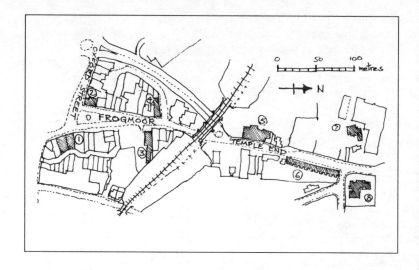

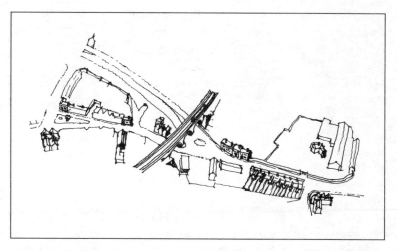

Figure 9.1 The Frogmore area of High Wycombe, Buckinghamshire (see footnote on next page)

number of sources to try and answer this question, including maps, the records of turnpike trusts, canal and railway companies, and town and specialist directories. As usual, many other sources will play their part, such as fieldwork, place names and publications. We start by walking the ground, noting down some of the features as we go.

The small area shown on the map is reasonably flat. The right hand 'prong', which rises to bridge a pedestrian subway, looks like a recently constructed by-pass. The brick railway bridge towers some 15 metres above the roadway and runs from SE to NW. It appears to date from the latter half of the nineteenth century – earlier bridges, for example on the Great Western Railway, were often built with more decorative brickwork. Recent repairs to the buttressing suggests that the bridge may have been wider than it is now, though both sides of the bridge itself look about the same age.

From the look of the houses just to the north of the area, and some buildings in Frogmore, the main roads date at least from the eighteenth century, probably earlier. Frogmore boasts a short sequence of 'old' buildings: there are a few from the seventeenth century, one side of Temple End has a good Georgian building, and the other side a row of attractive mid-Victorian terraced cottages.

There are a few actual dates displayed on buildings: 1861 (a modern plaque commemorating a nineteenth century business foundation) and 1909 on a Salvation Army Citadel foundation stone, both in Frogmore; also 1765 and 1888 on a one-time pub, 1876 on a disused police station, and 1892 on a past chair factory*: all three are on the edge of our study area.

We can see a few road names, and we must note these carefully, as they may offer valuable clues. When you are walking round any small area like this for yourself, other features to note are:

- unnamed courtyards
- open spaces
- street furniture
- buildings related to transport systems.

We might theorise, from what we have seen so far, that this was a crossing of some antiquity: a named road to a major city meets another containing houses dating back at least two centuries. Perhaps there was a temple (prehistoric/Roman/more recent?) somewhere near the northern part of the area. Somewhere near here a manorial dovecote may have stood.

---

* During the proofing of this book, the old chair factory has been demolished. This is typical of local history study: our record of this piece of High Wycombe's past is all that survives.

POINTS TO CONSIDER

Speculating on the meaning of names is always a good idea, but there are many ways that some names can arise. You will need to check early maps and other documents to 'prove' anything. For example, 'Ship Street' is often properly 'Sheep Street': the end of a drove road. Here 'Dovecote Road' provides another example:

◆ It could commemorate the site of an ancient (usually) manorial nesting site for pigeons, bred for the pot

◆ It could refer to a field of that name, itself probably derived as above

◆ It may once have had a pub nearby of that name; this may have been named at some past owner's whim, but again could refer to a real dovecote;

◆ bear in mind, though, that it may even be a wrong interpretation of some earlier name: for example, suppose a property once stood on this site called 'The Ducat' (referring for some reason to the medieval coin of that name), it is not difficult to imagine people saying 'Dovecote' years after the original building had disappeared.

The seventeenth century building in Frogmore is a pub, 'The Bell'; we must check to see if it has always had this name. Were there other pubs in this area? Were any of them staging posts for coaches or carriers?

The triangular area in Frogmore suggests a market. (Road patterns like this, even those where the enclosed area is built over, are often all that remains of an open market space.) There is no evidence of a market today. The street name and the lie of the land suggest low, perhaps boggy ground.

POINTS TO CONSIDER

Today's place names ending in -moor-/-more/-mere/-mer may come from Old English *mor*, meaning 'moor', 'waste upland' or 'fen'; or from *mere*, 'lake'.

Now we must start searching the records; we will leave our High Wycombe example for a moment.

— Transport systems: background —

For many hundreds of years, the only alternatives to walking were riding on horseback or on a cart. Heavy loads would be transported on packhorse trains, or moved ponderously by ox-carts; oxen were best suited to hauling dead weights slowly along roads either awash with mud, or baked into solid corrugated ruts. Only in the sixteenth to eighteenth centuries were coaches first imported (from the Hungarian town of Kocs). But at the time, few roads outside the main cities would have been fit to drive on. Both roads and transport which used them developed technically during the nineteenth century; the processes of improvement went hand in hand. A few steam buses were introduced as early as the 1830s, (see Figure 9.2). The public were worried about them on several counts, however, but a parliamentary committee ruled that they were acceptable as long as they did not exceed three tons in weight, nor run at more than ten mph; that way, said the committee, they were acceptable, as:

❝ they admit of greater breadth of tire than other carriages, and as the roads are not acted on so injuriously as by the feet of horses in common draught, such carriages will cause less wear of roads than coaches drawn by horses. ❞

Figure 9.2 One of Hancock's patent steam coaches, 1832

Early motorised vehicles used every conceivable drive system, though the problem of weight was not really solved until petrol engines evolved at the end of the nineteenth century. By that time the technology of rubber tyre manufacture had also developed.

Bicycles and tricycles (from which cars developed) evolved too, and as manufacturing methods standardised, large numbers could be produced profitably, spreading their use widely. Many districts had cycling clubs and, as photography had also developed into a popular hobby, most local history picture collections include records of their meetings.

Until the early 1800s, all river and canal and transport moved by sail, horse or manpower. The first steam boats (on the River Clyde in 1802) quickly established themselves. Within ten years, a passenger service was running and, a few years later, the joys of a steam boat trip down the river were expressed in ballad form

> ❝ The signal horn has call'd us now on board
> To warn the people, it is blown right loud
> While for the trip the steam-boat is well stor'd,
> The weather fine has brought a decent crowd
> The various luggage is in haste well stor'd
> Now strikes the hour, departure's pointed term
> The steam-boat flies, as of its cargo proud... ❞
>
> *The Traveller's Remembrancer*, 1812

The process of efficiency by enlargement meant that more and more river navigations reduced in length (as vessels grew larger their draft increased). Towns traditionally trading as ports, such as Rye, could be reached by fewer vessels. Trading by river would make an interesting local history study.

Perhaps the nineteenth century's greatest single change across the country was the advent of railways. The technical developments – from horse-drawn spoil trucks running in slots cut in stone, to the first class luxuries of the nineteenth century Pullman cars are well known and documented. However, local studies of the impact of the railways, and later of their closure, are still of value.

Finding out about evidence for transport systems

The sources most useful to us include maps; town records; parish surveyors' accounts; turnpike trust, railway and canal company records; newspapers; directories and various miscellaneous evidence.

Maps

Prepare a large-scale outline map of your area, and mark on it your evidence as you find it.

Find out what maps you have ready access to in your reference library or museum, and work backwards from modern Ordnance Survey maps, tithe-award maps, and back to any early maps you can find. Your local planning office may be able to help with town studies, and some solicitors hold old maps in their records.

Your CRO and the British Library Map Room in London will hold more maps, any one of which may contain a vital piece of information for your study. Inevitably, though, the further back one goes, the smaller the scale of roads shown, and before the sixteenth and seventeenth century, roads may not be shown at all.

As you discover a new feature, mark it on to your working map: for example side courtyards, water runlets, bends subsequently straightened, disused railway lines, and so on.

Names on maps

Street names provide a wealth of information. This may involve:

- the streets themselves (you can get a surprising amount of information from the qualifying part of a name, see box)
- trades which were once carried on (Cornmarket, the Shambles, Baker Street)
- places the street led to (not always identifiable as separate places today)
- institutions in the street (Ship Street may relate to sheep, as we have established; but make sure it doesn't refer to an inn of that name)
- owners of land (Gold Street, Saffron Walden, Essex, for example, once led to the house of a medieval merchant named Goul).

POINTS TO CONSIDER

A 'road' is somewhere to **ride** on. You may equate an 'avenue' with a tree lined road, but it is really anywhere for you to come along (French *à venir*, to come to); not unlike an 'alley', which is for you to 'go along' (French *aller*).

'Court' is from the Latin root **hortus**, a garden; and both 'yard' and 'gardens' come from the same Old english word *gyrd*, a wood where 'yards' (i.e. poles for ships' masts etc.) are grown.

Also of interest are the names people give to the little passages between and behind houses. 'Ginnel' or 'gennell' is a northern word. Other names include 'jigger', 'snicket', 'tewer' and 'wynd'. The Grander 'mews' referred originally to the place in London where the king's hunting birds were housed while they were moulting ('mewing', from the Old French *mouer*, to change, **mutate**); the name then transferred to the lane where these birds were kept, and then to any back lane.

Town records

Roads and bridges were the responsibility of the settlements they served. Much ill feeling was generated in the middle ages as the villager appointed surveyor of highways did his best to stir his neighbours into action. Unless they had commuted their service into annual cash payments, every landowner had to contribute actual labour working on the roads, and had an obligation to provide carts.

Town records established and maintained rights to create and preserve roads and bridges, and control the passage of rivers as they passed through the town. They also contain general registers of judgments concerning boundary rights, the malfunctioning of drains and any misdemeanours relating to land and the roads which bounded it.

Turnpike trust records

During the eighteenth century road improvements projects were put in hand, as the condition of roads had deteriorated with increased traffic. Broad-wheeled carriers' carts (the HGVs of the age) broke up the surface of roads, and being regular services, they did so continually. Drainage and road surfaces generally were so poor that travellers were often forced deep into private land bordering the roads to get through. (Today's walkers, coming across a footpath flooded from hedge to hedge, will appreciate the problem!)

POINTS TO CONSIDER

Not all roads ran through lowland farming country (the type which was run as open fields). Celia Fiennes travelled widely in England on horseback in the early eighteenth century, and describes roads which varied a lot according to the soils on which they were built. In Devonshire, the roads were narrow:

> ❛ I cannot see how... any horse can pass by each other [sic], and yet these are the roads that are all here abouts, some little corners may jutt out that one may get out of the way of the other, but this but seldom. ❜

By contrast, Sussex – where the going was so bad through liquid mud that London-bound timber caught in the autumn rains would be dumped by the roadside until spring – was:

> ❛ A pleasant place to ride in the summer and dry weather, but a sad, deep unpassable road when much rain has fallen. ❜

The Illustrated Journeys of Celia Fiennes, Macdonald, 1982

By the late eighteenth century, newly planted hedges restricted such detours, however. The enclosure act stipulated that roads going through the newly closed open fields must be bordered by grass on each side, so that vehicles could go around impassable lengths of highway. The total width from hedge to hedge was to be 40 feet (12 metres), with grass on either side of the 10 foot (3 metres) road. But if the road was impassable, how long would the verges have lasted?

A new surface, and new management measure, were desperately needed.

John Loudon Macadam's 1820 recipe was to top a bed of small, even-sized stones with flint or granite chippings, and to allow the traffic to crush it into place. The idea was taken up widely, and Macadam's surface continued in use for country roads for many years.

POINTS TO CONSIDER

On a broken stone, old flint road, the energy needed
to move a waggon weighing just over one ton is.. .. .. 65 lb

On a road of broken stone on a concrete base, and
on a roughly paved road, the equivalent force is.. .. .. 46 lb

But on a well-made pavement, all that is required is.. .. 33 lb

[Adapted from Thomas Telford,
Encyclopedia Methropolitana, (1845)]

In towns, too, paviors' previous use of stone or wooden slabs, setts or cobbles, was superseded in the middle of the nineteenth century with the tar by-product from coke making. Putting this flexible yet hard-setting surface on to Macadam's chips provided the surface we still today call 'tarmac'. So much for the physical surface, but who could control its use?

Entrepreneurial Georgian and Victorian landowners not only wanted to stop people crossing their property, but also to make money from travellers. So control of new road building and maintenance changed hands from parishes to turnpike trusts. These were groups of people who planned and – once the necessary parliamentary permission had been given – financed the building of new roads. Then, for a fee, travellers could pass the pole barrier (the turning pike) and benefit from several miles of good road – until they reached the next barrier.

The fees charged were (according to Richardson's *Local History Encyclopedia*) one quarter penny (old d) per head of cattle (that is to say about ten cows per 1p today!), and 6d per carriage horse (i.e. 5p for a carriage and pair). Local carts and traffic going to church or funerals were exempt.

Frequent dodging of the simple bar led to more permanent gates being installed with toll-houses nearby, in which the toll-gate keepers, or pikemen, and their families lived. These houses had to be secure; the money held by the toll-house keeper attracted raids from time to time. By 1821, 24,500 miles (40,000 km) of turnpike roads were open in the UK.

Many such toll-houses still exist, and names help to place others – ('Tolbooth'; 'Halfpenny Bridge'; pubs called 'The Gate' and so on. Such toll-gates operated until local authorities took over responsibility for road maintenance in the 1860s and 1870s, while the tolls paid to cross London's bridge were not cancelled until 1878–79.

Traffic using these roads was increasing. There was migration to the cities, an increasing population (and a consequent increase in the food, hay and wood needed to sustain them) and also a growth in the moneyed, trading class. These people had the wealth and time to travel, and became increasingly inventive in developing the means of making their journeys including such potentially destructive devices as Brunton's 1813 patent road locomotive. This used two steam-driven poles that imitated the hind legs of horses in an effort to 'punt' the vehicle along!

Records of turnpike trusts, and the acts of parliament which created them can give useful background information on existing conditions, local landowners, money-raising ventures, compulsory purchases, toll rates and many other things.

Not everyone agreed with what they saw as the commandeering of the public highway, and letters may be found in local newspapers making contrary views known.

Canal and railway records

Like turnpike trusts, the records of these companies can yield a lot of information about the areas through which they wished to pass.

Canals needed to be cut through whatever countryside lay on their contours. Cutting a swathe of clear level ground was a technical task which engineers were increasingly well equipped to undertake. But, as with today's motorway construction, the disruption to everyday life and property must have been considerable.

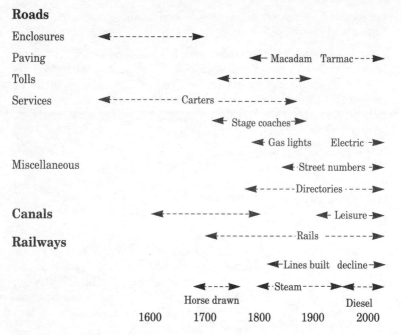

Figure 9.3 Timelines for transport systems

Not only was land appropriated and homes demolished, but bricks were often made on site, a smelly and smoky process. Heavy groundwork involved an influx of many hundreds of labourers. One can imagine that such groups could cause mayhem on occasions, even if they also spent money in the communities they worked in. Whole temporary villages of workers and their families are recorded in the 1851 and 1861 census even though most canals were completed long before this.

Canals were a huge improvement on hauling freight by road. On the latter, with a maximum speed of two to two-and-a-half miles an hour for heavy loads, the force needed to pull it is, as a proportion of the weight of the carriage and its load, 0.01. Compare the canal equivalent force of only 0.0001 – in other words, its costs a hundred times less force to draw the same load on water.

Canals were so much better than roads – but the new railroads were better still. At four miles per hour, the *Encyclopedia Metropolitana* physicist tells us, the frictional resistance of a load is the same, whether carried on a canal or taken by rail. At twice the speed, however, it costs

Figure 9.4 Puddling the Thames & Severn canal with clay – a repair of about 1904.

eight times more to pull the same load by water than by rail. At more than walking speed, the railways are by far the more efficient.

Canals had other disadvantages. Because they needed to travel on the level they had to follow longer routes than railways. The railway was able to haul loads up shallow gradients (even though this cost some of its efficiency advantage). Canal locks helped, but the cost of building them was high, and a great deal of water is lost when using a staircase of locks. As well as millions of gallons evaporating over the length of the canal, there were leakages along the bed. Also, whenever a lock opens, a body of precious water is pushed 'downstream'.

Canal and railway company records will tell you not just about their building, but about running them. For you need to establish why the authorities wanted to build canals and railways through your area. Case Study 3 in Chapter 11 provides a very good example, describing one of the very first canals.

The rewards from freight carriage, mail distribution and the carriage of passengers were great enough to encourage railway companies to fight for land and routes, and to make quite sure of securing them by buying up the canal companies and suppressing them.

POINTS TO CONSIDER

Exactly how much water is lost when a lock opens depends on its depth. But as an example, for a 5-metre fall, in a lock 10 metres wide and 40 metres long, no less than 2 million litres of water is moved: say 10,000 baths full!

Directories, newspapers and other printed sources

Lists of people who live and work on the roads in a town are useful in building up a picture of its expansion. For example, carriers used inns on main routes as their bases. Mail services did the same thing, as did stage coach companies. Plot these on to your working map, and try to establish the date range over which they operated.

Local newspapers list services such as stage and mail. But they were also a forum for editorial and correspondence discussion of many aspects of communications and travel. For example, when railways began, people were seriously worried about being asphyxiated by the rush of air at such speeds. Land was compulsorily purchased once acts of parliament had been passed granting building rights to canal and railway companies.

Secondary evidence, such as town and transport histories, includes much useful information.

Ephemera

As you walk round your area, and read about it, the ephemera you may come across varies a great deal:

- street furniture (traffic lights, signs, lighting, manhole covers, etc.)
- lighting systems
- old road surfaces: holes in the road may help. Unfortunately there is no rule of thumb correlating depth with passing years. The accumulation of soil depends on the degree of urbanisation – lots of people make lots of dirt. In Bath, Roman street levels about 2,000 years ago are a good six metres below today's surface. In many villages and towns, the entrance to some buildings is reached down steps: this is often a confirmation of the old age of a building
- past drainage systems: culverted streams and raised street levels
- masons' marks on buildings and kerbstones

- milestones
- cats' eyes (a modern invention in the UK, but the Romans set dia-
  mond-shaped white marble stones in Pompeii's pavements, to
  guide pedestrians in the dark).

High Wycombe: what research revealed

We chose a small intersection of two old routes in this town, by no
means the most important crossroads in the town. Research reveals a
number of facts about the area. Small courts ran off both roads: the
descendant of only one remains today. The most recent Ordnance
Survey map reveals that the right-hand road branch is newer than the
map. Until recently, the railway bridge was really two bridges, side by
side. From 1862 to 1906 it had been a single-track line going over one
bridge on its way from London to Banbury. The second bridge was
added with another track when expansion was being negotiated.

The tithe-award map of 1849 reveals water channels by the side of several streets in the area, and directories actually call the area 'canal' or
'canal side'. These were artificial runlets taking their supply from a small
river. The triangular shape turns out to be related to that river (almost
delta fashion) rather than a market, though there was indeed a market
here, and the name 'Frogmore' is obviously 'Frog marsh'.

These channels represent a look at real life: picture the rubbish
washed into the channels, and the subsequent blockages, floods and
smells, the scavenging dogs and vermin. Then imagine children pad-
dling, and yourself drawing water from the same source...

Maps suggest that two original roads have followed these lines for
many centuries. Both are trading routes into the medieval market
town, one a through road between London and Oxford, the other a
passage into the local hills. A steady trade went on throughout the
Civil War along the main road, even between Royalist Oxford and
Parliamentary London.

'Temple End', we discover from town histories, ties the ownership of a
local manor to the Knights Templars.

One of High Wycombe's earliest records, the so-called 'First Ledger
Book', dates from 1475, but begins by repeating earlier 'things worth
remembering' as the modern editor puts it. A selection of just three of

the several entries relating to Frogmore will show the value of this kind of source.

- On 4 November 1309 a small parcel of land was granted to Thomas le Warner, a tailor 'which lies in the street of Frogmore ... which land is 12 ft wide on the western side and 6 ft wide on the eastern side from the running stream'.
- In 1477 another piece of land is granted. A general glimpse of the area emerges. The streams are described as running through people's gardens. The new tenant is granted rights in the far side of one branch of the river from his house, provided he 'make and kepe a brigge in Frogmore over the same watir agenst a house that [be]longyth to the Chapell of the Holie Trinity in Wycombe'.
- In the 1650s, those bringing beasts for sale 'have laid ... Dung-hills or moynes [mounds] of Dunge in the streete near the market, and after such Dung hath layen long there to the common nuisans have att the takeing away thereof digged holes in the streete and carryed away as well the earth as the soyle [i.e. the dung] to the greate wrong of the Towne'.

In 1394 a curfew after 10 pm is mentioned, and in the seventeenth century bequests are made for 'the repaireing and amending of the high waies'.

10
CONTROLLING LIVES

In this chapter we will consider the following:

- government in the community
- the role of the church and aristocracy
- law and order
- the needy in the community
- finding the evidence for local controls
- finding out about the changing role of the local church
- finding out about local crime and punishment
- finding out about treatment of the poor.

Most of the information given in this chapter looks at the English situation. It was not always paralleled in Scotland, Wales and Ireland. Scottish central government records are housed at the Scottish Record Office in Edinburgh and include parliamentary, privy council, exchequer, treasury and supreme court documents prior to the 1707 union. The Scottish Office was created in 1885 and departmental records for home and health, agriculture, transport and education are housed there. Many local authority records and burgh archives are also kept there including sheriff's court and commissary court records as are the 796 parishes covered by the heritor's records (committees of landowners). At the local level in Scotland, one should not ignore the influence of the local laird in a community. Many families have deposited records either in the Scottish Record Office or in the National Library of Scotland.

Local community and government controls

Throughout much of history, national and other distant forms of control have existed for many local people. It is often the central or religious controls which have generated documentation of specific interest for the local historian. After all, the valuable *Domesday Book* was a national government, not a local, initiative.

Crown and central government impinging on the local community

Whilst a person might live in a local community, it would be unusual for them to go through their lives controlled and answerable to a single authority. Central government would be likely to intrude in most people's lives. The monarchs certainly had their officials at local levels including the sheriff.

Sheriffs, lord lieutenants

In the eleventh century, the sheriff became the most important officer in the shire. This was the main instrument for royal law and order until the office of justice of the peace developed after the fourteenth century. Another crown appointment was the lord lieutenant who had a responsibility for the militia. It should be noted though that some landowners had their own forces and courts and operated semi-independently, especially in areas such as the Welsh borders.

Justices of the peace

For the local historian, the most useful crown appointment may well be the justices of the peace (JPs). The office really dates from around 1368 when the crown appointed guardians of the peace to maintain internal order in each county, selected almost exclusively from the local gentry. Gradually their duties escalated and they met four times annually in Quarter Sessions. They summoned a 12-man jury and many other officers. In between sessions there were petty sessions. Any elected JP could also deal with minor problems personally. It was the sixteenth century that saw their real increase in power, a role they retained until the 1834 Poor Law Act and 1888 County Councils Act drastically reduced their authority. For years, therefore, they had many administrative and judicial powers. The latter included the right to deal with crimes of theft, damage, trespass and infringement of the poor law. Serious offences were usually referred to the Assize courts.

It should be noted, however, that the sheriffs did not disappear. They were still used between the fourteenth and seventeenth centuries for matters like royal taxes, organising the militia and parliamentary elections.

Away from central governments, most people came into contact with authority at manor, parish, borough or county level. In the nineteenth century, they might also have dealings with some of the statutory boards of health, poor law guardians and sanitary authorities.

Manorial controls

Manorial control might be local. Many estates were held by local landowners but others were under the control of people with a regional or even national influence. These included monastic landowners and important lay ones such as the Duchies of Cornwall and Lancaster.

A number of officials were often appointed to ensure the smooth running of manors. Many were appointed annually. In practice, the posts were not always popular and it was clear that they could not always be filled easily. Not all fulfilled their duties well. There are plentiful instances in court rolls of abuse of office. These posts varied from manor to manor: there might be a **reeve** whose duties included the organising of the daily business; the **hayward** who might ensure the good repair of hedges and fences, and look after the common animal stock; the **pounder** – the man in charge of the pound for stray animals; the **constable** and the **ale-taster**. Many court rolls show the regular appointment of jurors. Few women served in any of these posts and most were chosen from amongst the unfree tenants.

Parish control

It was under the Tudors in the sixteenth century that the parish became a unit of government, a position it really held until the nineteenth century when it gradually lost some of its earlier powers such as the relief of poverty (1834), the collection of church rates (they were abolished after 1866) parish and constable appointments (1872). After 1894 few responsibilities remained.

The vestry

The government of the parish was the vestry. Most were open, allowing all ratepayers to attend and take part on a one man one vote basis, but after 1818 an act re-established voting on a scale related to land ownership. The vestry organised local rates and charities and they appointed churchwardens, parish constables and the overseers of the highway and poor.

Churchwardens

Churchwardens had to deal with routine matters affecting the church such as the maintenance of the fabric, nave, belfry and churchyard, purchasing items for the church such as books, vestments and furniture, collecting and spending the church rate, allocating pews for worship, reporting any moral problems with the rector or parishioners to the archdeacon (the churchwarden was expected to attend), ensuring parishioners attended church regularly, gathering voluntary alms for the relief of the poor, assessing and receiving rates for the relief of maimed soldiers, prisoners in the county gaol and for those affected by personal or public disasters.

Constables

Constables' duties covered the maintenance of general law and order, the pursuit and arrest of criminals, maintaining the means of punishment such as the stocks and local lock up, sometimes inspecting alehouses and supervising the military arms supply and the provision of training for the local militia, assisting the churchwarden against those who did not attend church regularly, caring for the parish bull, helping at shipwrecks in coastal areas and in the early days responsibilities associated with the poor.

Overseers of the poor

After 1601 many of the duties associated with the poor were transferred to the overseers of the poor. This was not always an easy or popular job and many instances can be found of neglect of duties. Duties might include arrest of vagrants including superintending their whippings or escorting them to other parishes, relief of licensed travellers and the chronic sick and disabled. The overseer had, in general, the responsibility for ensuring that none of the parish starved to death and the needy had somewhere to sleep.

Many urban areas had their own forms of organisation although major regulation ensued after the passing of the Municipal Corporations Act of 1835 which, amongst other things, required the keeping of council minutes.

Nineteenth century reorganisation

More local regulations appeared in the nineteenth century as the role of parishes and justices of the peace declined. It also developed as a result of new legislation such as that relating to schools and the police. The 1835 Municipal Corporations Act provided for a uniform system of elected town councils. Local boards of health were set up in many places after 1848 and the 1875 Public Health Act established urban and rural sanitary districts.

County councils were established by the Local Government Act of 1888 with counties divided into electoral districts of equal size with one vote per ratepayer. Large towns with populations in excess of 50,000 were usually formed into county boroughs. Such county organ- isations took over many of the administrative functions of Quarter Sessions. They took over other functions as well, such as school boards, turnpike trusts and highways boards and after 1930 the duties of poor law guardians. Counties also gained powers over roads, lunatics, the poor, social services, leisure, police and fire services.

Urban and rural district councils were set up in 1894 taking over the duties of the old sanitary districts and boards of health. These lasted until 1974 when district councils replaced RDCs and UDCs and it may be possible to consult minutes, accounts, by-laws, plans, reports and correspondence. The system of district councils has held sway although the move towards unitary authorities in the 1990s may pro- duce further changes. After 1894 parish councils took over most of the civil functions of vestries.

Other controls over the community

Religion

One other form of control existed in many peoples' lives at least until comparatively recent times. It would be unwise for you to ignore the influence of the church on local communities. Apart from the fact that the landowners of a major part of the county were monastic or diocesan, people owed tithes and other taxes to the church. Wills were proved by the church and births, marriages and deaths had to be registered with the church. At other times and for certain people, there were oaths to take or fines to pay for recusancy. With so many people living in areas controlled by the church in medieval times, it was inevitably the case that they were subject to jurisdiction and administration by religious bodies.

After the Reformation, many denominations and sects were formed to exert their particular influences on people's lives. The history of the British Isles is studded with religious conflict and divided loyalties and, for many the everyday direction of their lives may have been influenced more by non-Anglican influences. In more recent times when religious influence is often supposed to have declined, there have been many forms of control and ways in which it has affected the lives of people in communities whether it be through registrations, church courts, parish councils, wills, church schools or land ownership.

Unofficial controls

Besides the statutory bodies controlling life, however, there is the less official. Many people's lives were controlled directly by their landowners who, certainly in the days before the 1872 secret ballot, exerted a tremendous influence on what people did. Many landed aristocrats and industrialists exercised at best a paternal approach to workers and, at worst, an autocratic tyrannical control. The example below illustrates this effectively. It appeared in the *Durham Chronicle* on 8 September 1837 and came from the local landed family, Lord and Lady Londonderry:

> ‘ We do earnestly entreat our Tenentry, as well as all Agents, persons and people employed in our Collieries and Works in the County of Durham of every description to come forward with the utmost zeal and ardent exertions at the present important crisis to return to Parliament for the Northern Division our excellent and valued friend the honourable Henry Thomas Liddell. ’

Law and order

The enforcement of law and order was not particularly successful until the nineteenth century.

A haphazard system

The haphazard approach to law and order through officers such as the elected parish constables was not an ideal system and much crime clearly went unpunished. A series of courts dealing with different aspects and different issues and circumstances added to the inefficiency. For example, there were manorial and borough courts, those dealing with minor and more serious crimes, those dealing with moral matters, some for unfree people and others solely for free citizens.

Assizes

Manorial and borough courts did not deal with all crimes. Felonies such as homicide, rape, serious theft and burglary, arson and breaking out of prison were usually dealt with in higher courts. Royal judges travelled to hold eyre and assize courts in medieval times hearing cases affecting the King's peace, revenues and civil pleas. Assizes were held from the mid-thirteenth century with justices hearing cases and sentencing. After 1800 the only cases to survive in these higher courts related to treason, riot, murder, sedition and conspiracy. The court of the archdeacon and bishop's consistory courts usually dealt with matters affecting the clergy, tithes and matrimony.

Quarter Sessions

Justices of the peace had much control over law and order. Statutory powers were given to them to build gaols and houses of correction for offenders or public asylums. They visited prisons and had control of the early police forces. Quarter Sessions became liable for maintaining gaols as early as the sixteenth century and were the real administrators by the eighteenth. In 1865 they became the sole prison authority although after 1877 all prisons were taken over by the state.

Capital offences

It is well-known that the number of capital offences was high in former times. The number rose considerably in the eighteenth century. In the early sixteenth century it was estimated that six crimes carried the death penalty. This escalated to 187 over the next century and a half, especially after the 1720s when it included crimes as ludicrous as blacking faces to plunder the deer park at Waltham. In truth, many of the crimes carrying the death penalty were commuted to transportation.

The establishment of a police force

Establishing a police force was not easy with many people seeing it as a form of tyranny. There was almost an acceptance of crime as a price worth paying for freedom although there were earlier attempts at crime prevention with organisations like the Bow Street Runners in London. It was the work done by people such as Colquohoun, Mackintosh, Buxton, Romilly and Wilberforce that led to a slow acceptance of the benefits. The Metropolitan Police Act dates from 1829 for London and the 1835 Municipal Corporations Act gave powers to incorporated towns to form a Watch Committee and a borough police force. Few bothered. A Royal Commission looked to extend police forces to boroughs in 1836. A permissive act of 1839 allowed the establishment of county constabularies but by 1853 only 22 counties had established police forces. It became compulsory after 1856.

The treatment of the poor and needy

The needy in society included: the old, the mentally ill, widows, orphans, illegitimate children, the chronically ill, the unemployed, the seasonally employed, the low paid and the lazy. The early history of their relief is shrouded in uncertainty. It is likely that the church and the local community played a part in looking after its more needy members.

Tudor legislation

One thing is certain though. The Tudors became increasingly concerned about poverty, vagrancy and begging. For example, in 1531 it was stated that any healthy person accused of begging should be 'tied to the end of a cart naked and be beaten with whips throughout the town ... til his body be bloody'. Those incapable of working had to obtain a licence to beg. In 1572 every parish was told it must be responsible for looking after its own poor and churchwardens took on much of this responsibility. After 1597–8 a poor rate was allowed, relief being divided into 'indoor' for those maintained in poorhouses and 'outdoors' for those in their own house.

Between 1485 and 1649 parliament passed some 24 laws. Poverty may have become worse as the sixteenth century progressed, exacerbated by the dissolution of the monasteries which had played some role in helping the poor, and there were also some negative effects from enclosure. Some historians estimate that one third to a half of the population lived in or near poverty in much of the sixteenth and seventeenth centuries, the result of many causes such as health, weather, too many children, too many widows and old soldiers.

Seventeenth and eighteenth century responses

It sounds a callous age with such legislation perhaps epitomised with a 1697 Act which required paupers to carry 'a large Roman letter P and the first letter of their parish on the shoulder'. Local historians will know that this was not completely true as the testimony of almshouses will demonstrate, as will the charity documents which can be consulted. An estimation for Norfolk suggests that 12% of charity money was given to the poor but this had risen to 44% by the later seventeenth century.

Further acts affecting the poor followed in the later seventeenth century. The 1662 Act of Settlement ordered that a stranger starving in a parish could be removed by the overseer if there was no prospect of work within 40 days. By-laws appear for many local communities. For example, one for Darlington in 1723 endorses placing beggars in a house of correction for a month's hard labour, and rewards those apprehending beggars.

Quarter sessions play their role in matters of poor relief. Justices of the peace who issued removal orders and settlement certificates and took examinations or statements of vagrants. Moreover, any disputes between parishes were dealt with in Quarter Sessions. The following entry speaks volumes about attitudes towards and the situation of the poor in the first half of the eighteenth century. It is taken from the Cornwall Quarter Sessions:

❛ it is ordered by this court that Thomas Davy a vagabond has been judged an incorrigible rogue. He is remanded to the prison to serve with hard labour for 3 months and also on Saturday next he is to be stripped naked from his middle upwards and be publically whipped at Truro until his body is bloody between the hours of 12.00 and 2.00 in the afternoon. In the following week he will be similarly whipped in the town of Bodmin. ❜

(1741)

Private charity continues to supplement official sources even into the twentieth century. Until the nineteenth century, however, there was little regulation.

As late as 1834 the investigation into the Poor Law noted that 'charities are often wasted and mischievous'. The role of the charity commissioners develops in the nineteenth century. For example, in 1860 the Charitable Trusts Act allowed charity commissioners to intervene to reorganise smaller charities.

Although the 1834 Poor Law Amendment Act represents an important development in poor law legislation, it is a fallacy to date the workhouses from that year. A fair number of parishes established their own buildings after the early eighteenth century. Overseers of the poor could erect a poorhouse at ratepayers' expense. The 1722 legislation encouraged parishes to form workhouses and for small parishes to join together. Gilbert's Act of 1782 tried to humanise workhouse administration with the appointment of inspectors and the decree that children under seven were not to be separated from their parents. Paupers were not sent to workhouses more than ten miles from their own homes.

The effect of such legislation was sometimes to increase poverty. In years of a bad harvest, the local rate could be intolerable. The French Wars in the later eighteenth century put a tremendous strain on the system and there was insufficient work for the rising population. One result was the Speenhamland system after 1797. It kept paupers above starvation level and linked relief to the price of bread. Seemingly humane, it tended to encourage idleness and discouraged savings as relief was provided. Large families produced greater relief, often resulting in unhappy marriages and poor treatment of children. Poor rates rose dramatically.

Workhouses and nineteenth century responses

By the 1830s the poor law system was in a chaotic condition. A commission concluded that withdrawing outdoor relief would make the poor more steady and diligent and encourage higher wages. The commission led to the 1834 Poor Law Amendment Act which largely abandoned outdoor relief except for the old and sick forcing many others to enter the workhouse which was to operate in the principle of 'less eligibility', i.e. it should be less attractive than the lowest paid employment. Parishes were to combine together and set up unions. All told some 600 were formed.

These unions were to be run by boards of guardians elected by the ratepayers. There would also be a Central Board in London with three Poor Law commissioners who sent out instructions over aspects such as diet. You may in the course of your research discover the unpopularity of such workhouses, the dreadful conditions, the division of families, onerous work, plain clothes, spartan meals and silence. As anticipated, it did reduce the cost of providing for the poor but not excessively. Nor did it always achieve its aim. Labourers' wages did not rise, it did not deal fairly with those who were out of work through no fault of their own, many people suffered exceptional hardship rather than go into the workhouse, outdoor relief remained and there were riots especially in the north.

On the whole, workhouses were worse in the south than the north of England. However, the sources show touches of humanity, treats, schools and evidence of medical treatment. The system continued in place until 1930 when the duties of the guardians were transferred to county councils.

Finding the evidence for local controls

'What kinds of local organisation have existed in my community at different times and how effective have these been?'

It is most unlikely that your community remained in the hands of a single controlling authority over a long period. The first task is to trace who the original 'owners' were. The *Domesday Book* may give the earliest clue to who the owner was both at the time of the Conquest and in 1086. Since many medieval documents are concerned with taxation issues, it should be possible to trace ownership. These early taxation records include the hundred rolls, the thirteenth century enquiries into those holding lands in hundreds; the various lay subsidy rolls compiled at various times in the medieval period and up to 1689 but especially valuable for 1290, 1334 and 1524–5.

Information about royal influence may also be obtained from medieval sources. The office of sheriff generated the pipe rolls, accounts rendered by them to the Exchequer which details rents and other Crown revenue from 1131 until the early nineteenth century.

Central records dealt with a great deal of local business. For example, Chancery records which date from 1199 include Letters Patent which deal with areas of Royal concern about local communities and might include charters, grants of land, appointments to office and privileges from 1201 to 1920. Close rolls follow a similar chronology from the early thirteenth century to the beginning of the twentieth. They cover deeds, aids, subsidies, provisions, pardons, quit claims, land conveyancing, enclosure awards.

For the post-medieval period, there are other central government records which can aid you. Association oath rolls were compiled in 1696 when all persons in England and Wales who held public office such as clergy and gentry had to sign a pledge of loyalty to the Crown. After the establishment of the Home Office in 1782, the local historian interested in law and order can also benefit from this source. The records are likely to include lists of indicated prisoners, transportation records, the police, aliens and naturalisation.

Manorial and estate control

Manorial records may also be very valuable for shedding light on medieval and post-medieval organisation and control especially where you are dealing with estates which produced excellent sets of accounts, rentals, court records, surveys and the like. Sometimes the records for estates have been printed. At other times, the originals may be available in local archives such as borough or county archives. The *Victoria County History* usually contains details of the descent of estates.

Manorial records will often indicate the way local organisation worked, especially sources such as court rolls which indicate the type of business enacted, the organisation of licences and by-laws, how land was transferred and managed, how people's lives were controlled, e.g. through different types of labour services, permission to travel and marry.

Church and parish control

The role of the church can also be deduced from a range of sources. Consistory court records may be particularly useful because they deal with the relationship between the church and local people. However, perusal of wills and chantry certificates will induce the extent to which lay people bequeathed to the church. Oaths and registers indicate the names of people but they say much less about the way that the church affected their everyday lives.

As far as parish control was concerned, you are advised to consult the long-ago written but still useful *The Parish Chest* by W.E. Tate. Good work has also been done on the role of parish officials such as Joan Kent's *The English Village Constable 1580–1642*.

A large number of records exist from these parish officials although it is unusual to find full sets in any one place. In some respects though one other parish document has proved even more popular amongst local historians – the parish registers. These are dealt with in more detail on pages 32 and 155.

Urban control

A good source for general guidance is John West's *Town Records*. Details of early development of towns can be obtained from sources such as charters and the *Domesday Book*. The medieval borough charters are likely to provide some detail about their organisation and jurisdiction such as their freedom from control, and their other privileges such as the right to hold markets. Many boroughs have published copies but they are also recorded on charter rolls. Individual town records are likely to be kept locally.

Another good source for the organisation of towns is the 1835 Royal Commission on Municipal Corporations which looked at 284 towns including their constitutions and histories. A later report in 1880 added details on other towns. Since most towns have a published history – even if these are of variable quality – there is a good chance that it will contain details of its constitution and organisation. It may be worth consulting the archival records as well as the reports of the Historical Manuscripts Commission which has calendared the records of many towns.

Most towns will have minutes of the meetings of their governing bodies although how towns were organised varied and this can be confusing on first investigation. Records can also be extensive. For example, the small Shropshire town of Ludlow has deposited in the county archives copies of various charters, eight volumes of minutes covering 1590–1835, six of draft minutes, a range of judicial records from the borough court such as action books (1509–1864), summaries of judgements (1580–1712), rolls (fifteenth century), files and papers, recognisance books (sixteenth and seventeenth centuries), entry books of debts, 247 items relating to the coroners court (1551–1839), records of the pie-powder court (1479–1794) with land tax assessments, 886 items related to the Council of the Marches of Wales (1556–1684), various boxes of the court leet and views of frankpledge listing inhabitants and jury presentments, files and bundles for general and Quarter Sessions and gaol delivery, a minute book (1752–1810), licensing records, oaths of allegiance and 342 sacrament certificates. Administrative records include those for the corporation officers, four files on the Assize of Bread (1727–1813), some bridge records, charities, gaol turnovers, a fair number of market papers, militia records including a muster book 1595–1617, Civil War papers and a box covering 1715–1839. Parliamentary returns cover 1583–1820 and there are further boxes on voters, nominations (1690–1849), a police charge book (1864–89) and several turnpike records as well as details of nuisances.

This list is included not because it is unique but as an illustration of the type and extent of documentation available about a town. Admittedly many towns will have fewer documents, but there are others with many more. For many places, it should be possible to extract minutes of meetings, accounts, borough court records, rates, deeds, leases and papers and, after 1835, minutes and accounts of councils and various committees.

Family papers

Family papers may give clues to the way that patronage and paternalism existed in the past. This is likely to come from local estate archives such as letters and diaries which could exist for fairly recent times. There might even be oral evidence available live or in recordings such as the Verney estate near Winslow in Buckinghamshire. Older generations may well be able to provide you with information about the explicit and subtle ways that local families controlled the lives of their tenants not just through property and employment but in other ways as well. The influence may be felt politically and an examination of poll books may reveal to you the control exerted by powerful local people. Newspapers, diaries, letters and autobiographies may confirm such impressions and add further detail perhaps not available officially – such as treats or help in times of hardship.

Statutory bodies

It would also be worth your while to examine the way that elections and appointments of later bodies were organised. For example, to the school boards, guardians of the poor, turnpike trusts, vestries, local improvement commissioners and later to police committees, county councils, parish, urban and rural district councils. The influence of local personalities and the lack of representation of huge sections of the population may become readily apparent.

Modern times

You may wish to investigate organisation in relatively recent times. Modern council records are extremely detailed. Some county councils have published materials and some historians have produced studies for some areas, e.g. East Sussex 1889–1974. There is an increasing body of oral evidence available. For example, Suffolk County Record Office now has interviews with early employees of Suffolk County Council. Their records cover issues as varied as the poor, burials, wartime invasion preparations, allotments, footpaths, rights of way, local celebrations and festivals, recreation rooms and playing fields and village greens. Newspapers and directories may also be helpful for providing extra detail.

__ Finding out about the changing __ role of the church

'How has the role of the established church changed within the local community over the centuries?'

Obviously the research cannot go back beyond the sixteenth century. For the church in Wales and Scotland, it is even later. The main areas that you are likely to be investigating is the church fabric itself, the incumbents and their work, the organisation, problems between laity and clerics, taxes, forms of control, the church's role in education and helping the needy, and attendance at church.

Starting point

An obvious starting point would be published work. There may well be useful information in the *Victoria County History* and even church guides although many published works devoted to churches are concerned with architecture and fabric.

Archival sources

Archival records can add much more detail although you may find locating religious sources to be a problem. For an example of the problems facing you, look at the Cornish records. The bishopric of Truro was created in 1877 covering the county and containing one archdeaconry, eight deaneries and 212 parishes. Some 30 of these churches were under the direct jurisdiction of the Crown, Bishop or Dean and Chapter. Many of the records were kept at the Diocesan Registry in Exeter, some were destroyed in the Second World War and most are now at the Devon County Record Office but some have been retained by the Cornish Archdeacons and can be found at the Cornwall Record Office.

Bishops' records

Amongst the documents which may be available to you, which give clues to religious control are the bishops' registers which record the bishop's daily business, although after the Reformation of the sixteenth century they become more of a brief diary of ordinations and consecrations. Most are in Latin. Many religious documents are not easy to use. More useful may be bishops' licences, dispensations and faculties for marriages, administration of an intestate's property, church repairs, licences to practise as schoolteachers, preachers, for laymen to eat meat in lent, for priests to trade, for midwives and surgeons – clear indications of the power of the church on people's lives.

Another good indicator of the influences on everyday life is the ecclesiastical court, the records of which are likely to exist locally especially from the sixteenth century. They describe relations between church and laity such as disputes over tithes and about the moral life of clergy and parishioners such as cases of immorality, drunkenness, neglect of duty by parish officials, misbehaviour on Sundays and holy days, dissent and wills.

Visitation records

An archdeacon visited each parish annually and the bishop also visited the parish of the diocese every few years. These visitation records are particularly useful for the period 1660–1860. From the seventeenth century, it was a requirement to send out articles of enquiry prior to a visit. The local clergy had to answer questions. The place to seek such useful information is in the visitation book, many of which have been published. They provide clues not just to church administration and organisation but also to religious views, the nature of services, lay morality, popular education and church possessions although you should not assume the information will be easy to use.

Wills

Before 1858 the vast majority of wills were proved in ecclesiastical courts, largely in the probate court covering the area of the testator's property although a higher court could deal with matters if the testator owned land in different places. The main authority in matters of probate from 1383 up to 1858 was the Prerogative Court of Canterbury. The location though can be difficult and you are advised to use a handy source such as A.J. Camp's *Wills and their Whereabouts*. After 1858 a principal Probate Registry was set up at Somerset House in London and the country was divided into district registries. Many wills have been published and/or indexed – you should go early on to the British Records Society indexes of many Prerogative Court of Canterbury wills to save any unnecessary journey to Somerset House. Do note that old wills in their original form are in Latin and that women were not able to use wills to dispose of property before 1882. Care also needs to be used with dating as dates used in calendars and indexes refer to when wills were proved which could be a long time after the date of death.

In practice a will was often proved in the court of an archdeacon or in a diocesan court which can be a boon to you as the archive is likely to be fairly local: either in the diocesan registry or the county record office, although copies also exist at Somerset House. Scottish wills were 'confirmed' at commissariat courts and the records from 1514–1823 are kept at Old Register House, Edinburgh. After 1824 jurisdiction passed to the sheriffs which, with the exception of Edinburgh, are kept amongst their records. In Ireland, Armagh Prerogative Court had jurisdiction for the whole of the country prior to 1858. Today only abstracts remain and they are located in the Public Record Office in Dublin. Accompanying probate records can also prove useful especially the probate inventories already referred to although after 1800 it is rare to find an inventory with a will. You should also remember that relatively few people made wills – perhaps no more than 10% of the population.

Parish registers and other documents

Parish registers are very well known to most local historians. Many can be found locally either in churches or in county archives. Registers can show the business done by the established church in the field of baptisms, marriages and burials.

Other parish records are likely to prove invaluable to you. Many everyday issues emerge in the documents compiled by churchwardens, overseers of the poor, surveyors of the highways and constables. Parish lists were made of householders for the purpose of levying rates, militia or juries and these can date back to the seventeenth century although most are eighteenth century. Vestry records can be fascinating documents giving insight into community life and behaviour as well as a good indication of the power of the church at such a level.

Clerical diaries

Local clerics were often profuse diary writers and using these can prove both an informative and fascinating experience. Many give a good insight into beliefs and attitudes and the influence the local church had on members of the community. Some are well known and have been published such as Kilvert, Woodford, Skinner and Holland.

Magazines and directories

For recent times, use can be made of parish magazines which cover issues as varied as local history, services, parish organisation, facilities, Sunday schools, businesses, local concerns and the attitudes of the clergy to particular issues. Survival though is uneven.

Also available may be diocesan directories, newsletters and *Crockford's Clerical Directory* which provides biographies of clerics and details of churches after it first appeared in 1855.

Finding out about local crime and punishment

'What types of crime have local people committed and what punishments have been meted out?'

Starting points

The starting point should again be any published work for a particular community and the guides advising on the use of crime records. For example, David Hawkins' *Criminal Ancestors: A Guide to Historical Criminal Records in England and Wales* or Philip Priestley's *Victorian Prison Lives: English Prison Biography 1830–1914*. There are also societies which can be utilised such as the Police History Society or local record society volumes.

Your main concerns are likely to be the organisation and effectiveness of crime prevention, types of crime, methods of punishment, prisons and their changing nature, types of criminal, attitudes to crime and the treatment of criminals, the development of the police force, the changing nature and seriousness of crime in different communities and the causes of crime.

Different courts

Part of the difficulty is the range of courts which dealt with different sorts of crimes, e.g. minor crimes, serious crimes, crimes against morality, debt and military crimes. Different groups of people at different times could be dealt with in very different courts and this causes problems to researchers. Occasionally, the records for some courts are good. A detailed series of manorial court rolls can give a good indication of minor misdemeanours. Felonies such as homicide, rape, serious theft and burglary, arson and breaking out of prison were usually dealt with in higher courts. Church courts also date from medieval times and cover cases of immorality, marriage problems and defamation, with bishops' courts dealing with clerical crimes. These records are not always well organised and catalogued and you may find them very difficult to use without practice.

In Scotland the supreme court for civil cases was the Court of Session and for criminal matters it was the High Court of the Justiciary. Court books cover criminal cases from 1493. The proceedings of the itinerant justices are covered in circuit minute books from 1576. Such documents are often interesting for the light they shed on particular attitudes and events such as witchcraft in the seventeenth century and the trials of radicals in the eighteenth. The local records of the sheriffs are usually deposited in the Scottish Record Office.

Quarter Sessions

From the sixteenth century, the Quarter Session records are obvious places to look for many misdemeanors and infringements such as those affecting the poor, vagrancy, roads and bridges, assaults, drunkenness, bastardy, recusancy, witchcraft, slander, debt.

Punishments are given in detail of which the common ones include fines, whipping, imprisonment, the pillory and later transportation. There should be information about the local gaols as JPs were the real, if not theoretical, administrators until taken over by the state in 1877. The first question you should ask when using these records is whether an index or calendar exists.

Records of serious threats to law and order

Sometimes the breakdown of law and order is serious, threatening the establishment order, and you may find this subject particularly interesting. Chronicles and other sources deal with serious problems in medieval times such as the problems faced by King Stephen, John, Richard II and the turmoils of the fifteenth century. Some useful documents have been transcribed and printed for earlier times such as the Devon gaol delivery rolls, or the fines imposed on prisoners who assisted the rebels during the Cornish rebellion and insurrection of Perkin Warbeck in 1497. State papers also deal with issues such as rebellions against Tudor monarchs such as the Pilgrimage of Grace in the north of England. It may even be possible for clues to be derived from building accounts and other sources relates to castles.

The Civil War generated a great deal of documentation including diaries and letters, sequestration orders, petitions, royal and parliamentary papers. Many of these have been thoroughly researched. You would benefit from looking at the bibliography for Civil War studies of many counties and smaller communities, or for larger areas, such as J.F. Rees' *Civil Wars in Wales*.

Threats to the established order continued into the twentieth century; you may be interested in investigating suffragette records, for instance. Home Office records can be useful sources of similar information. For example, E.P. Thompson in his well-known *The Making of the English Working Class* drew heavily on Home Office papers such as bundles relating to the London Corresponding Society as well as Privy Council papers and Treasurers' solicitors papers which contain details such as informers' reports and intercepted letters. Assize and other courts dealt with rural and urban discontent and crime such as Swing Riots and Luddism. Autobiographies and diaries can also be used as can early newspapers. Another source is family papers – especially for prominent people involved in activities such as local JPs and lord lieutenants. In Scotland, the difficulties caused by the Jacobites may be determined from the records of the Commissions for Forfeited and Annexed Estates. In Wales, some useful works have been established relating to the more serious disturbances such as D. Williams on the Rebecca Riots and G. Williams on the Merthyr Risings.

Nor should one ignore the many pamphlets, newspapers and periodicals beginning to emerge by the eighteenth and nineteenth centuries despite their obvious bias, such as Cobbett's *Political Register*, the *Patriot* which appeared in Sheffield, the *Mechanics'* Magazine and the

Northern Star. The list is enormous. Broadsheets can occasionally be used alongside such pamphlets.

Changing attitudes and circumstances

It is useful to trace the attitudes and response to particular types of crimes as they changed. As the eighteenth century progressed crimes against property are treated more seriously, and sources can be used to extract information about the types of crimes exacting capital punishment, the ages and types of people involved and the extent to which the full force of the law was carried out. Newspapers are another obvious source especially from late Victorian times.

One area which has produced a fair amount of serious research is the effect of economic conditions on crime patterns and the involvement of particular groups such as juveniles, Irish, Jews or women.

Central crime records

An obvious place to look for much information on crime and punishment is the county or borough archives but Home Office records from the later eighteenth century also dealt with crime and punishment such as calendars of prisoners' names, charges, verdicts and sentences, lists of convicts transported and in all prisons with details of ages, health, literacy and religion. In addition there are useful documents produced officially or by various societies, such as the various reports of the Select Committee of the House of Lords on gaols or the reports of organisations like the Committee of the Society for the Improvement of Prison Discipline. Both sets of records are useful for the earlier nineteenth century.

Prison records

Information about early prison records might come from comments made by the early reformers such as Howard and John Gurney. Other prison records can be useful, such as plans showing the development of different kinds of punishment such as separate cells. Prison organisation can be quite complex. For example, the 1819 select committee investigation discovered ten separate categories of prisoner in Worcester gaol. Areas for investigation can include the treatment of the prisoners, their cells, health, ventilation and lighting conditions, work, sentences, diet. Of more human concern are the details of the prisoners and the chaplains', surgeons' and visitors' reports can cast useful light on personal issues. Prison chaplains, in particular, regularly produced reports on prisoners and they can make fascinating reading often providing brief case histories of each prisoner as well as opinions on character and religious knowledge. Also useful might be sources from groups such as the Prisoners' Aid Societies in the nineteenth century.

The Shropshire records must suffice to give a taste of what types of prison records may be found in local archives. They include sources related to rules, diet, annual reports, plans and building reports on aspects such as heating, water, drainage and sewers. Also held are enquiries into the appointment and conduct of prison officials such as the prison surgeon, correspondence over issues such as treatment of the sick and insane and over military prisoners and charity accounts.

The nineteenth century generated many official investigations into all aspects of crime, criminals and punishment such as the 1819 select committee, the 1835 Report of the House of Lords inquiring into the present state of several gaols and houses of correction in England and Wales, the 1847 House of Lords inquiry into criminal law focusing particularly on juvenile offenders and transportation, the 1850 select committee on prison discipline and another on the same theme in 1869.

Police records

With the establishment of county and borough police forces, local documents were generated which often provide fascinating and valuable information. The range includes rules, regular reports from the county or borough constabulary committee and from the chief constables, information about the size of the force, employment, buildings, police committee minutes, accounts and charge books. There were also unofficial books and diaries kept by members of the force. Early police sources often demonstrate the force's unpopularity and the problems it faced. Local private organisations existed in some number – it is estimated there were some 500 acting as rivals to the police forces in 1839 – the records of Societies for the Prosecution of Offenders are often useful documents for those investigating law and order.

Modern times

In recent times the system of courts has altered. However, records of divisional courts such as petty divisional ones have often been deposited in local archives. Not all magistrates' records and police charge books will be released even to the bona fide researcher, although newspapers can help with more recent crimes. Many local papers devote considerable space to recording trials and crimes. They note punishments and occasionally reflect attitudes. Attitudes and extra information can also be derived from oral evidence from both criminals and law enforcers. For example, the Suffolk archives has a tape interviewing the first WPC.

Finding out about the lives of the poor

'How well have the poor been treated in the locality at different times?'

The researcher into the lives of the poor will find that the bulk of information will emanate from the period when central and local government became increasingly concerned about them. Trying to find out much about the very bottom tiers of society before the sixteenth century is very difficult. Any glance through manorial and central government documents will reveal few names of people who can be identified as paupers. At the same time, we know that the poor must have been extensive in number given the references to famine and starvation.

Starting points

Your main areas of interest are likely to include the extent of poverty, the causes of poverty, the types of people who were or became poor, attitudes to poverty and how these changed, types of poverty, ways in which local and central government attempted to solve the problem and the conditions faced by the poor. The effects of poverty can also be investigated, such as migration to London, emigration abroad and hardships in particular areas.

From the sixteenth century, you have available the information in the records of the parish officials especially the churchwardens and the overseers of the poor. Quarter Sessions dealt with infringements of the Poor Law and with issues such as pauper apprenticeship, workhouses, bastardy, vagrancy and disputes between parishes. Settlement papers can provide information about poor people, wages, jobs they have had and movement. A few towns had proper systems in place such as

Bristol where there was a Corporation of the Poor; Coventry has detailed minute books produced under the auspices of its directors of the poor. It was not always a heartless response and you may benefit from looking closely at charity records. Parish officials sometimes gave funds to those they felt deserving and some ran poor houses.

Charities' records

You could search for charities involved with the poor by looking at the records of the Charity Commission but this may involve visits to the relevant offices either in London or Liverpool, and not all files are accessible to the general public. The Public Record Office has the proceedings of the Commissioners for Charitable Uses from the later sixteenth century. A useful source is likely to be the *Reports of the Charity Commissioners* (1819–40 in 32 volumes) often known as the Brougham Commission.

Whilst official responses in local and national documents are likely to provide your main evidence, you may also care to look at specific self-help responses or individual attempts by particular places to help the poor. The records of Friendly Societies can be useful and it became a requirement after 1793 for registration of Friendly Societies to take place locally. Details can also be found in the abstract of the House of Lords Committee on the Poor Laws, along with details of the number of poor, existing workhouses and charities in the early nineteenth century. The Co-operative Movement sometimes gave funds to relieve distress, such as in Darlington in 1895 when they also provided bones for making soup.

Parliamentary records

Other useful information for the pre-1834 situation may well come from parliamentary papers for the late eighteenth and early nineteenth centuries. In 1777 information was published on the poor, poor rates, houses, houses of industry and workhouses arranged under hundreds and parishes. There were also reports in 1817 and 1818. A Digest of Parochial Returns to the Select Committee on the Education of the Lower Orders in 1824 lists the number of poor in each parish and poor relief expenditure for parishes is available for 1815 to 1835.

In Scotland, from 1535 each parish had been responsible for its poor, and the details of the administration of relief can be found in the records of kirk sessions which levied a local rate. A 1672 Act decreed that the poor fund of any parish could be supplemented by a levy, half on the heritors and half on tenants. Some early eighteenth century charity workhouses can be found in Scotland.

As in England, the system was under considerable strain in Scotland by the later eighteenth century especially in the rapidly expanding towns. The early 19th century was a period of real hardship for many in Scotland and this comes through in sources such as the Central Board for the Management of the Fund for the Relief of the Destitute Inhabitants of the Highlands who dealt with the effects of the Highland potato famine of 1836–50. A Royal Commission on the Scottish Poor Law has much useful detail in 1843 although the information derived from the larger towns is relatively poor. The 1845 Act set up parochial boards to direct the local administration of poor relief. If you are working in Scotland you can thus delve into the minutes of the parochial boards and their general registers which note the names, ages, genders, residences, religious denominations and relief of people concerned. The records cover 1845–94 but are of variable quality and better for rural areas. Most of the records are kept in the Scottish Record Office.

The workhouse system

The effects of the 1834 Act have generated much interest amongst local researchers especially where workhouses were established. Much has been published.

The new system set up led to masses of new documentation, much of it with a fascinating and human perspective. It is the wealth of the documents associated with the guardians that repay particular consideration. Although they contain many formal entries and the value varies from union to union, much can be derived from many workhouse records; for example, about diets, prices, produce and registers of births and deaths at the workhouse, the financial level at which families lived, the size of families, illness, and the accommodation thought suitable for the average labourer. Many have used the medical officers' reports, especially those that list treatments, and there can be useful information in the reports of the workhouse schoolteacher. There is also likely to be information about work and working conditions. Subcommittee reports commenting on aspects such as pauper children, lunatics and the like may survive, as may information about local crime, rates and public health.

There are other documents available to you besides the minutes of the guardians. Admission and discharge records, for example, provide names, birth dates, parish, occupation, marital status, able bodied or disabled, religion, dates of administration and discharge, the nature of relief and sometimes 'observations' which can be extremely interesting. Occasionally unusual angles can be found such as those relating to Belgian refugees at Atcham, Shrewsbury for 1914–15.

Although many workhouse documents will be kept locally, the Public Record Office has a sizeable proportion of poor law documents including the Poor Law Union Papers. These are arranged by counties and unions and contain correspondence between local and central including health matters. Sadly many of the post-1900 records were destroyed by German bombers. The Poor Law commissioners (and their successor bodies) produced annual reports, and it may also be possible to make use of other nineteenth century central documents such as annual returns and statements of paupers (which cover 1857–1948). Royal and other commissions occasionally investigated conditions and produced examples from particular areas, e.g. on the Aged Poor for 1894 and on the Relief of Distress 1909–10.

Although these unions continued until 1930, it may not be possible for you to inspect records less than 100 years old. Newspapers and oral evidence may help fill some gaps. You might also wish to examine the lives of those who did not have to go into the workhouse. A few diaries and autobiographies survive which can be useful for particular areas, such as the East End of London. People are still alive who experienced life in workhouses and some have produced accounts of their experiences.

11
CASE STUDIES

Research is possible from several starting points. You can begin with a theory, and then see if the evidence supports it. Alternatively, you can start with some interesting facts, and then spend your time investigating the circumstances which give rise to them.

In this chapter, we present seven case studies.

1 The medieval landscape
2 Marriage registers, Hughenden, Buckinghamshire
3 Bridgewater Canal, Lancashire and Cheshire
4 Lincolnshire's schools
5 Pest house/isolation hospital/Saffron Walden, Essex
6 North America: Grand Portage: Fur trade gateway to the Northern Great Plains, 1731–1804
7 New Jersey: Finding the opera house in the hardware store

These studies arise from different circumstances: the second, for example, discovers and analyses some unexpected behaviour. Others take physical subjects (some still existing and some not), and relate how they came into being and what they were like.

In some cases a surviving structure was the starting point; in the others only names or maps suggest the investigation.

Notice that these studies reach different conclusions. Descriptions can produce 'This is what we can see today' results; on the other hand, studying problems can only end with statements like 'This is what we have discovered so far, research continues'.

Case Study 1
The medieval landscape

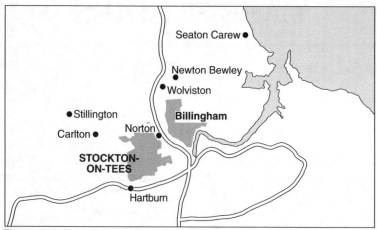

Figure 11.1 Places mentioned in the south-east Durham medieval case study

General comments

Trying to deal with a medieval community is unlikely to be easy for you if you are a beginner. The problem will include the paucity of evidence as well as the difficulty of interpreting the material that does survive – not just the language of the documents but also the unfamiliar content and the paleography. Despite this, it is a pity if the period, which is often so crucial in the development of a community, is left untouched. Although there may be difficulties, many of the sources may have been transcribed by others even to the extent of translating the medieval Latin into English.

The case study which follows is an attempt to give an indication of the riches of information which can be gleaned about the medieval landscape for a fairly small area. It should not be assumed that the medieval history of all places is equally rich, varied and accessible, but many areas had an interesting medieval history worth accessing if at all possible.

The area

South-east Durham is a fairly low-lying area bordered in the south by the River Tees which separated it for centuries from Yorkshire. In medieval times, the 60 square miles around the town of Stockton contained a number of communities shared between two large landowners and a smaller one. All three — the bishop of Durham, the prior of Durham and Merton College, Oxford — have bequeathed valuable sources providing insights into the later medieval period.

In this area by the later fourteenth century, the bishop had control of the communities of Stockton, Norton, Carlton and Hartburn; the prior had Billingham, Cowpen Bewley, Newton Bewley and Wolviston, whilst Merton College owned Stillington and Seaton Carew. County Durham in the later middle ages was the greatest liberty in private hands, with the bishop's power dominant at the expense of the monarch of England.

Through close scrutiny of the documentation it is possible to piece together a picture of this community in the century or so following the Black Death, which seems to have affected the area badly. The source material is considerable especially for the priory but also for the bishop's lands.

The sources

Although the sources are plentiful, they do present problems. Firstly, all the documents are in Latin, often abbreviated at that. Secondly, although the state of preservation is surprisingly good for much of it, it had become faded and difficult to make out in places. There are also many gaps making it impossible to gain a complete record of the period. To add to the difficulties, the documents are not kept together. Although the bishop's records have been kept in Durham for long periods, they were transferred to London in the nineteenth century whereas Merton College retain their sources in Oxford, leaving only the priory records in Durham.

Persistence though can pay off. For example, a perusal of the surviving documents for the 11 communities referred to above reveals over 630 place names, and this allows a reasonable reconstruction of the medieval landscape even if few of them can be placed with absolute certainty. Information about the bishop's lands comes from a large number of court rolls and accounts as well as some surveys such as Bishop Hatfield's of 1384. Merton College also provides us with over 50 accounts and indentures.

It is the priory documents though which are the stars and of national importance. Again the court documents are the mainstay – especially the thrice yearly halmote courts which a majority of villagers in each of the priory villages had to attend and which transacted all kinds of important as well as trivial business. A nineteenth century historian studying these excellent court rolls – some 99 full ones survive for the period 1364–99 alone – went so far as to state that 'it is hardly a figure of speech to say we have in them village life photographed'.

This was somewhat of an exaggeration – for a start, not all villagers had to attend – but they give insights into so much, and make many of the villagers come alive. They crop up time and time again in various guises: as officials, exchanging land, owing labour services to the prior, organising local matters, neglecting official duties, getting married, dying, obtaining licences and often getting in small amounts of trouble such as for trespassing, debt, slander or fornication. The courts also confirmed the by-laws made by communities as a way of ensuring the smoothest running of things. These are excellent ways into under-standing the way people organised work, especially farming, and their everyday lives. The four priory villages in south-east Durham between them produced some 430 by-laws in the century and a half after 1350.

That the court rolls can reveal much can be surely demonstrated by the fact that the nine villages belonging to bishop and prior yield together 10,123 entries for the 150 years following the Black Death.

There are other documents besides the court rolls, and the many different kinds of accounting sources can yield additional information about the period and the communities. For example, the priors' archives contain annual account rolls of the bursars, arrears books, debt lists, waste and decay rolls and rentals.

Other officials in these communities had to answer for their responsibilities. For example, the local collectors' accounts frequently reported renders owed to the lord, rents on buildings such as forges, common ovens and mills, court revenues and decayed rents. The bailiffs of the bishop accounted for the different parts of the fields, noting what should have been obtained. Stockton – which was already a borough – accounted for its tolls, the oven, a ferry across the Tees and the rents from the burgesses.

Evidence for land use

This area in medieval times seems to have been one of large open fields following the three-course rotation. The strips of the villagers seem to have been dispersed amongst the various fields. One field was always fallow and the two others often had wheat or barley and peas or oats. Another interesting insight comes from the accounts showing the various grain yields. It is probably a fair assumption that when prices were high harvests were poor. This enables historians to make educated guesses about medieval climate. How the land of individuals was distinguished is unclear, although a clue may be found in a by-law issued for Billingham – 'to stop people stealing other people's land, the prior insists that boundary stones called merestanes shall be put down'.

The number of land transactions also makes it clear that there was an active land market. At times rents were high and land at a premium, but the Black Death and subsequent plagues seem to have had the effect of producing a shortage of tenants. The result was the breaking up of the old three field system and much subdivision. Some villagers seem to have gradually built up sizeable holdings from modest beginnings.

The many land transactions might not make the most riveting of reading but they give an indication of the types of people buying and selling and often give clues to the conditions attached to land sales. For example, they show that women were quite actively involved in buying and selling, with widows having a fair number of rights – giving lie to the belief that women's rights really developed only in the nineteenth century. For example, in 1385 'Celicia widow of William Casson comes into court and takes all the land which her husband used to have. She is to hold this land by widows' right and she will continue to pay the old rent. Gilbert Hardgill and John son of Alexander say she is fit. She has to pay an entry fine of £1 6s 8d'. It seems that many elderly people gave up their lands on condition that they were looked after during their lifetime.

Evidence from farming misdemeanours and problems

The large number of offences and by-laws shed much light on farming practices and the fact that there were many cases of minor dishonesty. Animals seem a perpetual nuisance and there are constant references to people being fined for allowing animals to wander freely. For example in 1399 'John Osbourne and 6 others from Stockton were fined because they allowed their pigs to wander where they want amongst the open fields causing great damage to the people'. In Billingham two years earlier, 'John Luklin, William Wright and others will be fined 3s 4d if they do not ring their pigs immediately'.

It was not just pigs. There are many entries for horses, sheep, geese and other beasts. One way of attempting to control the situation was by restricting the number of animals that individuals could hold, largely in relation to their legal or economic status. For example, two later fifteenth century by-laws stipulated that 'no man who owns a cottage may have more than 5 sheep or else he will be fined 13.4d' and 'each person who has a land called a bondage tenement is allowed only one goose for every 20 acres of land he holds'. Other solutions included defining the times when animals could wander, as the following entry for 1394 testifies: 'It is essential that no one allows their mares and foals to go into the corn fields from August 1st until the corn is cut'.

There are even clues in the documents to dogs — which often seem far removed from the pets of today — as the following two entries testify: 'Robert Spurnhare of Carlton is fined 6d because his dog ate a foal' and 'John Swynherd's dog ate a pig belonging to Emma del Holme which was valued at 2s 0d and he is fined 6d'.

Much more happened in farming than animals causing problems. The following entry tells us so much about medieval farming and the potential problems.

❦ John Jenkinson of Billingham has received his lands in good condition three years ago but has not looked after them. In fact, during these three years he has not manured them at all preferring instead to sell his manure. This has meant that his lands have got into a dreadful state and weeds and other horrible things have spread from his lands onto those of his neighbours. ❧

Drainage was another problem as demonstrated by the fines for 'the villagers who own land at Southmeadow because the watercourses have been allowed to get dirty and other people's land has been flooded because of their carelessness' (1411). The court rolls also have many cases of villagers not looking after their hedges.

Evidence for building

Although farming dominated the local economy, the court and account rolls give clues to all aspects of life. In the absence of much surviving archaeological evidence about houses and other buildings, one again has to resort to the clues in the written sources. It seems the longhouse was the norm for most villagers, but there were larger buildings as there are references to people living in houses with seven rooms. Wood seems to be the main material strengthened with wattle and daub as the following entries strongly suggest: 'John Raynald broke into and entered illegally at night the lord's park at Bewley where he took away the branches of 17 oak trees which he used to repair his house'; 'The house of the vicar of Billingham is in a very poor condition and therefore it is ordered that he repairs his roof, the wattle and daub of his walls and the whitewash on the inside of his house'.

Houses seem to have stood in their own land probably often enclosed by a ditch, as indicated by the by-law for 1383 which stated that everyone had to 'build a ditch all around their houses so that the corn does not stray into people's houses'. The overall impression is of fairly constant repairs to buildings with many buildings falling into disrepair and the roofs often singled out for repair. This did not mean that the buildings were without any sophistication. The 1401 fining of four villagers from Cowpen Bewley for 'carrying away the door of a waste house consisting of the wood, a socket stone, iron hanging post, key, padlock, hinges and a latch' suggests that this was more than a primitive affair.

Although buildings cannot be placed directly onto the modern map, it does appear that most of these south-east Durham communities were nucleated, probably with streets up to 600 metres around a village green. The tofts rarely extended back 150 metres. The medieval streets with names such as Eastrow or Westkeville seem to correspond to the present alignments. The documents make reference to specialised buildings including the church, toll-booths, forges, watermills, dovecotes, a guildhouse and the common bakehouses where bread had to be baked.

Evidence for communications

Communications appear to have been primitive, although there are references to many roads and pathways. The following entries suggest that maintaining them in a good order was at best an uphill task: 'Robert Robinson of Wolviston stole a piece of the main road through the village which he then ruined by ploughing it. So he is fined 6d'; '13 villagers from Cowpen Bewley are each fined 6d because they have not used the proper road through the village. Instead they have made their own'; 'Many villagers are fined because their carts have totally ruined the road at Ravenswelburnleys'; 'The small road known as the longing is unrecognisable outside the properties of Robert Gibson and John Laweson and they are held to be responsible. They are each allowed one month to repair that bit of road outside their land'.

Evidence for attitude towards officials

The well-being of the community seems to have depended in large measure on the dedication and honesty of the unpaid officials selected from amongst their number to help maintain law and order. The main ones on the priory lands seem to have been the reeve, constable, collector and ale-tasters. Each were elected but they were not always desirable positions. For example, in 1361 it was noted that 'William Kaa of Norton has come into court and paid 2s 0d because he has been elected as the reeve but is too frightened to serve for the next four years. Fined 6d for every year he will not serve'. A few years later in the nearby village of Wolviston, a by-law orders that 'no one in the village is to use either horrible words to the reeve or to harm him in any way or else that person will be fined £2 0s 0d'. Nor was it only on the bishop's lands. In Cowpen Bewley in 1409 William Jonson was hauled up before the court because 'he had beaten the reeve so grievously that blood had been spilt from the reeve's body'.

There is evidence in the documents that the anger directed at some of the officials was justified, as there seems a sizeable number of occasions when the official took advantage of the perks of the post. For example, in 1401 it was stated that 'John Hodegeson, the constable of Norton, has been very dishonest to his fellow villagers. He is fined 6d because he frightened Alice Widowe into giving him 3s 0d which did not belong to him'. Likewise Robert Wilkinson, a later constable of Norton, went to the house of Richard del Well and warned him that unless he gave him 9s 0d he would have him arrested. Richard was most frightened and handed over the money. The same dishonesty seems to have affected the pounder of Stockton in 1401. The task of the pounder was to lock up stray animals in the local pinfold. In this particular instance, John Jenkinson, the Stockton pounder, broke into the yard of Richard Stanlawman where his horse was kept. He then took the horse and placed it in the village pound, saying that the horse had been wandering loose in the road and had caused great damage and upset to many people. He then told Richard he could only have his horse back if he paid a fine of 1s 0d. The outcome instead was a fine of 6d for the pounder.

The overall impression gained is of a community with many minor misdemeanours and problems but few very serious crimes. In reality, things in these south-east Durham villages seem to have run quite well. Many of the misdemeanours reported are trivial by our standard today. Some of them are almost incomprehensible to us. Quite why, 'the villagers of Newton Bewley are warned that they will be fined £1 0s 0d if they call another person a rustic', especially when the threatened sum is one of the severest penalties in any court roll, is a mystery. Likewise, it is difficult to believe that 37 villagers would be fined today for 'playing ball' as happened in 1386.

Evidence for anti-social behaviour

Anti-social behaviour was often frowned upon. In 1490 William Miryman was fined because 'he has provided lodgings for Margaret Capknytt who is not welcome in the village of Billingham'. A few years earlier it was noted that 'the wife of John Ireland is a gossip and a nuisance to her neighbours. She is ordered to get on better with her neighbours or else she will not only have to pay a fine of 6s 8d but have to get out of the village'.

While the majority of entries concerned men, women are not absent. One of the most intriguing of fines was 'leyrwite', for sex out of wedlock but payable only by the woman. How the crime was detected is uncertain – maybe pregnancy needed to result, but you might wonder what to make of an entry such as 'Alice Tewer for sleeping unlawfully with a man. This is the tenth time she is accused of this. Fine 6d'. The misdemeanours of women range as widely as that of men. For example, 'Alice of Bellasis brews ale but it is bad' in 1366 and in 1370 'Emma del Holme trespassed against Agnes Ster and caused 1s 9d damage, another trespass in the corn doing 2d damage, made a false accusation against Agnes Ster, made a trespass against William Ross causing 6d damage. She also took coal from Thomas son of William' or 'Elizabeth the servant of the vicar who married John Thorp and paid a merchet license fee of 2s 0d because she was unfree'. It seems Katherine Sharp of Stockton could give as good as she got as, in 1475 she was fined 3s 4d for assaulting Elizabeth the servant of Robert Burdon at which blood was spilt. She was fined another 2s 0d 'for shedding the blood of John Joyfull'.

Looking at the sources as a whole, this was not a primitive, anarchic community. It was generally well ordered and carefully controlled. Upsetting neighbours in the community at large was looked down on as evidenced by the by-law in 1378 which decreed that 'no one living in the village was to allow outsiders to cause a disturbance or else they risked being fined £2 0s 0d also payable by those who did not come to help or to warn the constable'. Other clues exist to the concern showed for the common good. The villagers of a nearby village in 1367 were ordered 'not to use the common well for washing their clothes' and in 1365 the villagers of Billingham seem to have had enough of the smell of fish oil coming from the house of the appropriately named Thomas Heringher. The outcome was that Thomas risked a 6s 8d fine if he made any more oil after Christmas. Finally, a portent of things to come when it was decreed in a 1460 by-law that 'no one is allowed to keep tramps in their house', a precursor of the harshness of such attitudes so well known in Tudor times.

[Researcher: Tim Lomas]

Case Study 2   Marriage registers, Hughenden, Buckinghamshire

Background

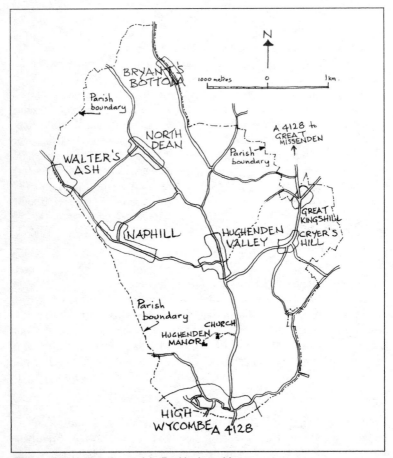

Figure 11.2 Hughenden parish, Buckinghamshire

The parish of Hughenden is entirely rural. Its 5,751 acres (7,200 acres estimated in 1797) lie in the Chiltern hills above High Wycombe, and its southernmost boundary actually takes in the outskirts of the town. It contains several settlements, some being little more than small strings of houses along the roads which cross the parish. None of these villages is large, and many were little more than hamlets until the twentieth century. The village closest to the parish church (Hughenden Valley) is modern. There is no settlement called 'Hughenden'. The parish takes as its centrepoint the Domesday manor of *Hvchedene*, with its group of estate buildings including the church, vicarage and church house (see Figure 11.2).

The marriage registers for many parishes in the country have been published. St Michael's and All Angels, Hughenden, begin in 1559, some 21 years after the original Henry VIII statute required registers to be kept. Partly because of the start of civil registers in 1837, and partly because only completed indexes were transcribed, the printed marriages in Hugheden close in 1812. Analysing the statistics of this register, a distinct pattern was clear, see Figure 11.3 which shows 25-year totals.

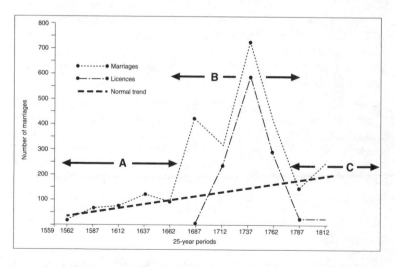

Figure 11.3 Marriages at St Michael and All Angels, Hughenden, Buckinghamshire, in 25-year totals

The entries in period A suggest a lightly populated area of modest size, exhibiting a slow growth as years passed. The third period, C, seems to confirm this, but something unusual appears to have happened during the years of period B.

This was recognised by the editor of the published registers, who adds two notes:

1662   Here the number of marriages become altogether disproportionately large.

1669   As an example of the remarkable proportions of this Register, notice that in 1669 there are 45 marriage entries and only 8 baptisms and 8 burials. The usual proportion for marriages is about ⅛ and burials ⅜ of total number of entries.

The second note is particularly useful, as it suggests a rough norm against which we can measure the Hughenden marriages: of every 100 events, about 52 are baptisms, about 12 are marriages, and about 36 are burials.

To explore these first impressions in more detail, the Hughenden marriages annual total was plotted. Periods A and C show no surprises. In the early years – when the idea of registering marriages was new and probably suspect – there was some under-representation. For example, in 1570 and 1573 and in the early years during the Civil War period, no marriages were recorded at all. The annual rate in period A predicts a probable level of about ten marriages a year by 1800. The pattern for period C does indeed follow that prediction.

Figure 11.4 plots the marriages in two-year totals during period B. There are two separate abnormal rises within the period. The first, from 1662 to 1680, peaks in 1669; but, after dropping to zero in 1685, a second longer bulge begins in 1703 and lasts for 50 years, reaching its high point in 1719. At its greatest total, in 1669, more then five times as many weddings were held in this little country church than the local population required.

Sources

To investigate this, maps, histories and ecclesiastical references were consulted, and enquiries made of other local historians. But first, the list of annual marriages was refined by extracting more data.

All occupations and residences given were noted; the way each marriage was authorised, i.e. by banns or by licence, and any general comments made in the register were written down. A few parishes are very rich in such extra information, although most only state the bare legal requirements from time to time. (You should consult a suitable book to understand the requirements; this can be found in many texts, for example *Using Local History Sources* listed in the bibliography.)

From parish histories, the names of the priests in charge of Hughenden during period B were identified, and three men were seen to dominate it, as shown in Figure 11.4. The same sources confirm that there have never been any dramatic population changes – it was rural in the *Domesday Book* and remains so today. Neither is the shape of Hughenden's marriage curve far out of line with the equivalent curve for the national population during this period.

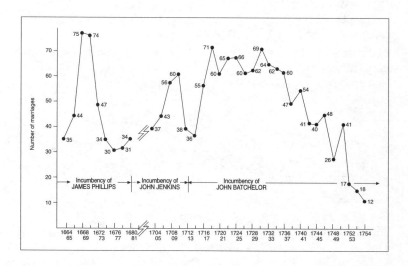

Figure 11.4 Marriages at St Michael and All Angels, Hughenden, Buckinghamshire, for period B

The geographical position of Hughenden church (see Figure 11.2) might lead one to look for a medieval village, later abandoned. Local histories, early maps and so on do not confirm this, however. Everything points to a quiet rural area, and this 'normality' only seems to be contradicted by the registers.

One piece of evidence from a published history of the parish appears to support our findings. It mentions a ring being tied to the door of St

Michael's church, to enable poor people simply to turn up and borrow the ring with which to be married without any further expense.

The detailed analysis of annual marriages does throw up two more pieces of information.

- The number of marriages by licence in period B mimics the curve of total marriages quite well, and represents nearly 80% of that total; whereas in period C, it falls away to only 13% (Figure 11.3).
- An astonishingly high number (987 marriages between 1700 and 1749) involved both brides and grooms coming in from parishes outside Hughenden to be married.

Furthermore, the distribution of these 'supplying' parishes – and there were no less than 101 of them – is quite evenly spread around Hughenden, see Figure 11.5. Plotting these marriages in detail throws up another fact. In many cases, both brides and grooms came from the same 'supplying' parish, while in others they came from parishes close to one other. So, for example, 13 couples both came from Aylesbury (14 miles from Hughenden); while in one case a couple came from Chipping Camden, Gloucestershire, over 50 miles away.

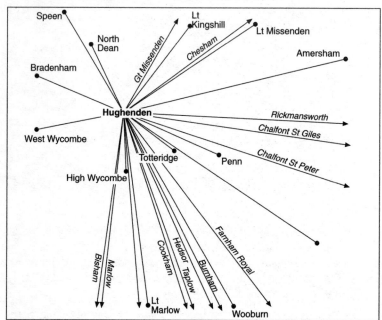

Figure 11.5 Some of the outlying parishes supplying one or both partners in Hughenden, Buckinghamshire, marriages

One cautionary note: there are so many entries marked as marriages under 'Licence' and others where one or both parties are mentioned as being widowed, that one needs to be aware that others may have been licensed or widowed too, the incumbent merely forgetting to add the necessary note in the register.

The evidence for 'why?'

Researching deeper, a number of general factors come to light which may have a bearing on the case.

- In 1640, a parliamentary committee was set up to consider, among other things, 'where there are men of more than one Benefice... [and] what such mens Revenues are reputed to be.' The enquiry was to cover the whole country, but the order actually says it is to address 'the Petition of the Inhabitants of Huyendam in the County of Buckingham and all other Petitioners of that nature'.
- An episcopal court, sitting in Aylesbury in 1662, ruled that John Tilbie and Mary his wife were never married, as Mary had been married to John's deceased brother Edmund. John's defence was that many people 'had of late years taken to wifes the relicts of their dead brothers'. He truly believed that it was legal to do this. The judge rules that they do penance in Hughenden church and Wycombe market place on several set dates (which normally involved appearing barefoot in a white sheet).
- In 1754, Lord Hardwicke's Marriage Act made many earlier forms of 'irregular' marriages illegal. For example, those performed in strange places (such as prisons); or those between parties forbidden to marry by church law (this category even included the widowed for some strict clergy, though most priests allowed them); or those for which a greased palm excused a lack of some required authority.
- Marriage licences were required to cover certain conditions (such as not wishing to wait for banns to be read). These were issued by diocesan chancellors (or registrars), and they sometimes appointed surrogates to issue marriage licences in their place. In Hughenden's case, the diocese was in those days that of Lincoln, and one might well expect surrogate appointments as far from the centre of the see as this. Hughenden parish lies in the diocese of Oxford today.

There were four incumbents in office during period B, but the unexpected numbers affects only three of them. The records searched revealed a little more about one of these vicars. The Rev. John

Batchelor held office for 52 years. His life style was typical of many Georgian clergymen: he was master within his world, and ran a house fitting to his station. The old vicarage still stands surrounded by the fields and parkland as remodelled by Benjamin Disraeli (who bought the manor in the nineteenth century and completely rebuilt it). Batchelor's home was of the size one associates with traditional Georgian vicarages, and must have required quite a large staff to run it.

Moreover, the Rev. Batchelor was a pluralist, also being rector of the nearby parish of Radnage. The impression of Radnage church and rectory too, is of a small church dominated by a Georgian rectory!

A terrier of Hughenden parish survives, made in the early part of the eighteenth century. It took the usual form of a perambulation around the boundaries, taking two days. At various regular points, a hymn was sung or a prayer said, and then the local landowner 'provided'. At one point, the fortification of such 'provision' was forgotton, and the parish clerk was quick to write a suitably scathing comment. And when, on the next day, the repentant landowner sent provisions to the next stopping point, the vicar refused to accept it.

Conclusions

This story has no definitive ending; most local history studies do not.

We do not know if the Rev. Batchelor and two of his colleagues were appointed surrogates to issue such licences, although it seems very likely.

If he did hold such an appointment, we can also only speculate as to the reasons why so many people needed to be married by licence. Research would be necessary into conditions in their own parishes. Did their incumbents refuse to marry couples who already had children? Or where one or both parties were widowed? What happened to the 'bulge' marriages later?

Perhaps it is uncharitable to ask also whether the Rev. Batchelor and the others really did take the view that they would marry anyone provided a fee could be produced. Such questions only serve to keep the local historian digging at what is a typically uncompleted case!

[Researcher: James Griffin]

– Case Study 3   Bridgewater Canal –

Background

The Bridgewater canal was one of the first narrow canals to be built in the eighteenth century. At that time the roads were in very bad condition, so moving goods by road was hazardous, time consuming and therefore costly.

Francis Egerton, the third Duke of Bridgewater (1736–1803) had coal mines at Worsley, ten miles (16 km) outside Manchester, and needed to transport his coal into the city for sale to the textile mills. He thought of a canal, having seen them working successfully in Europe. In 1758 he consulted the millwright James Brindley to see if the scheme was feasible. Brindley was a self-made engineer who used no written calculations or drawings. John Gilbert, the Duke's agent, was also involved.

Construction and operation over 250 years

The plan went forward and a section from Worsley to Manchester was completed. The canal went right into the coal face, so boats could be filled directly and then towed by horse into the city where the coal was sold. Small boats 47ft by 4ft 6 in. (14.3 by 1.4 m) were towed along underground tunnels. The canal was orange around the entrance of the mine due to the ochre seam colouring the water. The canal was a great success, enabling the Duke to sell his coal for half the price.

Soon the Duke was considering an extension of his canal. James Brindley was consulted again. The main difficulty was how to cross the River Irwell. Brindley suggested a masonry aqueduct lined with clay to hold the water. This was achieved successfully at Barton, although many people were sceptical when it was suggested. Figure 11.6 shows the original canal running south-east into Manchester, and the second phase which extends in a south-westerly direction. The canal crossed 38 ft (11.25 m) above the river, as shown in Figure 11.7.

The unique feature of the Bridgewater canal is that it has no locks. Brindley made use of contours, and built embankments to construct a waterway that enables narrow boats to travel freely. The Bridgewater canal and the Barton aqueduct were completed in just three years from 1759–61. James Brindley's reputation and his skills were in great demand.

The canal now went into the area of Manchester known as Trafford Park. Here it splits: one branch goes into Salford and joins the Rochdale canal; this last link was completed in 1805. The other branch continues south through Stretford, Sale, Altrincham, Dunham Massey, Lymm, Grappenhall, Stockton Heath, Preston Brook and finally arrives at Runcorn.

Quays were constructed along the route. Boatyards and the aftermath of the industrial uses of the canal can be seen today.

Communications between Manchester and Liverpool were improved considerably, so that goods were carried directly along the canal. The cost was reduced from 5s to 2s 6d (25p to 12.5p) per ton.

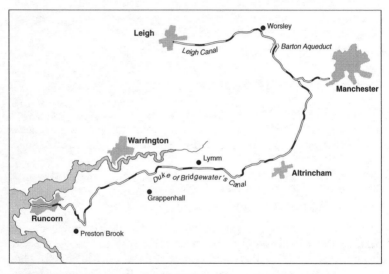

Figure 11.6 The route of the original Bridgewater canal and its extension

The original Barton aqueduct was replaced by a steel swing aqueduct in 1894, and this goes over the Manchester ship canal.

Parts of the route followed by the Bridgewater canal is in the countryside, encouraging leisure boats to use it today. Boats, painted in the traditional canal colours and decorated with roses and castle designs, carry holidaymakers to such local attractions as Durham House near Altrincham, Lymm, a picturesque Cheshire village and Preston Brook, which has a modern marina with all facilities.

[Researcher: Anne Thorn]

Figure 11.7 Brindley's aqueduct at Barton, near Manchester, 1761–1893

Case Study 4
Lincolnshire schools

One of the most common areas of research by local investigators is the history of education in their community. This example is taken from the rural county of Lincolnshire and is designed to illustrate some of the possibilities and pitfalls of pursuing such an investigation.

One of the advantages of an investigation into the history of a local village or urban school is that much can be done without having to seek out centrally held records. This case study therefore focuses primarily on what can be obtained by using sources of information available in the community itself.

Background

Lincolnshire is fairly typical of many rural shire counties. The area is large and predominantly rural. There are only six settlements with

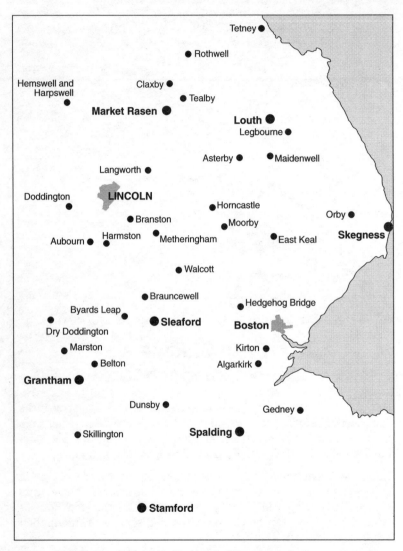

Figure 11.8 Places mentioned in the Lincolnshire case study

more than 15,000 people and 300 villages have fewer than 200 inhabitants. Like many other rural areas, there has been a significant amount of rural depopulation resulting from mechanisation and the waning influence of large landowners. The peak of the population was probably in the mid-nineteenth century.

Foundation of schools

A noticeable feature is the comparatively early date of foundation for village schools in Lincolnshire. Many investigators see the 1870 Education Act as significant, but a large number of Lincolnshire villages had schools before this date. Some were charity schools. Of the 170 parishes in Kesteven, 59 had a charity in the eighteenth century. There were certainly school boards set up in Lincolnshire following the Act, and some schools transferred to the boards. Many of these boards were small and always remained short of money. Educational provision improved in the nineteenth century. Only 17 of 170 parishes in Kesteven had no elementary school by the late nineteenth century and a few parishes combined to form a united school. For example, the isolated school serving scattered communities at Dunsby Fen was known as the 'United District School'. Documents and memoirs of these schools demonstrate that they often served as the social centres of communities. The isolated school in Metheringham Fen, which drifted on until 1980, was also licensed for church services.

Some schools grew up serving a collection of scattered hamlets or farmsteads with no noticeable centre of population, for instance in fenland communities such as Dunsby or Branston Fen. Road junctions were sometimes favoured as can be seen at the long-closed Byards Leap near Cranwell.

Subsequent changes

Very few schools in Lincolnshire have retained exactly their original structure. Even on the same site, the school is likely to be an amalgam of different buildings.

Many schools have amalgamated. These sometimes involve the closure of one or more sites and a concentration on one of the other sites where facilities were better. In other cases a new site has been selected. To avoid local argument, names are sometimes changed: a recent example is the closure of small village schools at Legbourne and South Reston, resulting in the opening of a new one on a new site in Legbourne diplomatically called East Wolds.

Religion and patronage

A few villages possessed more than one school. The background to this can sometimes be found in differing religious affiliations. Lincolnshire possessed a large number of those linked to the Church of England, partly because of the prominence and comparative wealth of the diocese of Lincoln but also through the large landowners operating through the church. Prominent local families were often closely connected with certain schools (and still remain so) such as Lord Yarborough in the north of the county, the Thorolds at Marston and Lord Brownlow at the closed schools at Belton and Manthorpe.

Tracing old schools

Old school buildings have proved popular with house purchasers. In Lincolnshire, the majority of former schools have not been demolished. Some such as Algarkirk near Boston are of architectural interest and have survived for this reason. Others have been retained with many different functions. Most are now private residences often easily identified with names such as 'Old School House' as can be found at places like Asterby, East Keal, Pickworth and Moorby.

Others have proved ideal as village halls when the schools closed as can be seen in places like Hatton, Hemswell and Harpswell, Skillington and Rothwell. Myriad other uses have been found for former village schools – industrial or trade uses such as lorry parks (Kirton Holme), television repair firms (Orby), potteries (Swaby); a youth hostel (Claxby) and an outdoor centre for the handicapped (Maidenwell). The delightfully-named 'Hedgehog Bridge', isolated in the fens near Boston, became a scout centre.

Despite this it is not always easy to trace exactly where a school once stood. In several cases the schoolroom has gone, leaving only the school house which is not always recognisable as an educational institution.

Others have plaques or house names. The isolated school at Brauncewell is identified today only by 'School Row'. Rather more distinctive is another isolated school at Kirton Skeldrake now serving as storage for a farm but recognisable with the sign above the door 'Board School for Infants'.

Oral evidence

Many schools in Lincolnshire have closed in comparatively recent times.

Kesteven closed some of the very smallest schools in the late 1930s, such as Rowston, but many small schools lingered. In 1946, for example, there were 43 one-teacher schools and 53 two-teacher ones. Kesteven closed 32 one-teacher schools between 1959 and 1973 some very small. The Annual Report of the Director of Education for example shows the small size of some at the start of the autumn term in 1960 with five pupils on a role at Branston Fen, six at Doddington and seven at Dry Doddington. The following year revealed just three pupils at Branston Fen.

A research task which still awaits is to seek out the people associated with these schools to collect their memoirs. Those who taught in schools in the 1960s and 1970s are retiring or dying, and many have tales to tell which add humanity to what are often formal, official documents.

Besides the teachers, other people such as educational officers, advisers and inspectors can reveal interesting information. Discussion with such people in Lincolnshire has brought to light stories of staff continuing to remain isolated from each other when two schools amalgamated, of the permanent smell of Bovril at one school, and of another school's reputation and numbers plummeting because of poor teaching, personality problems and of one case where sexual scandal proved the final nail in the school's coffin. More frequent are the fascinating tales of making and mending when official bureaucracy inhibited urgent repairs and refurbishment.

Attendance

Attendance always seems to have been a problem in schools such as those in rural Lincolnshire. A perusal of the log books for Tetney, a school near Grimsby, reveals many reasons for both longer- and shorter-term absences. They include many factors connected with the farming year, especially harvest time but also planting crops such as potatoes. Illness also loomed large notably measles, whooping cough, ringworm and influenza. The Sleaford Catholic School noted for 11 November 1908 'one girl with gangrene of the head will be absent for a long time'.

It appears that local events and visits were also usually accepted reasons for absences, especially fairs. The log book records the reasons for the high number of absentees at Tetney School for August 1867 as 'fatigued by the previous day's pleasure – Annual Trip to Cleethorpes'. New technology was also a draw as demonstrated by the lateness of four boys from Tetney in the 1860s because they went to see a 'steam cultivator'.

School was open for many more days than today and one can perhaps have some sympathy for pupil absence when one finds entries such as that for Christmas Eve 1895 at Tealby: 'We intended to continue teaching till this evening but the number present was so small that we left at noon'. Likewise the log book for Walcott, a fenland village school, notes in the 1 January 1883 entry 'as the parents did not respond to the request I made to send the children to school the day after Christmas Day, it was impracticable to keep the school open'.

On the other hand there were also many official closure days. Walcott, for example, closed for royal coronations, weddings and funerals, church events, harvest holidays and Empire Day. Many schools also served as polling stations. There was even closure for the '750th Anniversary of Magna Carta'.

Sometimes the school was affected by more calamitous events. Most of the entries for Tealby are dominated by moans about poor attendance but this is suddenly replaced by one for 9 February 1889 noting that

❝ this morning a little after 6 o' clock Mr James Taylor discovered the schoolroom to be on fire. The fire had at that time already made considerable progress... soon a number of people were already on the school premises... but they could only observe and deplore the conflagration which quickly spread throughout the main building and the beautiful and ornamental roof, handsome windows of coloured glass, the floor and every article of furniture – desks, forms, maps and books – hardly a vestige remained. ❞

Calamitous though this was the 26 February entry records how 'today we attempted to re-open the school with scanty appliances'.

School conditions

Controlling temperature in these old schoolrooms must have been problematical. Mrs S.M. Bond recalling her schooldays at Walcott noted 'I remember how bitterly cold the winter months were and if it was your misfortune to sit next to the passage end, any excuse was made to get to the teacher's desk for a warm up, the teacher's desk was of course situated next to a large black coke burning stove'. The documents at Tetney corroborate the poor condition of many schools. There were 100 in some classrooms and the log for 20 February 1871 refers to the poor ventilation, and greatly smoking chimney which 'caused the scholars to cough very much'. The same school's entry for 21 January 1881 – 'reading was taken instead of writing as the ink in the inkwell was frozen' – is not the only such entry in Lincolnshire school log books at this time. The Walcott school entry for 13 May 1927 recording that 'a dozen mice were killed in the classroom' highlights another problem.

Equipment

An analysis of the equipment in log books and inventories not only reveals the deficiencies in many schools but also the technological development and changing attitudes to education. At Tetney, for example, the earlier records are characterised largely by slates, jumping apparatus and a few books. The first typewritten letter appeared in 1895. A radio is mentioned in 1948, a record player in 1962, a roneo duplicator in 1967 and television programmes in 1968. The order at Tetney in 1895 for 'five dozen fans of the infants for fan drill' is amongst the more unusual entries.

The curriculum

The curriculum offered was heavily dominated by the 3 R's especially when these were examined, and school funding partly depended on success in these areas. However, the curriculum broadened as the grant was extended to other subjects such as singing. One can sometimes make inferences about the teacher's favourite curriculum areas from the tone of the entries. Clearly geography was not a labour of love for the Walcott head teacher on 1 October 1882 when he noted 'I have had to talk geography till I am weary at the end of the lesson... it seemed the progress made has not been equal to the exertions made'.

Scotter school near Scunthorpe had, amongst the lessons in the February 1863, numeration, the geography of the British Isles, journeying of the Israelites, commandments, a parable and the rivers of Europe, homework, spelling, an examination or two, the capitals of Europe, the alphabet, sewing, learning a couple of songs ('Busy Bee' and 'The Violet') and the lives of Moses and Abraham.

Standards

As has occurred throughout the ages teachers lamented the standards of pupils in their charge. This became a significant issue when school funding depended partly on success. Entries by despairing teachers abound such as one for Gedney Church End, on 22 July 1881: 'I examined the whole school this morning. I found the numeration throughout the school careless'. Those unlikely to succeed in the tests were not always entered for the examinations. Reasons given for non-entries at Tetney in 1880 include 'imbecile', 'young and dull', 'delicate' and 'imperfect utterance'.

Behaviour

Whilst many older citizens today can recall monitorial jobs like being ink or milk monitor, the lives of some pupils were more onerous and can hardly have enhanced school life. For example, Tetney school used boys to do heavy manual work such as carrying sacks of coal and one can only feel sorry for the boy posted in December 1903 by the door to brush the boots of all pupils as they arrived.

Perhaps it is not surprising that pupils were not always well behaved. The following situation seems to have prevailed at St Mary's Roman Catholic School at Sleaford in 1903. In April the head, K. Rockford, arrived noting that 'the children are exceedingly fidgety and inattentive and it has been impossible to follow the timetable correctly today'. By June 1903 the head had resigned. The successor, Mary Cullen, arrived on 8 June but departed on 3 July noting 'I find the scholars do not know what discipline or order is. Their rule seems to be "do not obey and do not tell the truth!" To attempt to follow any timetable or give any lesson is quite an impossibility. Considering all this I tender my resignation.' It seems incongruous that the new teacher was observing by 16 September of that same year 'the children are docile and easily managed... they march in and out to music and fall into their ranks orderly'.

Punishment books and log books attest to many problems. At Tetney there are 142 entries in the punishment book between 1900 and 1996 with misdemeanours including stealing, cutting hair off girls' heads, damaging furniture, spitting, unladylike and ungentlemanly behaviour, pulling faces, teasing the village cretin, exhibiting to other boys, throwing various objects including apple cores and half bricks, letting off fireworks and touching the mains electricity switch.

Responses from teachers to children's bad behaviour varied. Sometimes the culprit was sent home. One can probably guess why Joseph and Frank Robinson, for example, were sent home on 7 March 1864 'to wash themselves'. At other times, the response from teachers could be brutal and many are the references to corporal punishment even with young pupils.

Teachers and governors

It was not easy to attract the best teachers to small rural villages where the community may not have had the highest regard for education. Some of the pupil teachers 'failed' and the turnover in many of these Lincolnshire schools was fairly high. The reasons given were many – moving home, frustration, getting married, illness and death or occasionally, as at Tetney with Maria Manby on 28 September 1883, resignation 'on account of her immoral conduct'. Other staff could occasionally give problems. The School Board Minute Book entry for Tetney in November 1897 noted 'classroom set on fire by cleaner by leaving a bucket of red hot cinders on floor'. The entry continued laconically 'Board did not feel justified in retaining the cleaner's services'.

The relationship between teachers and governors was not always amicable. It can have been no easy time for the head of Sleaford St Mary's Catholic school having to deal with the school manager, Reverend Father William Lieber. Although he is stated to be a benevolent and popular local priest, he came into conflict with the school head teachers on a range of issues in the earlier part of the twentieth century including the misuse of the premises for dances, dog excrement, his dog knocking down the head and the freedom he allowed Belgian refugees during the First World War to do as they liked within the school.

[Researcher: Tim Lomas]

Case Study 5   Pest house, Saffron Walden, Essex

National background

Before medicine developed detailed knowledge about the transmission of diseases, people realised that getting away from the threat was the best thing to do. However, if a neighbour contracted a dread disease, it was easier for the community to force him to leave than for the community to do the moving.

When people or communities **did** run away from disease or anything else (poverty, crop failures, lack of work) social problems were created. Even in the fourteenth century, vagrants were sent back to their birthplaces if they couldn't work. By the beginning of Henry VIII's reign, those on the run who were capable of work were subjected to harsh penalties, such as losing their ears or even hanging.

Various improvements were made, from the sixteenth century onwards, to the way the poor were looked after.

- The Poor Law Act of 1563 required the appointment of people to gather a community's piecemeal charity together, and to apply it for the benefit of the poor.
- The 1602 act formed such people into overseers of the poor, and suitable accommodation for the needy was to be provided by them – that is, workhouses. The act also called for houses of correction to be built, into which vagrants were to be put.
- At the same time, a very few enquiries were being made into what caused disease. Only the rich, benevolent and enquiring were able to do much. The poor were too busy surviving; the hard-hearted did all they could to get rid of the problem.

However, the first stirrings of industrial activity created a need for more manpower; and the population began to gather in the larger towns. Also, the incidence of disease, especially bubonic plague, became acute and widespread. The London plague of 1665 may be the best known episode, but it was only one of hundreds which occurred across England before and after that date.

Many towns were affected. The disease spread across the land in waves, and again it is ironic that an agent in the ultimate cure of dread diseases and one possible source of infection may be loosely connected. Paper was needed for the books and newspapers from which a few people developed and worked on their theories of disease. Yet the rags used to make this paper were stripped from the plague-dead in cities, and transported by the cartload to paper mills. Here, the poor worked in cold, damp and extremely foul-smelling conditions knocking dirt from the rags and cutting them into shreds in the first stage of papermaking.

The emergence of pest houses

By the early eighteenth century, scientific investigation had developed in several directions.

- Gentlemen had begun to enquire into and look for causes of unusual events.
- Parishes had grouped themselves into unions, so that communal help could be given to the very poor (by definition often the sick). The resulting workhouses were neither free nor generous. Those physically able to work were driven out to labour on roads or the parish land. In exchange they received the barest of subsistence. Families had to be desperate indeed to be forced to rely 'on the parish' in this way.
- It seems likely that workhouses were not healthy places.

By about 1720, pest houses were being built to which those suffering from certain diseases could be sent. ('Pest' in this sense is derived from the Latin *pestis*, meaning 'plague'.)

Background to the study

In the late 1950s the isolation hospital in Saffron Walden, Essex, closed. It had been established by the town's union but the formation of the National Health Service had created a more central administration, and it made medical sense to treat those suffering from diseases like scarlet fever and tuberculosis in larger centres.

Thus, the buildings comprising the isolation hospital were redeveloped as flats and houses, and what has been called Isolation Lane was renamed Hill Top Lane. I moved into this road in 1995, and began this particular case study.

Sources

Maps and histories of the area, and extensive archives in several places, have yielded tantalising information. Brief flashes of information on the establishment, development and use of the hospital are surrounded by years of silence. There are abundant records for Saffron Walden hospitals, but very few relate to this one. (There were two other hospitals in the town). The search for relevant information continues.

However, from the references I have found so far, the beginnings of a picture can be sketched in.

The pest house

The building used by the overseers was an old brick-built farmhouse in what was then called Well Green Lane. The conversion was made before 1750, one source giving the specific date of 1744. The first such hospitals in Essex had been built in the 1720s, and despite Saffron Walden not being mentioned on one list of the country's isolation hospitals, the mid-1740s is a quite plausible date.

The farmhouse chosen stood, surrounded by fields, on a modest ridge (so the breezes could blow away 'the pestilential atmosphere of its occasional inmates', suggested a local historian a century later). It was, of course, 'isolated'. The site is within the town's built-up area today, but even in the early twentieth century was nearly a mile from the centre and three quarters of a mile from the outskirts, to the south of the town.

From a very early date – at least since 1400 – this area appears to have been where wrongdoers were executed. Two separate field areas, each called Gallowsshott, suggest that a warning scaffold stood by two of the town's entry routes. (Today these sites are linked by 'Seven Devils' Lane', which is perhaps suggestive.) Not only that, a nearby wood echoes another early name, Burnt Woman's Plantation, and that may recall the results of witch hunting.

An east–west lane led to the farm from the highway. It stood beside a pond, with various cottages nearby. The choice of this for an isolation hospital was no doubt strengthened by the sinister nature of the area. Well Green Lane played its part in this, for one small field running alongside it was called Hangman's Close.

Probably long before the 1841 census, the name of this land had changed to become Pest House Lane; in 1845 a 'bricket' hospital is described as reached up a lane lined by young poplar trees. 'Bricket', a word not given in SOED, is assumed to mean 'brick-built'.

Changes

The nineteenth century saw different diseases come to the fore. The plague had played itself out; but to counterbalance this the population grew apace, and diseases associated with overcrowding and poor water supply took over. However, the best treatment for many of these (typhoid fever, diphtheria, scarlet fever, etc.) was still to isolate them. Thus the old pest house continued to be used, and in 1860 the Saffron Walden union reported that they had a 16-bed hospital for smallpox and other infectious complaints.

Between the 1860s and the end of the century, various other developments occurred. One medical officer of health report states that the old farm house was bought in 1877; maybe this means that the health authorities of the day acquired it from the Saffron Walden union. A search for the hospital records continues, which may confirm this.

In 1894 a new block was built – described in 1910 as 'of modern type' – as well as an administrative cottage. Later these were named the Scarlet Fever Block and the Matron's house.

What was it like?

The historical snapshots, which today's surviving evidence provides, can be put together to build up a shadowy picture. The whole site occupied one and a quarter acres, see Figure 11.9. It was surrounded partially by corrugated iron and spiked railways. A length of this spiked fencing remains today near one of the isolation hospital gate posts, mostly buried in a hedge, Figure 11.10.

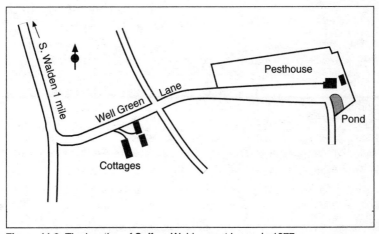

Figure 11.9 The location of Saffron Walden pest house in 1877

Figure 11.10 Some evidence, 120 years later, of the Saffron Walden isolation hospital

An official 1871 report states that water was drawn from a pond, whereas in 1910 it is said to have come from a shallow well. The latter report is highly critical of the quantity of water available, and also says that 'there is no sewer near'. The reference to a well may reflect the original name, Well Green; but the Old English *wella* meant 'spring or stream', and could just as easily have referred to the pond.

The two buildings shown in Figure 11.9 were the original farmhouse and a smaller outbuilding. As late as 1910 this was used as a washroom and mortuary, two functions which hardly seem to go together!

The nineteenth century censuses tell us something of the households who lived there. In 1841, there was only one, that of the caretaker. Two were shown in 1851, which may imply a second building.

Patients were attended in the hospital by two types of people. No doubt they were visited from time to time by medical men, but their daily needs were supplied by residents. However, as waves of disease passed, these caretakers would have reverted to general or agricultural labouring. For example, in 1867 the annual Saffron Walden hospital report says that there were 'no cases of infectious disease sent [from the main hospital to the isolation hospital], and the district has generally been free from fever and other similar complaints.' The following year, however, several cases of fever were admitted, some of whom died.

In 1871, the attendants were a man (described as a labourer) and his wife. Neither could write, though the man could read.

Perhaps in about 1877, when some administrative changes were being made, the name of the lane leading to the hospital was changed. Instead of reflecting a disease, its new name reflected a treatment. It became Isolation Hospital Lane, and not long afterwards simply Isolation Lane.

Figure 11.11 shows the scarlet fever block and administrative building in 1902. Both of these buildings were built after 1877.

Figure 11.11 Saffron Walden isolation hospital around 1902

In 1910, the hospital proper consisted of a two-ward block containing six beds, and an administrative cottage. The original farmhouse was then used to isolate diphtheria cases. Amongst the hospital's shortcomings, reported the medical officer of health, were a lack of hot water; no indoor bathing facilities; no guards for the fires; and no telephone.

By the time the hospital was closed, the buildings had risen to eight. There were two main ward blocks, an administrative building, the original farmhouse and its nearby one-time mortuary, a new bungalow in which the matron lived, and two smaller buildings.

Today, the two wards have been converted into flats, and the matron's bungalow is privately occupied, though much enlarged. The original farmhouse, the mortuary, and indeed the pond which served them, have been superseded by new houses.

Memories

Many older people in the town have recollections associated with the isolation hospital, to which they or their friends were transported by 'the fever van'. When that happened, boys and girls who lived near the infected house were purged with Epsom salts!

Just before it closed, a trainee teacher developed mumps, and remembers being sent to the isolation hospital. Her main memory is of having to leave the relative warmth of the ward to reach outside toilet facilities.

What next?

Like every local history study, this research continues. I have a number of suggestions of helpful contacts still to reach; and several local sources and county archives to search. It would be useful to find more maps, and I continue to hunt for the elusive records of the isolation hospital board itself.

[Researcher: James Griffin]

Case Studies 6 and 7 are from the United States of America and Figure 11.12 illustrates the location of each area.

Case Study 6 North America – Grand Portage: Fur gateway to the – Northern Great Plains, 1731–1804

National background

Five interconnected Great Lakes are located along the southern side of the ancient Precambrian Shield and drain to the Atlantic Ocean through the Saint Lawrence River. This 1,200 mile east–west water route through the Great Lakes enticed European traders and explorers into the interior of the North American continent by the 1630s. Soon they focused on the north shore of Lake Superior and its westward flowing rivers as routes to the unexplored north-west. One route began in Thunder Bay and went up the Kaministiquia River. Another commenced about 45 miles to the south-west in Grand Portage Bay.

Little known until the 1730s was a nine-mile-long portage connecting a sheltered bay on Lake Superior with the westward flowing Pigeon

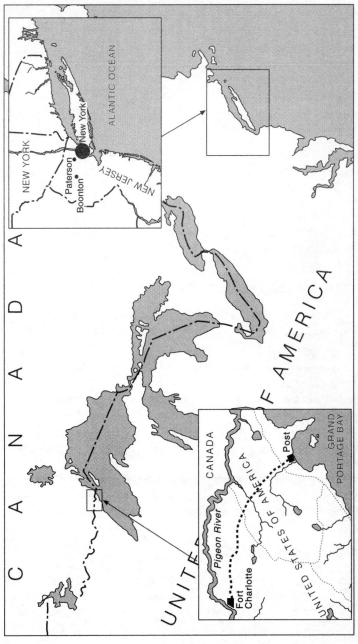

Figure 11.12 The location of Case Studies 6 and 7

River. This was the legendary Grand Portage that provided a passage around rapids and falls in the lower Pigeon River. [Morse; Woolworth, 1982]*

The Grand Portage was surpassed only by Hudson Bay as a natural route into the heart of North America during nearly two centuries of the fur trade. This historic portage was strategically located between Lake Superior and a series of lakes and streams leading to the Northern Great Plains, the Rocky Mountains, and the fur rich Athabasca Country. These geographical advantages led to the creation of a great inland fur trade depot at the head of Grand Portage Bay. This depot was the headquarters of the British North West Company and its fur trade empire which spanned the continent by the late 1790s. Nowadays, Grand Portage National Monument includes the partially reconstructed North West Company depot, an eight-and-a-half mile portage, and the site of Fort Charlotte at the western end of the portage. [Woolworth, 1982]

Geographical features of the area

Three key geographical features of the Grand Portage locale made it the best water route between the Great Lakes and the north-west. These were:

1 a sheltered bay on the north shore of Lake Superior with level land for erecting trading facilities
2 a relatively easy portage around the impassable lower Pigeon River; and
3 the Pigeon River, an excellent waterway to the north-west.

Significantly, the portage rises almost 700 ft during its eight-and-a-half mile course from Lake Superior to the Pigeon River. Lake Superior is approximately 602 ft above sea level, the Pigeon River at the upper end of the portage is a bit less than 1,300 ft above sea level. [Woolworth, 1982; US Geological survey]

Cultural background

Centuries prior to advent of Europeans, woodland Indians developed technologies to create light birchbark canoes. They also made tumplines to balance heavy loads; and portages to form an intricate network of

* See page 229 for references

connected rivers and lakes. Other Indian technological innovations were directed towards subsistence in a relatively harsh environment. Most prominent were processes to harvest, dry and store wild rice; and to reduce maple sap into storable sugar. Still another Indian creation was pemmican which became a fur trade staple on the prairies. [Woolworth, 1993]

Pierre La Verendrye and his sons

Recorded French fur trade over the Grand Portage began with the immortal Pierre La Verendrye. On 26 August 1731, he landed at Grand Portage Bay with his sons; a nephew, La Jemeraye; the Jesuit Father Mesaiger; the indispensable Cree guide Auchagah; about 40 voyageurs and many canoes. Encumbered by heavy packs of trade goods, supplies and canoes, they started over the long, rough, little used portage. Then came Minnesota's first recorded labour strike. The men mutinied and loudly demanded that they turn back.

A few voyageurs went on to Rainy Lake with La Jemeraye, but La Verendrye returned to Thunder Bay. In June 1732, La Verendrye came back to Grand Portage, traversed the portage and went to the Lake of the Woods where he built Fort St Charles. En route they 'took great care to improve all the portages and waterways' by reducing them from 41 to 32. These measures improved travel, took less time, and reduced transportation costs. [La Verendrye]

From the Lake of the Woods, La Verendrye's sons quested westward for an elusive 'Sea of the West'. They explored to the Red River; the Mandan villages on the Missouri River; and the Arikara villages further south. Finally, they went up the Saskatchewan River to the vicinity of Prince Albert, Saskatchewan. The years 1740 to 1745 were the peak of the French fur trade over the Grand Portage. [La Verendrye; Gilman]

The Verendrye family travelled over the Grand Portage until about 1750. They were succeeded by Jacques Legardeur, Sieur de St Pierre, who used the Grand Portage until 1751. Then Chevalier de la Corne directed trade until 1755 when he closed the posts of 'La Mer de l'Ouest'. In 1759, trade to Lake Superior and the west was ended. [Gilman]

The British conquest

Superior British logistics and arms triumphed over the French on the Plains of Abraham outside walled Quebec in 1759. Enterprising

British and Scottish merchant traders moved swiftly from New York to revive the moribund trade. Alexander Henry the Elder traded into Lake Superior soon after the British conquest, and other British traders followed in his wake. By 1767 British traders secured permission to winter among tribes of the north–west. Jonathan Carver visited Grand Portage in the summer of 1767; even then it was an important fur trade rendezvous and entrepôt for traders. [Carver]

Great Montreal canoes were used to carry trade goods and supplies to Grand Portage early in the British era. By 1772, a trader suggested using Montreal voyageurs to take goods over the Grand Portage. A year later, they were required to carry six pieces across the portage and return to carry baled furs down to the lakeside posts. By 1775, 60 north canoes [i.e., Canadian birch-bark] laden with goods from Grand Portage were competing with the Hudson Bay Company in the north-west. [Thompson; Wallace, 1934; Hearne]

Large scale British trade to the north-west via the Grand Portage began about 1775. Alexander Henry the Elder came there in June 1775 with provisions and trade goods valued at £3,000. He had 16 canoes and 54 men in his brigade. Seven days of 'Severe and dangerous exertion' moved canoes, provisions and trade goods over the portage. Other data indicate that 41 canoes manned by 241 men went to the Grand Portage this year. [Henry; Wallace, 1954]

By 1776 Grand Portage had supplanted Michilimackinac as the advance supply depot for the north-west fur trade. This year saw 70 canoes with cargoes valued at £49,000 pass over the Grand Portage. Traders to the rich Athabasca Country garnered 12,000 beaver pelts along with quantities of otter and marten furs. John Askin at Mackinac shipped bulky cargoes such as barrels of rum and bags of dried corn by sailing vessels over Lake Superior to the Grand Portage. [Thwaites; Rich; Askin]

Fierce competition led to the formation of a North West Company of 16 shares in 1778. It reorganised in 1784 under Benjamin and Joseph Frobisher. Soon, it had an investment of £50,000 in the trade to Grand Portage. Two sets of men were involved, with one half employed in the transport of goods from Montreal to the Grand Portage, and the other engaged in the north-west trade. [Thompson; Innis]

Dynamic Benjamin Frobisher spent large sums of money in about 1784–87 to build a great inland fur trade depot on Grand Portage Bay, and to expand facilities at the upper end of the portage. He died in

April 1787, and was succeeded by Simon McTavish who dominated the firm until his death in 1804. The North West Company grew and prospered into the first decade of the 1800s. The remarkable geographic discovery by Peter Pond of the Athabasca Country, and Alexander Mackenzie's epochal overland journey to the Pacific in 1793, led to the company's expansion across the continent. [Mackenzie]

An advanced depot at Fort Charlotte on the Pigeon River housed food, supplies, north canoes and in-bound furs. Each summer fur brigades outfitted there and then began the long journey westward to Rainy Lake, the Red River of the North, Lake Winnipeg, the Assiniboine River, the Saskatchewan River, the base of the Rocky Mountains and the Athabasca Country. Much of the early fur trade of the Northern Great Plains originated at Grand Portage up to 1802 and Fort William after that date. Here John Macdonell and many others went from posts on the Assiniboine River south-west to the Mandan and Hidatsa villages near the mouth of the Knife River where it joined the Missouri River. [Wood]

Pemmican became a staple west of the Red River. Compact and highly nutritious, it was made from dried, pulverised buffalo meat mixed with hot buffalo grease and poured into a buffalo hide bag. Normally it was edible for more than a year. 'Pemmican posts' on the Assiniboine and Saskatchewan rivers made or traded for it with plains Indians. Then it was issued to passing canoe brigades. At times it was eaten dry, but more often it was boiled with water to make a soup called 'rubbaboo'. [Nute]

By 1797, North West Company policies had estranged many ambitious young traders, who formed the rival XY Company. With Sir Alexander Mackenzie as leader they fought a savage trade war with the North West Company until the death of Simon McTavish and a merger in late 1804.

During the summer of 1797, an Indian told a North West Company officer about a route to the north-west along the Kaministiquia River. It had been used by Indians for generations and by French traders before the Grand Portage was developed into the major entrepôt to the north–west. This discovery led to the speedy abandonment of Grand Portage and the development of a new depot at the mouth of the Kaministiquia River in British North America. By 1804 the North West Company facilities at Grand Portage were removed or demolished. Historic Grand Portage then lapsed into obscurity. Fort William on Thunder Bay, British North America, flourished until the company's merger with the Hudson Bay Company in 1821. [Woolworth, 1993]

[Researcher: Alan Woolworth]

Case Study 7   New Jersey:
Finding the opera house
in the hardware store

Background to the study

The Boonton hardware store has been standing on the top of Main
Street in Boonton, New Jersey, for better than 100 years, and for the
last century the structure has housed the Boonton Opera House in its
second storey [i.e. 'first floor' for English readers]. The building looks
very much the same as when it was built in the summer of 1890 by
Mrs Sarah Green. Quite by accident, I took the elevator from the
hardware store on the first floor to get at some lumber [timber] on the
second floor of the building which I was going to use for sets on the
stage of the local High School. Much to my surprise I found the lumber stored on the floor of an old theatre! The upstairs 'Opera House'
had been left intact after its doors had been closed in the early 1920s.
The discovery piqued my curiosity, as I then knew very little about
the structure of small town theatres of the 'gilded age'. I started with
general histories of theatres of the day, and also with the Historical
Theatre Association, and soon discovered the basic information about
performing troupes and spaces of the day.

The majority of the population of the United States during the closing
decade of the nineteenth century was centred in the small towns.
Middle class people were carrying out the traditions and ideals of a
'democratic society'. The increasing productivity of an industrial society created a new leisure time, which in turn caused a need for
activities to fill it. Theatres flourished in the small towns across the
country. Between 1880 and 1900 there were over 500 travelling companies. Each town had its own unique performing space, and although
the structures were similar, each building was stamped by its creator
with a local and very distinctive stamp that caused it to fit easily into
the local community. These performing spaces were often called 'opera
houses', perhaps to lend a more respectable and cultural name to a
theatre. Operas were rarely performed in them, and although travelling companies toured through the towns, these houses became centres
for lectures, graduations and political conventions as well.

The structures were erected on the second floor of many buildings so that the lower level could be used for shops, and many are still extant in the United States. Many more have been converted into restaurants and office buildings, while still retaining the architectural look of the nineteenth century building.

Finding the sources and evidence

Although there is some general information about the life of the 'opera houses' of this period, there seemed to be little history on the life of individual institutions, and little information on what actually went on there from week to week. This particular theatre still retained its structure, so that at least one could imagine performances on the stage if one knew where to find records of plays and musicals that had passed through the town. These could be matched to company records and scripts of the day. The best place to start would be the local library and historical society.

Boonton's mayor at the end of the nineteenth century lived in a large mansion on the main street of the town, and his family donated the house to the town which, coupled with the fifty dollars they received from Andrew Carnegie, started the local library. At the time of my research, the library had also been left to reflect a gentler time of books and browsing in dusty stacks. The back room yielded the complete issues of the local paper *The Boonton Times* on ageing but readable microfilm.

The historical society was housed in a condemned historical building, and as a result entry was difficult. However, by reading the newspaper and copying the theatrical entries, I was able to link the theatre to severally historically interesting people. The information was not lodged in one place. The paper listed town council meetings that dealt with the construction of the 'opera house', and the licensing of all professional performances. A trip to the Town Hall yielded the original minutes of these early meetings often done in pencil in a lined copy book. I also found that, by asking historical society members and local residents about the theatre, I was able to get more information, although much of it was hearsay and needed foundations in fact. By matching the newspaper information with records of theatrical companies and biographies I was able to substantiate some of these tales.

Research about the life of the town revealed a small town in Morris County, New Jersey, situated 35 miles west of New York City, which is divided in half by the Rockaway river. The town has one 'downtown' section, composed of a single main street. 'Old Boonton', now submerged under the Jersey City reservoir, was the site of industry as early as 1747. In 1830, the New Jersey Iron Company purchased acreage between the then newly-formed Morris Canal and the east bank of the Rockaway river (the Hollow). The company erected an ironworks, with rolling mills, furnaces, a trip hammer, a slitting machine and a small foundry. Housing for factory workers was built on the hillside. The iron works executives constructed elegant octagonal shaped houses, with walls of slag iron, on the top of the hills. When the railroad reached Boonton, the town flourished industrially and by the 1860s and 1870s, the population had increased dramatically. During the 1890s, housing for the wealthy citizens was constructed alongside the 'iron mansions'. These homes were occupied by notable bankers and businessmen who commuted by train to and from New York City. When at the end of the century the iron works closed and immigrants began arriving looking for work, the community began to struggle financially.

During the golden years at the turn of the century, theatre flourished. The newspaper accounts list two major theatres in town. Mrs Sarah Green, wife of one of the industrialists, built the opera house in 1890. The doors opened on 29 November 1890, with a performance by the Boonton Concert Band.

[Researcher: Peter T. Lubrecht]

12

MAKING THE BEST OF THE HARD WORK

The options available

One of the most difficult tasks facing you is deciding when to stop the historical research and when to organise it into some historical product.

There are those people who see the joy of the task lying exclusively in personal research. Just satisfying curiosity and wanting to know is sufficient. Despite this, your desire to investigate accurately should never be compromised.

You may wish to contribute to the local store of historical knowledge, but not in the finished form of article or book. Your work will probably take the form of records or jottings. Your local library or archive will usually appreciate your material especially when its reliability is recognised. Until recent times, records were invariably in printed form but the computer age has moved things on. Already, the build up of large databases of documents such as censuses are a reality. The internet clearly offers numerous, exciting possibilities.

You may be a third type of investigator, one doing it for an educational or social purpose. Even young people are undertaking quite sophisticated research. In recent years, the number of A-level students in England carrying out high quality personal studies on local topics is testament to the high standards. Adult education groups, WIs and others have produced research which demonstrates the benefits of collaborative work.

You may wish to publish your work. Some researchers seek a publisher but the large number who publish privately indicate that many do not necessarily need a large commercial market.

Other researchers wish to contribute more directly to the academic debate. These people, wish to undertake a microcosmic investigation of a debatable national historical issue. The section below is largely concerned with producing this type of work whether its final format be an article, a contribution to a series of papers or even a book.

You should not assume that such work is only possible for those with a historical training and a high level of education. School pupils have made genuine contributions to historical knowledge as have many adults whose qualification extends no further than passion and interest. Frequently the missing ingredient is confidence. The feeling that the amateur dabbler has little of worth to contribute is natural but unfounded!

——— Organising the material ———

Most local investigators quickly gather masses and masses of material. It can be organised in different ways and there is no ideal or perfect method. Much depends on what you feel comfortable with.

Moving beyond the notes

Moving to the next stage is difficult: many have their own preferred methods. You could organise the archive material as soon as possible, writing it up neatly, organising it with a card index system. Get into the habit of noting specific references every time you use a source. There is nothing more infuriating than finding an important piece of information central to the final product and not having the precise reference.

Your desire to organise and publish should not be an urgent and rushed process. Since few serious historians wish to be belittled or criticised by those reading their work on the grounds that the work is inaccurate or unreliable by being based on too little evidence, the majority of local historians keep on gathering and checking their evidence.

Yet at some stage a decision has to be made and it is often only you who can make that decision. One criterion is that you have some confidence in the judgements and generalisations you make from your evidence – and that can seem quite vague.

Using the work of others for background

It is more than likely that someone else will have been working on a similar theme to yours for a different place or time or maybe the same theme at a different time. Dipping into various books and articles at various stages during your own investigation can prove useful and stimulating.

The secret is to start with publications giving general background information and move through to the more specific works as your own research progresses.

Before long that may mean dipping into the *Victoria County History* series which has been referred to often in these pages.

There is much worthy competition to this series. Specialised county histories are sometimes of excellent quality such as the County of Lincolnshire series. Many towns have their own publications, some of which can only be described as magisterial. Winchester is a good example here but many towns and cities, especially those fortunate enough to retain archaeological and research groups, are producing a stream of high-quality publications. A glance through the shelves and catalogues of a local studies library will reveal the vast range of materials.

The early period is likely to have been covered through archaeological surveys and reports. Many places have a specialised volume or two on the pre-Norman period. The local *Domesday* will be in print and many towns and counties will have specialised books and articles on aspects of the medieval period and early modern period. The Civil War period has produced a wide range of local studies. So has the Georgian period but that tends to be overwhelmed by the vast number of specialised local studies on the agrarian, industrial and transport changes of the last 150 to 200 years. The major themes of so many twentieth century local publications are the two world wars and childhood memories, but few areas have not been touched.

Another source which may be worth dipping into at some stage is the unpublished thesis. Over the years thousands of local historical theses have been produced largely as part of a qualification – anything from GCSE to doctorate level and even beyond.

—— **Preparing the final product** ——

- accuracy
- efficiency
- persuasiveness
- coherence

- clarity
- relevance
- interest.

These attributes are not the province solely of the professional.

Consider your audience

You need to make an early decision as to the form of the final product. You may want to produce a multi-media display, with text, photographs and charts, for your town or village hall. You may be aiming to produce a guidebook or a brochure. Your readers may be professionals, those with an interest in local history or the general reading public.

Drafts

The first draft can be disillusioning – sometimes almost to the point of despair. You may find yourself feeling that you cannot convey the interest of the research you have done or that it is criminal to leave anything out; or that generalisations and conclusions fail to reflect the data. It is also likely to be incoherent and poorly organised. In short, the first draft is often a low point. The consolation is that it gets better although the best advice is not to leave too long a gap between one draft and another.

Keep things simple and clear

The real skill lies in putting over complex ideas in a straightforward language that can be understood by others. That is not the same as popularising. Good local history is not about sensationalising and omitting the ordinary in favour only of the juicy bits. It is about selecting significant issues, backing them up with telling and relevant evidence and coming to clear conclusions based logically on the points made. It is also about being tentative and not dogmatic in the communication.

Drawing conclusions

Do not be afraid of drawing conclusions. Good local history often needs to extend beyond a set of statistics or uncontroversial information. Whilst there may be some who believe that it is not the duty of the local investigator to give out conclusions preferring to leave the reader to draw their own, this is not a commonly-subscribed-to view.

This means that your local history work should be characterised by a fair bit of analysis and evaluation as well as description, reconstruction and uncritical narrative. Features which may be worth heeding include the following.

Source evaluation

Be aware of the problems associated with the sources. It is always dangerous to accept source material at face value. Even if comparatively few documents set out with the deliberate intention of lying or deceiving, many were compiled by those representing a particular viewpoint. It also pays to be conversant with the problems the compilers of sources faced and impediments to reliability such as access to uncertain data or not being present at the events described.

This is not to suggest that you should be over-critical of such source material. Being aware of the problems and issues associated with particular sources is not a matter of being defeatist but of being healthily sceptical and tentative.

Explanation

Give sufficient attention to explanation. This is a frequent shortcoming on what otherwise are painstaking and accurate reconstructions.

If you are brave, you may want to offer some commentary. Often this means explaining why things happened. It also means going beyond the evidence to make educated guesses or inferences. For most events and issues in history there is insufficient source material. It is also likely to be distorted and, even if there was information about everything which happened in the past, there would not be the time to look through it all. There will therefore always be gaps. What has to be called for is a judgement not based on a fanciful flight of the imagination but on the basis of probability resulting from the evidence that has been used. It may be that you are wrong in making your judgements. Other investigators may soon be able to come up with alternative and perhaps more convincing conclusions, but this is how historical scholarship progresses.

In many cases there may well be differing interpretations and viewpoints. It is always useful to consider how different people at the time may have felt and reacted to issues as well as later commentators. One thing so often forgotten by local historians is that, just as today in any local community, there is rarely one single viewpoint about any feature, event or issue.

Context

Place findings in context. This provides not just a background but a framework to fit your own findings into. This is an area in which many amateur historians lack confidence, feeling that they cannot be expected to have the historical awareness which easily allows them to place findings in a wider geographical, thematic and chronological context.

Convincing the reader

Having urged you to go beyond the evidence to make inferences about the reasons for happenings and to comment about events and come to conclusions, it also has to be said that a string of unsubstantiated sweeping assertions is bad local history. In many respects, your final product **will** be heavily selective. It will need to adopt shorthand in the form of generalisations and conclusions. There will also be a need to miss out much of the material so that it can be coherent to those reading it.

Paradoxically the most convincing work does not necessarily result from swamping an argument with myriad data. A good piece of work is one where the reader or viewer can follow the discussion, arguments and points clearly and not get bogged down with detail which seems to confuse.

Good writing

This is not the occasion to tell you how to write. Clarity is often helped by good headings, syntax and punctuation. The best writing establishes clear argument in well organised paragraphs and the meat of the argument is held together between good introductions and conclusions. Sentences are often short and simple. Sentences and paragraphs follow logically from each other. Care is taken to focus on the relevant.

Some local historians believe in quoting extensively from sources and there may indeed be many occasions when material from particular sources should be referred to frequently. If your work is to be analytical and evaluative, extensive quoting can affect the flow of argument and add a fair amount of material which is not centrally relevant to the argument.

The conventions of the local historian

One important way of producing convincing work is to follow the accepted conventions such as footnotes, bibliographies and acknowledgements. Whilst some might regard the slavish adherence to many of these conventions as unnecessarily pedantic, they are a valuable aid not only to scholarship but also as references to further investigation.

Footnotes

Publishers often dislike too many footnotes but it is sensible to resist attempts to prune them excessively. Footnote references should be sufficiently detailed to allow the serious reader a relatively easy opportunity to locate the full reference. This means noting details such as:

- the initials and names of the author
- the full title of the book
- the place and date of publication (possibly also the edition where appropriate)
- the page number
- the title of the article if in a journal or magazine
- the title of the journal or magazine
- the volume number and date of the journal or magazine
- the page number of the article
- the accession number of an archival document along with its folio or page reference
- the name of the archive.

Appendices and glossaries

Some believe that appendices and glossaries can fulfil a useful purpose and there may be advantage in including information in extensive appendices if it is likely to yield valuable data for scholars. In too many cases, however, it is the place where you throw all your research findings to avoid the heartbreak of leaving out the fruits of hours of work.

Visual material

Many local history books and articles contain visual material. Often this serves a valuable function but it should not be assumed that a good local history book must be accompanied by lots of local pictures and photographs. The criterion is fitness for purpose and the good book can stand independent of pictorial sources. It is important to talk to any potential publisher about what is needed.

Maps

It is easy to forget that a locality may well become very familiar to a dedicated researcher but others may be much less conversant with places. Few works of local history do not warrant at least one map and often several such as those marking contemporary names as well as features relevant to the time period being covered. It is worth putting in the effort to ensure visual attractiveness and accuracy. At the least they should have clear lettering, a scale and appropriate legends.

Tables and graphs

Tables and graphs form part of many local history books and articles. They are an effective way of organising data and an appropriate graph can give a clear message even more effectively than a well-honed paragraph. One failing is to include such material largely independently of the text. The main value in including them is to back up generalisations and conclusions being made. If there is no cross-referencing then their value is diminished considerably.

Acknowledgements and bibliography

Acknowledgements, a bibliography or reading list need not be detailed but it is a courtesy to recognise particular help given.

There may be some who see the bibliography as superfluous when the footnote referencing is full. However, a detailed bibliography is a good checklist for those interested in following up information or extending their own reading on the subject. Some publishers may prefer a reading list to a bibliography.

—— Getting something published ——

You will not be able to dump a mass of research notes in front of a publisher and expect a completed and polished product back. One of the hard lessons to learn is that you will frequently have to compromise over form and presentation even when this is to your own satisfaction.

In many instances that involves shortening things. Publishers and editors of journals have their house styles and guidance on books and articles. The degree of control authors have over their work will vary from publisher to publisher, but respectable publishers and journals rarely accept anything totally at face value. The material will usually be passed to readers who comment on its worth and reliability. With many local history magazines and journals appearing only once a year, you may need to await your turn patiently. There may be conditions imposed. Apart from the need to prune – sometimes whole sections – there may also be a need to adopt the format of the journal in terms of footnotes and such like.

Few write local history with the intention of getting rich. There is a local history industry but there are few people who make anything more than pocket money. Many make nothing from the venture and some even pay to have their work in print.

—— Where to get things published ——

Local history articles are rarely commissioned although a serious monograph may result from putting a proposal to one of the history publishers. If you are seeking a publisher you may not find the main academic publishers the most fruitful starting point. More often than not, they reserve the slots for academic historians looking at a national or international issue from a local level.

National publishers

There are other national publishers, however, who specialise in local history publications and a major piece of work which adopts the conventions of academic research may be worth submitting to them. Amongst these companies are Phillimores, Batsford, Alan Sutton and David and Charles. It is usually more beneficial to have a finished draft to present to them and, even then, there can be no guarantee of publication. At best, it is likely to involve considerable adaptation of manuscripts.

Local publishers

With recent advances in technology, there has been a surge in small publishing companies in recent years. Their market is always small and many specialise in particular places or themes such as transport. A glance through local bookshops and even the branches of major chains reveals a large array of books available only within that locality. Many will be booklets rather than full-scale books.

Some towns and areas have their own publisher working to establish either a town history or a collection of publications covering different aspects. Sometimes the publisher will be the local library, archaeological society, council, WI or archives and it may be worth checking to see whether groups are active in publishing materials. An option for some may be a collaborative group task.

Articles

It may be that the publication was never intended as a book or even a pamphlet. The scope for publishing articles is large. It is as well if those interested in having something published are aware of the most suitable places. In part this depends on length and the degree of academic rigour. If it is short, interesting and chatty, local newspapers may be appropriate. So can local magazines which often appear monthly. They may represent a particular county or locality (many have the title ... *Life*) or there may even be scope for a national heritage or history magazine such as *This England* to publish some local history material.

Local societies

Most counties and many towns have their own local history societies. Some date back well over a century and are respected institutions. In many cases, especially with the older established county journals, the articles tend to be academic ones written by professionals and carefully referenced. Even so there is scope for the well-fashioned article written by a non-professional. Such articles tend to be submitted rather than commissioned.

Not all local history journals are of this type. A number of towns and areas have their own local history organisations. Nearly all produce some publication ranging from a glossy, professional-looking one to home-made typescripts. Many also produce newsletters besides an annual journal. They often provide a home for brief articles or summaries of recent research. Another possibility is the various publications either of local museums, research units, archaeology groups and archives or the Friends groups associated with such institutions.

Thematic studies

Almost every conceivable branch of history is covered by a national journal, for instance education, economics, business, agriculture, social and gender issues, types of industry and transport, religious, theatre, cinema, various aspects of leisure – the list is enormous. Different religious denominations have their own historical societies and publications. Another possibility lies with the many publications produced by local and national family history societies.

Specialist local history journals

National journals and organisations also add to the scope. Two journals *Local History* and *The Local Historian* (formerly the *Amateur Historian*) cater for the interests of local historians generally and contain a good blend of learned articles, news, book reviews, new publications and shorter articles. The latter journal is obtained through membership of the British Association of Local History which produces a growing range of books and publications. A parallel organisation is the Historical Association which has a local history committee responsible for a wide range of local history publications. Their *Guide to Records* is particularly popular but their range of pamphlets is impressive and covers areas as diverse as the gas industry, puritanism, education and vernacular housing. Some Historical Association branches have been particularly active in local history pamphlets for their area.

———— Building on the work ————

It is now many years since G.M. Trevelyan reviewed A.L. Rowse's *Tudor Cornwall* and condemned local history with faint praise. The review heaped compliments on the book and felt that the author was now skilled enough to move on from local history. The professional-isation of local history helped by academic departments in universities has long since shattered this view. W.G. Hoskins and the work of the Department of English Local History at Leicester may be the best known but it has certainly not been alone. The local history world is now able to embrace the enthusiastic lay person as well as the most academic, professional historian.

The majority of local historians get a bug they find difficult to shake off. Look at those working in archives and you will see a cross-section of types, ages and experiences of researchers. The joy of local history work is that it can not only be approached at different levels but that you can pursue it deep into old age. Nor is it a requirement or even expected that you progress to a more academic type of local history. There is room for the merely interested as well as for the professional.

Local history offers inspiring opportunities for individual and collaborative work. It can be a most sociable activity, fostering new friendships for you far and wide. There is the scope to develop further your original work or to embark on something new. You can get out and about or work in libraries and archives but there will also be work to do in the comfort of your home. There are always new avenues and new questions. It uses your brain, fires the imagination and satisfies a natural curiosity. In short, it allows us all to probe and recall our ancestors' past. We owe them this and thankfully everyone can enjoy the activities involved in pursuing this end.

GLOSSARY

The following list defines words local historians may come across. Often part of our understanding of a word is reinforced by knowing its origins. Accordingly, where it seems helpful, a definition is given of the word itself as well as its historic use.

Administration something done for someone else as his servant (Latin *minus*, less), see next word

Admonition something one has been required to do (Latin). Both this and the previous word are used to cover the legal documents appointing someone to act for another person who has died intestate

Archive a place where public records are kept (Greek)

Artefact anything that has been made (Latin). Also **artifact**

Athenaeum literary or scientific club (after the Greek temple to the god Athene, where professors taught and poets rehearsed)

Badger One who buys corn, etc., to resell. He used to wear a badge of office. Other names for such dealers include **cadger** (originally a carrier); **forestaller** (who stopped people taking produce to the market by buying it himself); **hawker** (an itinerant trader); **higgler**, **huckster** (who haggled over dairy produce before buying it)

Benefice ecclesiastical appointment (enabling him to 'do well' Latin *bene* + *facere*). See **incumbent**

Bills of mortality a formal document (Latin *bulla*, a seal) listing the number of deaths in a period and their causes

Bishop's transcripts from 1676, copies of births, marriages and deaths registers sent to the diocesan chancellor's office.

Board schools Schools run by boards of guardians (who sat round a table), from 1870

Boon unpaid service due by a tenant to his lord

Bordar smallholder farming five acres and living in a **bord** (ultimately linked to 'board', so the sense: a simple wooden house)

Broadsheet a large sheet of paper, printed on one side only, i.e. a poster. It preceded newspapers. Also known as a **broadside**

Bye-law a law local to a *by* (Old Norse, a habitation)

Cadger see under **badger**

Calendar a register of documents (originally a list of accounts due on the calends, the first day of each Roman month)

Calotype an early photographic method (*calo*, beautiful + type, impression). Also called **talbotype** after W.H. Fox Talbot who invented it in 1833 (though only publishing it in 1839)

Canal Artificial water course (Latin). Also found as **kennel**. It has the same root as **channel**

Cartulary see **chartulary**

Champaign open-field (q.v.) country; also **champion**. Latin: *compania*, a plain)

Chantry school one run by a body of priests (who had been appointed to chant masses for the soul of some person)

Chartulary a collection of charters (or charts, a word linked to 'card'), Latin

Cinque Ports five (French) defence ports on the English Channel: Hastings, Sandwich, Dover, Romney and Hithe. (Rye and Winchelsea were added later)

Clapper bridge a simple stream crossing made by laying a slab to span two piles of stones (Latin *claperium*)

Cobbles large, rounded pebbles (cf. 'cob' nuts) useful as paving. Also called **setts**

Consistory court governing court of the chancellor of a diocese (Latin *sistere* to stand up)

Constable Latin 'count of the stable', an early French court officer. This developed into **marshal**, q.v. The local peace keeper was originally called the 'petty constable' or the 'parish constable')

Court baron originally 'court of the baron'. A meeting of the freehold tenants under their lord or his steward

Court directory a list, in town directories, of gentry

Court leet a meeting of the residents of a hundred (q.v.), district or manor, under a lord or his steward (cf. **lathe**)

Court rolls the records (originally scrolls) of a court, stored in cylindrical tubes

Culverting covering over a stream or ditch

Curate see **incumbent**

Custumal a written record of customs

Daguerreotype   early photographic method, invented by Louis Jacques Mandé Daguerre (1789–1851)

Demesne   the land belonging to the lord of the manor (Latin, *dominus*)

Dike   ditch (Old English); but also 'embankment'. The process of digging a trench naturally produces a pile of spoil. Also **dyke**

Diocesan chancellor   church dignitary whose duties involved authenticating by sealing commissions, etc. In his name the bishop's records are kept.

Dole   distribution (a 'dealing out') of charitable gifts

Dredge   to clean out the bed or a river, originally using a 'dredge' (a piece of equipment for dragging up oysters)

Driftway   a road along which animals were driven. Or **drove road**

Enclosure   fencing in common land for personal use

Entrepôt   a place to which goods are brought for onward distribution. (Originally a storehouse where things were placed; Latin *inter* + *positum*)

Enumerator   the official who collects details about people in a particular area. Latin: he who counts

Extent   the assessment and valuation of land, etc. The Latin sense is to examine all that is 'stretched out' before the assessor

Eyre Court   circuit court held by judges 'on tour' (Latin *iterare*, to journey)

Factory   where things are made (Latin *facere*); a **manufactory** was where they were made by hand

Faculty   a licence to do something (Latin *facilis*, to make things easy), especially one issued by an ecclesiastical superior, to enable something that would otherwise be illegal

Feet of fines   the court's section (at the foot) of a three-part indenture (q.v.), paying a sum to end ('finalise') a tenant's application to his lord, or some other medieval final payment

Ferry   where you travel (Old English *ferian*) across a river. Linked to the words 'farewell' and 'thoroughfare')

Forestaller   see **badger**

Frankpledge   the Old English law system where everyone stood guarantee for everyone else. Originally *Frithborh* (peace pledge), this was apparently mistranslated by the Normans as frank, that is 'free'

Geld   tax paid to the Crown before the Norman Conquest. The word is akin to 'yield' meaning to give up (and has no connected with 'gold')

Gild   an association of people formed for their mutual aid and benefit. The word is linked to 'geld' above. Also spelt **Guild**

Glebe   land (Latin for 'soil') granted to a clergyman as part of his benefice

Halmote court The court of a lord of the manor, held in his hall. A variant of 'hall moot'

Hawker see **badger**

Hayward officer in charge of hedges and enclosures (sometimes of cattle feeding on common land). Old English *hay*, meaning 'hedge' + *weard* 'guardian'

Heriot a render, qv., due to his lord on the death of a tenant. Originally a service of arms or equipment (Old English *here*, army + *geatwa*, equipment)

Heritor an heir (in Scotland the owner of a heritable object)

Hide the land needed to support one free household (Germanic root *hiw-*) and their dependants. The measure was that amount of land that could be ploughed by one plough in one year. A hide was divided into 100 acres, but the area of one acre varied locally

Higgler see **badger**

Housling people those who receive the Eucharist (Old English *husl*)

Huckster see **badger**

Hundred a division of many English counties, with its own court. At specified places **moots** (meetings) were held to discuss community matters, their results being recorded on rolls.

Incumbent the holder of a church **benefice**, i.e. a priest with a particular appointment. The **rector** owned the rights (Latin) to the great tithes. The **vicar** standing in place of (Latin *vicarius*, a substitute) the rector when he is an absentee is only entitled to the small tithes. A **curate** has the cure (care) of the souls of his congregation. A **priest** is an elder (Greek *presbus*, an old man) of the church. A **pastor** shepherds his flock (Latin *pascere*, to feed).

Indenture any documentary agreement between two people. It was divided by a wavy or tooth-like (c.f. denture) cut, so that both parts matched exactly

In-migration movement of population into an area (but not necessarily from another country)

Inventory a detailed list, with values, of a deceased person's belongings. It was drawn up by his neighbours (i.e. not by specialists). Latin *in* + *venire*, to come upon or find

Journeyman Having served a full apprenticeship, a person qualified at his trade is ready to be hired for a day's work (Old French *journé*, a day). Compare a 'journey', which was a day's travel

Kennel see **canal**

Kidder a huckster

Lathe a county division used in Kent

Lay subsidy rolls   records of non-ecclesiastical taxes (levied by the monarch). Originally Latin *sub* + *sidere*, of troops 'sitting behind' the rest (i.e. reserves)

Lea   land lying fallow, grassland. Also lay, ley. The ultimate sense is woodland opened up to the light

Letters patent   open (latin *patent*) letters from one in authority to anyone reading them, granting particular rights to the bearer

Leywrite   variation of 'lairwite', a fine (*wite*) for adultery (Old English *leyer*, lying)

Liberate rolls   legal records delivered to a county sherriff to recover lands etc. held as security. Latin *liberate* ('Deliver ye') was the first word on such records

Linchets   strips of green land between two ploughed fields (often terraces on a slope). Old English *hlinc*, a slope, is akin to 'lean' (i.e. not level). Also **lynchet**

Low bells   catching birds at night by frightening them with cow bells

Manufactory   see **factory**

Merestones   stones set up as boundaries (Latin *murus*, a wall)

Marshal   an official at court, in law, etc. Originally one who looked after horses (Teutonic roots: *marcho*, horse + *skalko*, servant).

Merchet licence fee   a fine paid to his overlord by a tenant wanting to give his daughter in marriage. (Akin to 'market')

Metalled roads   from 1806 (just before Macadam's method was first used). The sense is merely that a well compacted road was as hard as metal

Microform   any way of presenting photographically reduced images: on reels of **microfilm**, or on separate **microfiche** sheets

Monitors   senior school pupils who had duties to keep order and occasionally to teach smaller children (Latin *monere*, to warn)

Moot   see **hundred**

Muniments   title deeds (which protect one against false claimants, etc.) Latin *munire*, to fortify

Murage books   Books recording tolls collected to build or repair town walls (Latin)

Navvy   short for 'navigator', one who steered the canal he was digging along its route across country

Open field system   late eighteenth century phrase describing **champaign** country, i.e. unenclosed land

Out-migration   Migration of people from a population one is studying, not necessarily overseas

Overseers of the poor   officers appointed each year from 1600 to 1834

Palatinate   a district ruled by a nobleman granted special privileges by the monarch. Originally an officer at the Imperial Palace on the Palatine Hill in Rome

Pastor   see **incumbent**

Pemmican   Cree Indian, from the root word *pime*, fat. Dried and pounded lean meat mixed with melted fat and worked into cakes

Pest house   a hospital for persons suffering from any deadly disease, but especially bubonic plague (Latin *pestis*, plague)

Pie powder court   a summary court – making quick decisions on the spot – held at markets and fairs to administer justice to itinerants (Latin *pede* + *pulverosus*, a dusty footed person)

Pinfold   from 'pound fold', a pound (circular structure not unlike a 'pond') in which stray animals were folded

Pipe rolls   records rolled up and stored in tubes

Pluralist   a person holding more than one **benefice** at once

Poll books   records of votes (where one counts heads, Dutch *polle*)

Population trees   Christmas-tree-like bar-charts for comparing populations of different age groups

Port books   town records of maritime trade through ports

Portage   carrying boats and goods from one navigable water to another (Latin *portare*, to carry)

Postern gate   A small back door (in a castle or town), from Latin *posterus*, what is behind. Originally 'posterle'

Pot hanger   an adjustable metal device fixed in the chimney, with which to hang pots over the fire

Pounder   a person in charge of a **pinfold** (or **Pinder**)

Primogeniture   the right whereby the firstborn inherits property from his parents (Latin)

Probate   a thing proved (to test it, to see that it is good, Latin *probus*), especially a will, to make sure that it is genuine

Probate inventory   see **inventory**

Puddling   lining with 'puddle': clay and water taken from a ditch (Old English *pudd*) or furrow

Quarter Sessions   sittings (Latin *sedere*, to sit) of courts on the first days of the four periods into which the year was divided. In England and Ireland, Lady Day (25 March), Midsummer Day (24 June), Michaelmas (29 September) and Christmas (25 December). In Scotland, on those days appointed by statute

Quit claims   declarations of freedom, discharges. (Quit, originally 'quite', from Latin *quietus*, to make quiet)

Ragged schools   Schools for those at the lowest level of society

Rector   see **incumbent**

Recusant   One who refused to attend Church of England services, (he objects about [re] the cause)

Reeve   a medieval officer, originally with high office appointed by the Anglo-Saxon kings; later, a local magistrate

Render   a return of money owed by a tenant to his superior

River   Something that flows (the word 'arrive' is linked). People living on opposite banks were 'rivals'

Rubbaboo   water added to **pemmican**, making a soup

Sasine   Scottish law giving possession of property. Originally 'seisin'. This was from 'seise', from the Teutonic root meaning 'a holding' (cf. 'seize' in its modern sense)

Seneschal   a steward (Teutonic root for 'old' + 'servant')

Serf   one who serves: a slave or bondman

Skillet   small cooking pot, usually with legs and a handle. Perhaps 'bell-shaped', Old French *eschelette*

Spoil   waste material thrown up during mining; root sense is what is wrenched out of the earth

Stowball   variant of 'stool ball', a country version of cricket where a stool was used as a wicket

Subsidy roll   records of parliamentary finance for the monarch, see also **lay subsidy rolls**

Surrogate   a deputy appointed by a bishop to issue licences in his place (Latin *sub* + *rogare*, to offer instead)

Surrogate measures   Substitutes, which may be used, with some adaptation, when the ideal measures are not available

Survey   an enquiry made for some particular purpose, Latin *super* + *videre*, to look over

Tailings   The refuse that results when trimming a product to size (to 'tail' is to cut). Used of the waste from any process

Tarmacadam   Material used to make a road by Macadam's method (compacted layers of loose stone), topped with a layer of tar

Terrier   an inventory of property, late Latin *terrarius liber*, the book of landed estates (*terra*, land). Often takes the form of a perambulation around, and record of, the boundary of the property

Tithe   tenth part (Old English *teo÷a*). Great tithes, the rector's share, are of the main crops of the area, e.g. corn, hay, wood and fruit. Small tithes are the vicar's share of any minor crops not taken by the rector

Toft   a homestead on its land (Old Norse)

Troll madam   (Variation of 'trou madame', from French *trou*, a hole). A ladies' game like bagatelle

Tumpline   a strap placed across the forehead to help support a pack carried on one's back

Turnpike   a barrier across the road, from the late seventeenth century as a toll bar. Originally, a set of pikes set into the ground butts downward, to create a hedge of spikes

Valor ecclesiasticus   a listing and valuation of all monastic property, made in 1535, before the dissolution

Vestry   the place in church where vestments (clothes) were kept. In this room parish business meetings were held. From the late 1600s, the word also referred to people attending such meetings

Vicar   see **incumbent**

Villein   a peasant working entirely subject to his lord. Originally this word and 'villain' both meant 'a labourer who worked at the villa'

Visitation   an inspection, especially by a church official, of the current state of a diocese, parish, etc.

Vital statistics   those chief events that relate to life (Latin *vita*), particularly birth and death, but also marriage

Wake   a public holiday. Originally staying awake before the feast day of the local church's patron saint, an occasion for drinking and rejoicing

Watch committee   those controlling the town guard, who watched out for the safety of citizens

Wattle and daub   rods (Old English *watul*) set up vertically between the wall beams of a house, interlaced with springy twigs to produce a basketwork surface. On to both sides of this are smeared a daub of plaster, etc. (Latin *de* + *albare*, to whiten down)

Weir   a holding back of water in a river, to create a useful pool, but also to protect (Old English *werian*) lower areas from flooding

Wharf   A waterside structure at which boats can unload (Old English *hwerfan*, to be busy)

READING LIST

The following brief list will be augmented in your local library by a wealth of material relating to your own area of study.

General and relating to England and Wales

Barber, P. and Board, C. (1993) *Tales from the Map Room*, BBC Publications, London.
Brunskill, R.W. (1992) *Traditional Buildings of England: An Introduction to Vernacular Architecture*, Gollancz, London.
Cipolla, C.M. (1978) *The Economic History of World Population*, 7th edn, Penguin Books, London.
Emmison, F.G. (1967) *How to read Local Archives,* Historical Association, London.
Gooder, E. (1978) *Latin for Local History*, Longman, Harlow.
Griffin, J.R. and Eddershaw, D.G.T. (1996) *Using Local History Sources*, 2nd edn, Hodder & Stoughton, London
Haigh, C. (1985) *The Cambridge Encyclopedia of Great Britain and Ireland*, Cambridge University Press, Cambridge.
Hey, D. (ed.) (1996) *The Oxford Companion to Local and Family History*, Oxford University Press, Oxford.
Higgs, E. (1996) *The Clearer Sense of the Census*, HMSO, London.
Hindle, B.P. (1988) *Maps for Local History*, Batsford, London.
Historical Association (Reprinted 1994) *Short Guides to Records, numbers 1–24, first series*, ed. L.M. Mumby, introduction revised by K.L. Thompson and G.C.F. Forster.
Historical Association (1993 onwards) *Short Guides to Records, numbers 25–48, second series*, ed. K.L. Thompson.
Hoskins, W.G. (1982) *Fieldwork in Local History*, Faber, London.

EXPLORING LOCAL HISTORY

Hoskins, W.G. (1984) *Local History in England*, 3rd edn, Longman, Harlow, Essex.
Hoskins, W.G. (1992) *The Making of the English Landscape*, 2nd edn, Hodder & Stoughton, London.
Hurley, B. (ed.) *The Book of Trades or Library of the Useful Arts, Parts I, II (1811) and III (1818)* reprinted 1991, 1992, 1994 by Wiltshire Family History Society, 21 Elizabeth Drive, Devizes, Wilts SN10 3SB.
Local Population Studies (twice yearly journal), Tawney House, Matlock, Derbyshire DE4 3BT.
Munby, L. (1988) *Reading Tudor and Stuart Handwriting*, British Association for Local History, Phillimore, Chichester, West Sussex.
Oliver, G. (1989) *Photographs and Local History*, Batsford, London.
Perks, R. (1990) *Oral History: An Annotated Bibliography*, British Library National Sound Archive, London.
Pevsner, N. (various dates) *Buildings of England*, (county by county), Penguin Books, London.
Richardson, J. (1986) *The Local Historian's Encyclopaedia*, 2nd edn, Historical Publications, London.
Shaw, G. and Tipper, A. (1988) *British Directories: A Bibliography and Guide to Directories Published in England and Wales (1850–1950) and Scotland (1773–1950)*, Leicester University Press, Leicester.
Stephens, W.B. (1981) *Sources for English Local History*, Cambridge University Press, Cambridge.
Tate, W.E. (1969, reprinted 1983) *The Parish Chest*, 3rd edn, Phillimore, Chichester, West Sussex.
West, J. (1997) *Village Records*, revised edn, Phillimore, Chichester, West Sussex.
West, J. (1983) *Town Records*, Phillimore, Chichester, West Sussex.
Yarwood, D. (1956) *The English Home*, Batsford, London.

Scotland and Ireland

Cory, K.B. (1990) *Tracing Your Scottish Ancestry*, Polygon, Edinburgh University Press, Edinburgh.
Cox, M. (ed.) (1992) *Exploring Scottish History (A Directory of Resource Centres)*, SLA, Scottish Library Assoc., Motherwell.
Daiches, D. (ed.) (1981) *A Companion to Scottish Culture*, Edward Arnold, London.
Evans, E.E. (1957) *Irish Folkways*, Routledge and Kegal Paul, London.

Foster, R.F. (ed.) (1989) *The Oxford Illustrated History of Ireland*, Oxford University Press, Oxford.

Grant, I.F. (1951) *Highland Folk Ways*, Routledge and Kegal Paul, London.

Grenham, J. (1992) *Tracing Your Irish Ancestry*, Gill and Macmillan Dublin

Helferty, S. and Refausse, R. (eds.) 2nd edn. (1993) *Dictionary of Irish Archives*, Irish Academic Press, Blackrock, Co. Dublin.

Institute of Irish Studies *Ordnance Survey Memoirs 1830–39 (Ulster)*, Belfast.

Lyons, F.S.L. (1979) *Culture and Anarchy in Ireland*, Oxford University Press, Oxford.

Macafee, C.I. (1996) *Concise Ulster Dictionary*, Oxford University Press, Oxford.

Macleod, Martin and Cairns (eds.) (1988) *The Pocket Scots Dictionary*, Aberdeen University Press, Aberdeen.

Moody, D. (1986) *Scottish Local History*, Batsford, London.

Moody, D. (1989) *Scottish Family History*, Batsford, London.

Ritchie, G. and A. (1991) *Scottish Archaeology and Early History*, Edinburgh University Press, Edinburgh.

Sinclair, C. (1990) *Tracing Your Scottish Ancestors (in the Scottish Record Office)*, HMSO, Edinburgh.

Sinclair, C. (1994) *Tracing Scottish Local History (in the Scottish Record Office)*, HMSO, Edinburgh.

Smout, T.C. (1969/1986) *A History of the Scottish People, 1560–1830* (1969); *1830–1950* (1986), Fontana Press, London

Wilkes, M. (1991) *The Scot and his Maps*, SLA, Scottish Library Assoc. Motherwell.

Leaflets can be obtained from the National Library and National Archives, Dublin; and the Public Record Office of Northern Ireland.

Case Study 6

Askin, John, (1928) *The John Askin Papers*, Milo Milton Quaife, Detroit Library Commission. 1918–32, two vols, Detroit.

Carver, Jonathan, (1976) *The Journals of Jonathan Carver and Related Documents, 1766–1770*, ed. John Parker, St Paul: Minnesota Historial Society Press.

Gilman, Carolyn, (1992) *The Grand Portage Story*, Minnesota Historical Society Press, St Paul.

Hearne, Samuel and Turnor, Philip, (1934) *Journals of Samuel*

Hearne and Philip Turnor, ed. J.B. Tyrell, Champlain Society, Toronto.

Henry, Alexander, the Elder, (1901) *Travels and Adventures in Canada and the Indian Territories Between the Years 1760 and 1776*, ed. James Bain, Little, Brown, Boston.

Innis, Harold, (1956) *The Fur Trade in Canada: An Introduction to Canadian Economic History*, revised 1930, University of Toronto Press, Toronto.

La Verendrye, Pierre Gaultier de Varennes, Sieur de, (1927) *Journals and Letters of Pierre Gaultier de Varennes, de la Verendrye and his Sons*, ed. W Kaye Lamb, Cambridge University Press, Cambridge.

Mackenzie, Alexander, (1970) *The Journals and Letters of Sir Alexander Mackenzie*, ed. W Kaye Lamb, Cambridge University Press, Cambridge.

Morse, Eric, (1968), *Fur Trade Canoe Routes of Canada, Then and Now*, Queen's Printer, Ottawa.

Nute, Grace Lee, (1941) *The Voyageur*, Minnesota Historical Society, St Paul.

Rich, Edwin E. (1966) *Montreal and the Fur Trade*, McGill University Press, Montreal.

Thompson, Erwin N. (1969) *Grand Portage: The Great Carrying Place*, National Park Service, Minnesota.

Thwaites, Reuben Gold, ed. (1892) 'Trade in the Upper Country', *Wisconsin Historical Collections*, 12.

US Geological Survey, 1960 etc. Cascades and Grand Portage Quadranges, 7.5 Minute Series.

Wallace, W. Stewart, ed. (1934) *Documents Relating to the North West Company*, Champlain Society, Toronto.

Wallace, W. Stewart, ed. (1954) *The Pedlars from Quebec and Other Papers on the Nor'Westers*, Ryerson Press, Toronto.

Wood, W. Raymond and Thiessen, Thomas D, ed. (1985) *Early Fur Trade on the Northern Plains*, University of Oklahoma Press, Norman.

Woolworth, Alan R., (1982) 'Grand Portage: The Great Carrying Place' in Gilman, Carolyn, *Where Two Worlds Meet: The Great Lakes Fur Trade*, pp 110–115; Minnesota Historical Society Press, St Paul.

Woolworth, Alan R., (1993) *An Historical Study of the Grand Portage, Grand Portage National Monument*, for the National Park Service, Minnesota.

USEFUL ADDRESSES

Local and family history societies

For the name and address of your nearest local or family history society, contact the local studies (or local history) department of your county or county council library, or the county record office.

The following associations will be able to provide you with the name and address of their member societies in your area:

England :   The Administrator, British Association for Local
and Wales   History, Shopwyke Hall, Chichester, West Sussex
                  PO20 6BQ.

Scotland: The Secretary, Scottish Local History Forum, 128
                  Gowanbank, Livingston, West Lothian EH54 EW.

Ulster :   The Secretary, Federation for Ulster Local Studies,
(nine counties)   8 Fitzwilliam Street, Belfast BT9 6AW.

Ireland :   The Secretary, Federation of Local History Societies,
(excluding Ulster)   c/o Rothe House, Kilkenny.

All the above associations produce journals on a regular basis.

Contacts for family history societies often change, and if your local library service or CRO cannot help, then contact:

The Administrator, Federation of Family History Societies, c/o The Birmingham and Midland Institute, Margaret Street, Birmingham B3 3BS

Aerial photographs

The following can supply copies of aerial photographs for a fee.

Wildgoose Publications, The Reading Room, 46 Dennis Street, Hugglescote, Leicestershire, LE67 2FP

Aerofilms Ltd, Gate Studios, Station Road, Boreham Wood, Hertfordshire, WD6 1EJ.

INDEX

In the following list, bold entries relate to descriptive coverage in Chapter 2. See also the Glossary.